Health Insurance and Psychiatric Care: Update and Appraisal

Health Insurance and Psychiatric Care: Update and Appraisal

STEVEN S. SHARFSTEIN, M.D.
SAM MUSZYNSKI
EVELYN MYERS

Foreword by
JOHN A. TALBOTT, M.D.

Appendices by
JO BRADY

American Psychiatric Press, Inc.

1400 K Street, N.W.
Washington, D.C. 20005

Printed in the United States of America.

Library of Congress Cataloging in Publication Data

Sharfstein, Steven S. (Steven Samuel)
Health insurance and psychiatric care.

Update of: Health insurance and psychiatric care/Louis S. Reed, Evelyn S. Myers, Patricia L. Scheidemandel. 1972.
Bibliography: p. 211
1. Insurance, Mental health—United States. I. Myers, Evelyn S. II. Muszynski, Sam. III. Reed, Louis Schultz. Health insurance and psychiatric care. IV. Title.
[DNLM: 1. Costs and cost analysis. 2. Insurance, Psychiatric—United States. 3. Mental health services—Utilization—United States. W275 AA1 S555h]
HG9387.S5 1984 368.3′82 84-2981
ISBN 0-88048-153-6

Contents

Appendices

Foreword

The funding of mental health services was until recently of interest to only a few in the field of psychiatry. Now, it has become *the* paramount issue for most of us. Whether in private practice or salaried positions, whether concerned about inpatient or outpatient care, and whether involved with direct or indirect services—we have had to look first and foremost at how our services are financed.

The methods and mechanisms of financing psychiatric services have undergone great shifts in recent years, as the face of psychiatry itself has changed. No longer do many patients pay their own bills, now others share in the risks through insurance; no longer do private monies constitute the majority of funding sources, now public monies predominate; no longer is the solo practitioner the modal deliverer of outpatient service, now psychiatry is increasingly practiced in "organized settings." No longer are we undergoing great economic expansion, now cost-containment and resource-shrinkage are common; and no longer do the vast majority of episodes of illness receive treatment in inpatient settings, outpatient care is now more prevalent.

In 1972, Louis Reed, Evelyn Myers, and Patricia Scheidemandel published their landmark work, *Health Insurance and Psychiatric Care: Utilization and Cost*. It was the first attempt to examine comprehensively the insurance funding of psychiatric services in this country, and it provided those of us in the field interested in the area the first specific look at such issues.

At the time, cost/benefit and cost/effectiveness were economic concepts well known to industry but almost unknown to us. As the health portion of the gross national product grew, however, questions were raised about "spiraling" health costs and strategies were proposed to control them. For a variety of reasons, some based on bias and stigma, psychiatric services were often singled out for scrutiny and reduction.

Peer review and claims review of insured benefits became commonplace and closer looks were taken at the utilization of psychiatric services.

By now, we are all aware of the universal attempt to cut costs through various schemes—public expenditure "caps," pro-competitive strategies, and benefit trade-offs. The American Psychiatric Association, through its public education and government relations arms, has been in the forefront of those advocating for more favorable and equitable funding of psychiatric services for the mentally ill. But it is only with an accurate data base and a clearly articulated series of policy options that such advocacy efforts can succeed.

This volume, updating Reed, Myers, and Scheidemandel's effort, provides this foundation. Written by three of the Association's most informed staff members, it enables all of us to understand the basic, important issues involved with financing mental health services today; enables those of us involved with public policy issues to have a compact and comprehensive summary of financing trends and opportunities; and enables those who design our insurance programs and make our laws to isolate and study the specifics of insurance for psychiatric illnesses.

It should be read by every psychiatrist in America, known to all who effect decisions about funding mental health services, and regarded as basic reference material by all who are in leadership positions in labor, industry, or government. The future of insurance for psychiatric services is a critical issue—our future patients will need care that they cannot predict they will need in advance, and therefore do not adequately advocate for—and it is only through a coalition of citizens and physicians, armed with data such as those contained in this work, that adequate care will be provided and financed.

JOHN A. TALBOTT, M.D.
President, American Psychiatric Association

Preface

This book was written to provide a full update to the landmark American Psychiatric Association publication of 1972, *Health Insurance and Psychiatric Care: Utilization and Cost*, by Louis S. Reed, Ph.D., Evelyn S. Myers, and Patricia L. Scheidemandel. Only one of the authors of that book (E.S.M.) participated in writing this one, but we hope we have preserved continuity with the empirical approach developed by Dr. Reed, which established the basis for rational discussion of the insurability of treatments for mental illness.

Our method has been to summarize the most pertinent work of the last decade, thus providing an up-to-date empirical basis for the maintenance and expansion of private third-party financing of psychiatric care. We believe that psychiatric care is both necessary and effective, although economic barriers to its accessibility persist to a greater extent than to care for general medical disorders. Indeed, the cost containment imperatives of the 1980s may be making the disparity between insurance coverage of mental disorders and of general medical disorders larger rather than smaller.

The book has two main parts. The first is a narrative exposition of the field today, leading to an agenda of cost policy and cost research issues for the next decade. The second part consists of appendices for those readers who want detailed data on utilization and costs and related issues for further study.

Although we are full-time staff members of the American Psychiatric Association and this work was done as part of our APA day (we receive no royalties), the book expresses our opinions and does not represent official Association policy. Our intention is to offer technical assistance to individuals and groups in psychiatry and in other professional and political arenas to aid in the search for better financing of psychiatric care.

The APA Board of Trustees established a Work Group on Competition/Legislation in December 1981. One of the group's principal tasks was to develop information and data which could be used by the Association, its District Branches, and other parties to facilitate efforts to maintain and expand third-party financial resources. Third-party insurance is a most urgent priority for the APA and for the patients who are treated by psychiatrists. Although not a representation of official APA policy, this book was written in response to this urgent Association priority.

We wish to thank the APA library staff, particularly Zing Jung, for timely support; Helen Roberts and Sandy Ferris for clerical support; and Dolly Gattozzi for developing consistency in style and thought. For helpful editorial and substantive criticism, we thank Donald Hammersley, M.D., Deputy Medical Director of the APA; Jay Cutler, Special Counsel and Director, Government Relations, APA; and J. F. Follmann, Jr., former Director of Information and Research, Health Insurance Association of America.

Thanks are also due to Melvin Sabshin, M.D., Medical Director of the APA; Allan Beigel, M.D., Chair of the Competition/Legislation Work Group; and George Tarjan, M.D., President of the APA. All were generous in their support and encouragement.

STEVEN S. SHARFSTEIN, M.D.
SAM MUSZYNSKI
EVELYN S. MYERS
JO BRADY

CHAPTER 1

Introduction to the Issues

Treatments for mental disorders are not reimbursed by third-party payers in the same degree or manner as general medical disorders. Although coverage of psychiatric care has improved during the 50-year history of health insurance in the United States, private insurance to cover the costs of psychiatric care is only about half as available as it is to cover general medical costs.

Reed and associates made this estimate in 1972 in the American Psychiatric Association's first major book on insurance, *Health Insurance and Psychiatric Care: Utilization and Cost.* The authors were cautiously optimistic that coverage of treatment of psychiatric illness would continue to improve. "There is some evidence that the insurance carriers are beginning to . . . realize that no program of health care benefits can be considered adequate or truly comprehensive if it does not take into account the need for treatment of mental or emotional disorders" (Reed et al. 1972).

Publication of the work of the economist Louis S. Reed and his associates Evelyn S. Myers and Patricia L. Scheidemandel signalled a sophisticated new awareness of the inequities and inadequacies of third-party financing of psychiatric care. It was a landmark study, a compilation and analysis of data from more than 40 private and public health insurance plans or organizations. The book undoubtedly helped to educate insurance carriers, major purchasers of health insurance, and psychiatrists themselves, and thus contributed to the subsequent expansion of coverage. In the Foreword, Walter Barton, the APA Medical Director, pointed out the purpose underlying the Association's concern with insurance issues as follows: "Some might look upon these efforts as primarily self-seeking. . . . But I like to think of our purpose as a much broader one—one directly related to the primary objective of this Association as stated in its Constitution: 'to improve the treatment, rehabilitation, and care of the mentally ill. . . . '"

As this sequel to update the data base and appraise the contemporary scene is being written, virtually everything has changed *except* the Association's purpose in continuing the study of insurance issues. And the changes are such that any degree of optimism would seem misplaced. A very different political and economic climate prevails today from that of the early 1970s. Then we were still in an era of rapid growth of both the health care establishment and the health insurance industry. Today the watchwords are cost containment, and the psychiatric profession is being challenged more urgently than ever before to define precisely the nature of psychiatric care and the appropriate role of third-party financing.

Not that pessimism is in order. Nowhere is regression to asylum psychiatry seen as acceptable. Nevertheless, current cost-containment approaches represent an historical discontinuity. The gradual improvement of coverage characteristic of the past shows signs of being stalled by contrary forces of market and government. Clearly, it is no longer realistic to assume a growing health care industry, with coverage of psychiatric care expanding as medical care and insurance themselves expand. Rather, new assumptions stemming from cost-containment imperatives are key to recent events and are shaping the future. An understanding of these new assumptions is needed to guide an effective agenda for the 1980s.

Before examining the current political scene, it may be of interest to review briefly both the reasons for the historical discrimination against the mentally ill in insurance plans and the efforts made by the American Psychiatric Association to overcome that discrimination.

APA Efforts to Overcome Insurance Discrimination

When insurance coverage for inpatient medical treatment first became widely available in the 1930s, it seemed acceptable for a number of reasons to exclude coverage for treatment of mental disorders. At that time, a diagnosis of serious mental illness usually meant long-term, perhaps even lifetime, hospitalization in a public mental institution, where custodial care rather than active treatment was the norm. Psychiatry was an institution-based specialty, for the most part out of the mainstream of medicine.

Beginning in the late 1940s, a series of dramatic developments propelled psychiatric care into the medical mainstream. To cite some of the most remarkable changes, the sharp decline in the number of patients resident in public mental hospitals, the development and wide acceptance of several classes of effective psychoactive drugs, the shift in locus of care from remote institutions to community-based settings, and the growth of psychoanalytic approaches to outpatient care. Much of this care now takes place in psychiatric units in general hospitals and community mental health centers, and in the offices of psychiatrists in private practice, who not only treat patients with disorders which would not have required hospitalization in the past, but also maintain in the community many persons with psychoses who formerly would have been hospitalized, often for entire lifetimes (Appendix II-A).

During the same period the health insurance industry experienced phenomenal growth. In 1940 only about 10 percent of the U.S. civilian population had any private insurance for hospital care and insurance for out-of-hospital care was negligible. By 1970, 78 percent of the population had some inpatient coverage and 43 percent some coverage of physicians' office visits under private insurance plans (Reed et al. 1972). As of 1977, approximately 87 percent of the population with private insurance had some coverage for mental health care (National Center 1981). Notwithstanding this long period of sustained growth and diversification, discrimination against the mentally ill—by limiting insurance reimbursement for mental illness beyond the limitations for treatment of general medical illness—has remained the rule rather than becoming the exception.

The American Psychiatric Association was in the forefront of efforts to reveal the scope of this discrimination as early as 1951, when its Mental Hospital Service surveyed 48 Blue Cross plans and found that 38 of them discriminated against patients with mental disorders and 22 totally excluded such patients from coverage.

In 1954 the APA Council (now called the Board of Trustees) went on record opposing discrimination and urged members and District Branches "to do all they can to see to it that the same coverage is provided for nervous, mental, and emotional disorders and for psychiatrist services as for other conditions." The APA statement also called attention to a problem related to insurance limitations: To protect patients' ability to use their insurance benefits, psychiatrists were often forced to report disguised diagnoses on claims forms.

A symposium to explore the problems of health insurance and psychiatric care was featured at the Association's 1957 annual meeting. Questions raised then are still pertinent today, as will be seen. From then on, the APA's activities steadily increased; a few of the most notable events and publications are described below.

- The APA, with the National Association for Mental Health, co-sponsored a study in 1959-1961 funded by the National Institute of Mental Health. Group Health Insurance of New York carried out the project, the purpose of which was "to test the feasibility of financing short-term ambulatory treatment by offering prepayment coverage of such treatment free of charge to a sample of otherwise medically insured subscribers." The findings, reported in *Psychiatric Insurance,* allayed the fears of those who expected long waiting lines at psychiatrists' offices. The author concluded that, "in the present stage of acceptance of psychiatry, there appears to be little danger that the costs of insuring the extent of coverage offered by the project [up to 15 office visits, up to 30 inpatient days] would be prohibitive if spread over an average cross-section of the 1960 population" (Avnet 1962).

- In 1963 the APA initiated discussions with the United Auto Workers, which was seeking improved health insurance for its members. The union successfully negotiated ambulatory psychiatric benefits for 4.2 million workers and their dependents, who, upon entering treatment, made no initial payment but became responsible for an increasing share of the cost as treatment continued.
- In 1965 the APA initiated a series of workshops held cooperatively with the National Association of Private Psychiatric Hospitals and the National Association of State Mental Health Program Directors and attended also by representatives of insurance carriers, the U.S. Civil Service Commission, NIMH, and employers. A set of principles was developed by the conferees and published as *APA Guidelines for Psychiatric Services Covered Under Health Insurance.* The document addressed such questions as "What is mental illness?" and "What are the accepted forms of treatment?" A second edition was published in 1969 following workshop discussions with representatives of diverse groups.
- The Joint Information Service of the APA and the National Association for Mental Health published *Health Insurance for Mental Illness* in 1968 (Scheidemandel et al.). The book reported the results of two studies, one on coverage of hospitalized patients and the other on coverage of patients seen by psychiatrists in private office practice. The latter study, the first of its kind, revealed that 26 percent of the patients seen had insurance that reimbursed at least some part of the psychiatrist's fee.
- In November 1969 the *American Journal of Psychiatry* published a Special Section titled "Insurance Coverage of Mental Disorders," which was made available as a separate reprint and was used extensively by the APA and the National Institute of Mental Health in documenting the case for improved coverage.
- In 1972 the APA published the landmark work by Reed et al., which provided data on more than 40 plans. The authors concluded: "The cost of providing insurance coverage of mental conditions both in and out of the hospital is relatively low—a few dollars per covered person and a small proportion of the cost of coverage for all conditions. From the standpoint of cost, insurance coverage of mental health care is feasible."

One of the plans given detailed scrutiny in this study was the high option of the Blue Cross-Blue Shield plan for federal employees. A word may be in order about why this plan especially merits research attention. The Blues have long underwritten the lion's share of the business in the populous marketplace of the Federal Employees Health Benefits Program (FEHBP). About 140 insurance plans and organizations participate in the FEHBP; they compete once every year during what is called "open season" for the business of 10 million federal workers, dependents, and annuitants. In the early 1970s the Blues high-option was a model plan, offering nearly nondiscriminatory coverage of mental disorders.

Reed continued studying the cost and utilization data from this plan (the FEHBP requires data collection of the insurers) and was able to make an important observation. "The upward trend in utilization of benefits for mental disorders, which had characterized the plan virtually since its beginnings in 1960," Reed reported, "appeared to have ended and leveled out in 1973 and 1974" (1975). This leveling continued; moreover, another APA study also found consistency in the use of mental illness benefits. The investigator looked at the experience of eight plans, covering about two-thirds of all federal employees and their dependents, over the four-year period 1976-1979. He reported that the data revealed "a surprising consistency in the propensity to use mental health services, both geographically and over the time period studied" (Krizay 1980).

- In 1977 the APA established the Commission on Psychiatric Therapies to consider general principles of evaluating efficacy. In 1982 the Commission published *Psychotherapy Research: Methodological Issues,* which dealt with the complexities of psychotherapy research and placed the evidence for the efficacy of psychotherapy in a favorable light by providing a clinical perspective to existing research. Turning next to a review of therapies, the Commission prepared two books (publication date, May 1984), *Somatic Therapies* and *Psychosocial Therapies,* that describe not only traditional therapies but the known new ones. Following completion of the Commission's assigned tasks, a new APA component, the Task Force on Treatments of Psychiatric Disorders, was established; it will develop a Psychiatric Treatments Manual (expected publication date, 1985 or 1986).
- Over the last 30 years APA efforts have also included a plethora of government relations. Major lobbying activity can be pegged to the initiation of the national health insurance debate. Since then countless pages of testimony and hours of discussion with key federal and state policy makers and related legislative efforts of advocacy for equality of reimbursement for the mentally ill have been logged.

• Peer review activities must today count as a major part of the APA's efforts to combat discriminatory coverage. Actually, psychiatry has been a leader among medical specialties in regard to peer review. In 1971 the Association established a task force on peer review that mapped out a collaborative program with both local and national components. Each District Branch proceeded to develop a peer review committee. The first edition of the *Manual of Psychiatric Peer Review* (1976), written in collaboration with the American Psychoanalytic Association and the American Academy of Child Psychiatry, was intended to provide "a set of guidelines for District Branches and their peer review committees which should be adapted and modified in terms of local criteria, standards, and practices."

In 1977, the APA signed a contract with the Civilian Health and Medical Program of the Uniformed Services (administered by the Department of Defense), which decided to apply peer review of its psychiatric benefits program on a national basis after pilot projects had shown the way. (A similar contract pertaining to psychologists' services was made between CHAMPUS and the American Psychological Association.) The contracts required the professional associations to establish a retrospective system of peer review for CHAMPUS claims for mental health benefits. Details included developing a set of review criteria and training CHAMPUS claims processors to appropriately handle mental care claims and case reviews.

As of 1983, the APA Office of Peer Review also had contracts with more than 20 commercial insurance carriers, Blue Cross-Blue Shield plans, and third-party administrators, including such industry giants as Prudential, Mutual of Omaha, and Aetna. The development of psychiatric peer review as an effective tool of cost accountability has proceeded apace, as will be discussed in Chapter 4.

GROWTH OF MENTAL HEALTH CARE

Writing in 1981, the economist McGuire observed that users of mental care services—traditionally designated as "patients"—had begun to behave more like "consumers" of the commodity called mental health services. The change of designation seems partly warranted as a brief recounting of the radical transformation of the past quarter century will show. The fundamental change was an attitudinal one, the according of legitimacy to the use of professional care for personal problems (Veroff et al. 1981).

The 1960s and 1970s were decades of tremendous growth for mental health services. The growth was fueled by ever-expanding public and private third-party financial resources. Substantial amounts of federal dollars were funneled through categorical support, especially community mental health center and training programs, and through third-party programs, especially Medicaid, or Title 19 of the Social Security Act (Appendix II-C). Not only did the number of patients seen in the general health and specialty mental health systems increase dramatically, but citizens of all socioeconomic backgrounds had access to new opportunities for services in an array of treatment and rehabilitation programs (Regier et al. 1978).

From 1955 to 1977 the number of inpatient and outpatient care episodes in specialty mental health facilities almost quadrupled, from 1.7 million to 6.4 million (Appendix II-A). After accounting for population growth, the patient care episode rate per 100,000 tripled in 1955-1977. (Patient care episodes are defined as the number of residents in inpatient facilities or patients on the rolls of non-inpatient facilities at the beginning of the year plus the total additions to these facilities during the year.) Total admissions during the year include new admissions, readmissions, and returns from long-term leave. Thus, patient care episodes count some individuals more than once, and do not count psychiatric care delivered in private office practice of psychiatrists and mental care professionals, general medical practice and clinics, and other settings such as neighborhood health centers, general hospital medical services, and nursing homes.

Part and parcel of the growth of sheer numbers was the shift in the settings in which care episodes occurred. Three-fourths of all patient care episodes in 1955 took place in inpatient settings. By 1977 this portion was down to one-fourth. Thus, even though the total number of patient care episodes increased by 40 percent, there was a proportional decline in inpatient episodes in state and county mental hospitals, where such episodes decreased from about half of all episodes in 1955 to only 9 percent in 1977. On the other hand, there was a ten-fold increase in patient care episodes occurring in outpatient settings, attributable in large measure to the federal funding of 788 community mental health centers from 1963 to 1977 (Witkin 1980).

Looking again at the inpatient sector, we see that the number of beds in state and county mental hospitals decreased by 70 percent in the period under review (although closings of such hospitals produced only a 2 percent decline in their number). The steep decline here was offset in some degree by the addition of psychiatric beds in other sector components, notably psychiatric units in general hospitals (some of which had separate units and some of which did not) and inpatient services of community mental health centers.

The number of mental health professionals also increased during these years, especially those trained as psychologists and social workers (up 300 percent) and psychiatrists (up 183 percent). NIMH training grants subsidized this growth (Appendix II-B). Fenton and colleagues, reporting on their study of trends in psychiatric practice 1965-1980, regarded the supply of practitioners, the economics of practice, and the structure of the service delivery system as major factors affecting trends in practice. Their study revealed a view of psychiatry in 1980 as "a profession that is far more diversified than it was 15 years ago. . . although office-based practice has remained the core activity. . ." (Fenton et al. 1984).

The emergence and expansion of a mental health system in our society depended on joint private and public financing—for example, federal "seed money" for community mental health centers and alcohol and drug treatment programs. Other major sources of funds included Medicaid, private health insurance, and federally subsidized insurance programs such as the FEHBP, or Federal Employees Health Benefits Program (Appendix II-C). Notwithstanding the positive features of this historic development, by the mid-1970s the upward trend in the cost of all health care became a focus of concern for both government and private funding sources.

The current era of retrenchment, even retreat, of financial support for psychiatric care should be viewed in the larger context of reaction to soaring health-care costs. The rationale for cost containment is compelling: As a share of the gross national product, health care expenditures between 1965 and 1982 increased from 6 percent to 10.3 percent (Appendix 11-C). Health care spending increased by a factor of six during this period. After adjusting for inflation, per capita spending for health care doubled. To what extent this growth represents an appropriate response to need and demand in contrast to representing inefficiency in the marketplace is an interesting but increasingly moot issue. The point is that irresistible cost-containment forces are at work and must be reckoned with in the decade of the 1980s.

Further, because the stigma of generations is not overcome in a few decades, it is not surprising that psychiatric care is more vulnerable to cost-containment tactics than the care of other medical specialties. Specifically, current patterns of insurance coverage for psychiatric care may be particularly vulnerable to cutbacks due to the prejudices against psychiatric medicine as compared to other medical specialties. Insurers and corporations are prepared to take more action to control costs in mental health than in other areas of health care, especially with regard to benefit design. The problems that insurers have covering mental disorders are discussed at length in later chapters.

CURRENT COVERAGE IN INDUSTRY

Data recently collected in studies supported by the APA reveal the current status of coverage of psychiatric disorders in plans enrolling many and diverse employment-related insurance groups. Employers are the source of most private insurance. In 1977, for example, 89 percent of the privately insured population under age 65 and 85 percent of the entirely privately insured population were enrolled in employment-related group plans. A survey conducted in 1977 by the National Center for Health Services Research showed that, of the 137.7 million persons under age 65 with any employment-related coverage, 77.8 percent were covered for outpatient psychiatric care: 7.7 percent had coverage identical to other outpatient physician benefits, and 69.9 percent had coverage that was discriminatory (Wilensky et al. 1983).

We will report here three studies performed by the APA directly or by others under APA contract. In the first category, Muszynski et al. (1983) surveyed health insurance benefits provided by a cross-section of major private sector employers. The 300 plans in the study sample covered, as of April 1983, a total of 33 million workers and dependents employed in such corporations as IBM, General Motors, and Exxon. A picture of benefit design emerged from this work.

All of the 300 plans provided some level of inpatient coverage for mental illness. Translating this coverage into numbers of employees revealed that 49 percent were protected for mental illness expenses on the same basis as any other illness, while the remaining 51 percent were covered at a reduced benefit level. Plans having the same benefits were most likely to be associated with a medium- to large-size employee group, to have an insured or self-insured financing arrangement, and to provide coverage under a comprehensive major medical arrangement. Plans having reduced benefits were most likely to be associated with small employee-group size, to be under Blue Cross-Blue Shield auspices, and to have coverage provided under a basic/major medical model (Appendix I-C).

With reference to outpatient benefits, 98 percent of the plans, enrolling more than 99 percent of the employees, had some coverage of outpatient expenses for mental illness treatment. However, only 10 percent of the plans provided benefits on the same basis as other covered conditions; 69 percent imposed a higher patient coinsurance than for other illness, 35 percent imposed maximum charges per visit, 29 percent imposed a maximum visit limitation, and some plans imposed two or more of these so-called inside limitations.

A similar benefit-design picture emerged from the two studies commissioned by the APA. One was an analysis of 1981 data gathered by the Bureau of Labor Statistics, U.S. Department of Labor, from 1,505 medium- and larger-size businesses employing 24 million full-time workers in eight major industry sectors. The investigators, Krizay and Brawn (1983), constructed a stratified sample of full-time employees so as to enable valid projections of the data to be made (Appendix I-A).

The study revealed the following features for inpatient care of mental illness. Virtually all employees in the establishments surveyed had some coverage. For 58 percent of the employees, the coverage was equal to the coverage for other illness: Commercial carriers insured about two-thirds of those with equal coverage, while Blue Cross plans accounted for 16-17 percent, self-insured plans for about 16 percent, and health maintenance organizations for only 0.3 percent. Fewer blue-collar workers than professional/administrative or technical/clerical workers had inpatient coverage. Among industry sectors, construction had a higher percentage of participants with equal coverage, followed by wholesale trade; at the low end was mining.

With reference to outpatient care, about 90 percent of all employees were covered for some treatment by psychiatrists, but over half the participants were in plans requiring 50 percent copayment by the patient and nearly two-thirds, including some of those with a 50 percent copayment requirement, were covered by plans with specific dollar maximums. Fewer blue-collar workers were covered for outpatient treatment by psychiatrists. Among industry sectors, the wholesale trade industry had the highest percentage of outpatient psychiatric treatment coverage, followed by the construction industry; the services industry was at the low end.

The final study on coverage to be reported here was a 1982 survey of the psychiatric benefits provided by 575 companies, 220 of which were industrial and the rest in the financial and service sectors (Appendix I-B). Of the 575 plans, 308 (54 percent) provided the same basis of room and board coverage for in-hospital psychiatric care under the basic plan for psychiatric as for other confinements, while 204 (35 percent) had the same basis of coverage but a separate maximum (most commonly, a 30-day limit); 36 (6 percent) had no coverage; and 27 (5 percent) had totally different coverage. Thirty-six percent of the plans provided coverage in a facility other than a hospital (Hay-Huggins Group 1983). Information on coverage of outpatient psychiatric care was reported by 720 major medical plans. The great majority—626, or 86 percent—were subject to the overall plan deductible and 20 (3 percent) were not subject to any deductible; 56, or 8 percent, did not cover outpatient psychiatric care. Seventy-one percent of the plans with outpatient psychiatric coverage had coinsurance different from the overall major medical coinsurance: In 405 plans (85 percent), the plan paid 50 percent of charges, while nine plans paid 60-70 percent of charges, 27 paid 75-80 percent, two paid 90-100 percent, and 22 paid another (unspecified) amount.

Forty percent of the 258 plans had a dollar limit on eligible charges for each visit: A surprisingly high 26 percent of the plans had a limit of $20 before application of coinsurance; 15 percent had a limit of $21-$29;

14 percent had a limit of $30; and 19 percent had a limit of $31-$49 per visit. Few plans limited the maximum number of visits; those with a maximum usually limited visits to one per week.

The Changed Political Climate

In 1984 it takes those with a long memory to recall the optimistic prospects for passage of national health insurance that flourished a decade ago (Upton 1983). In 1974 there were in the congressional hopper no fewer than 12 major proposals. These ranged in scope from the American Medical Association's "Medicredit," a voluntary plan with tax credits provided against individual income taxes to offset the cost of private health insurance, to the Health Security bill (sponsored in the Senate by Edward M. Kennedy), setting up a compulsory plan financed by a payroll tax and general federal revenues, to be administered by the federal government and to cover the entire range of personal health care services with no coinsurance or deductibles. In any event, however, the galloping inflation of health care costs came increasingly to preoccupy policy makers, crowding out favorable views of a program likely to increase demand and exacerbate inflationary pressures.

Health care has been (and continues to be) one of the most inflationary components of the Gross National Product. In every year for the past 25 years the rate of rise in its price outstripped that of the composite Consumer Price Index. One consequence was that, compared to 1965, in 1981 the country as a whole was allocating nearly 60 percent more of its resources to health care.

Businesses, which underwrite a great deal of health care costs, moved from a relatively permissive to a critical posture in response to the rising costs they were incurring. Businesses today are increasingly involved in local decision-making about health care (Pelletier 1984). The growing involvement of business is significant, for company representatives thereby are able to play a major role in restructuring employee health-benefit packages to assure coverage for lower-cost treatment alternatives and to require appropriate levels of cost sharing. Indeed, given the potential for change of business activities, some wonder whether business will be the next "regulator" of U.S. health care.

In the 1980 presidential election the national political consensus made an about-face. In the health care arena, both public and private policy makers today focus on ways to achieve cost containment. There are efforts to make providers and consumers more conscious of prices in the health care market because, as Sharfstein and Beigel have pointed out (in press), "one culprit in the rapid rise of medical care costs has been the almost total insulation consumers have felt from the escalating prices of modern medicine." As private insurance and such federal programs as Medicare lowered or eliminated financial barriers to care, they provided an incentive to greater utilization. The rising level of expenditures and resulting increases in premiums and budget allocations prompted first private insurers, then the Medicaid program to attempt to contain costs by increasing out-of-pocket payments by consumers.

Recent developments in the FEHBP are illustrative. In 1981 the Blue Cross-Blue Shield plan, the largest participating insurer, changed the copayment under its high-option from 80 percent paid by the plan to 70 percent. In 1982, it went much further and decreased the number of physician visits a year from unlimited to 50 for all purposes. At the same time, basic hospital benefits for treatment of mental illness were reduced from 365 to 60 days per year. (In 1984 the outpatient mental benefit was increased slightly: 50 outpatient visits are now permitted for treatment of mental disorders in addition to outpatient visits for other conditions.) In 1982, 13 of the 17 employee-organization plans in the FEHBP also reduced their mental benefits; in many instances, the copayment for office visits was decreased from 75-80 percent to 50 percent. In addition, about half of the health maintenance organizations (HMOs) in the program, which already had quite limited mental illness coverage, further reduced their benefits (APA 1982).

Along with recent cutbacks, "pro-competitive" legislative proposals have appeared. Encompassing a variety of approaches, they all aim to make providers and consumers more cost-conscious about health care purchases (Wilensky et al. 1983). The most direct approach mandates cost sharing. Another approach requires employers to offer choices to their employees in order to allow employees who prefer less coverage and/or more cost sharing the opportunity to purchase such "bargain-basement" plans. However, according to Wilensky et al., about 80 percent of individuals with employment-related health insurance were offered no choice among different packages.

There are dangers to psychiatry and mental patients in each of these approaches. For example, "capping" tax benefits would encourage employees to buy less comprehensive coverage. Since coverage for mental disorders has traditionally been utilized by only a small percentage of covered populations, and often only for catastrophic situations, it is a likely target for cutback. Further, since much mental coverage, especially for outpatient care, is a fairly recent development, such coverage could be reduced in a medical corollary to the rule of industrial employment, "last hired, first fired" (Sharfstein et a1. 1983a).

CHALLENGES FOR THE 1980S

The amount and quality of data on insurance coverage of mental disorders has vastly increased since 1972, the year of the APA's last major book on the subject. Psychiatrists must interpret this knowledge base in the light of the changed political and economic scene. As noted above, there is an historical discontinuity in current events in that market and government forces now threaten deterioration—rather than support improvement—of prevailing patterns of coverage of psychiatric care. It is no longer appropriate to assume further growth and expansion. Instead, what is required today is a limited, clear, economic, and soundly based agenda that aims to make the full range of psychiatric treatment an integral part of private and public third-party programs.

The psychiatric profession must show that care for mental illness under insurance is marketable—that is, that consumer demand makes this coverage not a frill but a necessity. Psychiatrists must make some hard choices as they promote nondiscriminatory coverage for treatment of mental disorders. Their capacity to hold colleagues accountable for the quality and cost effectiveness of treatment through peer review programs and other mechanisms, along with their willingness to contribute to the definition of "packages and products" of psychiatric treatment, will determine the future of the profession and the opportunity of the mentally ill to receive quality care.

There is a need to counter new versions of the old myths about the nature of mental illness and its treatment. At the symposium on insurance at the 1957 APA annual meeting, Albert Whitehall, associate director for health insurance of the Life Insurance Association of America, raised the questions of moment. After commenting that insurers felt that a lack of precise information in relation to treatment for mental illness was the key impediment to broadened coverage, he challenged the profession to work on these questions: "What is mental illness, its nature and causes? What are the various forms of treating it? What are the incidence and duration of utilization of services? What will be the future trends in the incidence of mental illness, its treatment, and rates of recovery?"

Whitehall's questions are as much of the moment today as they were 27 years ago. Psychiatry is being challenged anew to specify what treatments and what kinds of patients should be eligible for third-party reimbursement of treatment costs and to assist insurers to calculate the probable use and cost of variously designed benefit packages.

There are old issues and there are new issues. The growth in number of for-profit psychiatric hospitals, many of them operated by investor-owned multihospital chains, has raised questions of potential conflict of interest between profit considerations and optimal patient care (Levenson 1982). The increase in number of nonpsychiatrist mental health care providers and the development of a mini-industry of mental wellness has caused some to question the medical necessity and appropriateness of all services delivered outside the hospital. The diversity of services being offered contributes to public policy confusion and third-party disgruntlement over instituting or continuing reimbursement.

Further, the pro-competitive and consumer-choice benefit models being offered have generated problems of "adverse selection," a kind of skimming of customers for health insurance that puts great pressure on all carriers to match or better the products of competitors (Sharfstein et al. 1982). Such models create incentives for trading on the consumers' denial of their possible need for psychiatric coverage, encouraging them to opt for more popular needs such as dental and vision care, which are of greater general public interest and demand.

To approach these issues in a systematic manner, psychiatrists must underscore the predictability of utilization patterns. They must remind purchasers of insurance and public policy makers of the "offset effect"—that providing an appropriate package of psychiatric benefits tends to reduce a population's use of general medical services. They must state with clarity and precision the proper role of third-party reimbursement in the financing of psychiatric care, i.e., what should and should not be covered.

The issues will be taken up in turn in the chapters to follow. The next three chapters are meant to be an antidote to arbitrary cost-containment tactics affecting health insurance and psychiatric care. Chapter 5 deals with issues of equity that emerge in the wake of the case for adequate coverage. Emergent trends in the field are described in Chapter 6—diagnostic-related groups systems, preferred provider organizations, and other signs of "pro-competition." The last chapter outlines an action agenda for the future with consideration to such matters of special concern as coverage of intensive psychotherapy, including psychoanalysis, and long-term hospitalization in an era of cost containment.

CHAPTER 2

Insurance Underwriting and Psychiatric Practice

From the insurers' point of view, coverage for mental disorders presents difficulties under the three general headings of predictability, effectiveness, and accountability of costs. Many of the issues arise from the absence of universally accepted definitions of the nature and treatment of mental disorders. Addressing psychiatrists, Aetna's Medical Director wrote: "Good criteria must be developed to assist the carrier in evaluating diagnoses and treatment. . . . We need your help in differentiating between those who have mental disorders and those who simply have problems" (Guillette 1977).

A broken leg presents clearly defined conditions of disorder and treatment; a "broken mind" raises a host of questions about observable disease, necessary and appropriate treatment, reliable prognosis. In the long run, attainment of adequate health insurance for psychiatric care depends on breakthroughs in research that expand basic knowledge of mental health and illness. In the near term, reasoned argument based on the best available data can counter arbitrary cutbacks prompted by today's cost-containment imperatives and prevailing myths about mental illness and its treatments. An understanding of the principles of health insurance is the foundation.

Principles of Insurance

Insurance is an arrangement for transferring and distributing risk. It is an arrangement under which one party, an insurer, contracts to do something of value to another party, an insured or beneficiary, upon the occurrence of a specified harmful contingency. Insurance allows the individual insured to pay a small, definite cost, a premium, for protection against paying for a large loss which might occur. The arrangement enables the fortunate many who escape loss to compensate the unfortunate few who suffer loss. Because insurance assuages anxiety about potential loss, it provides the insured both pre- and post-loss utility.

A successful insurance plan is a business like any other in that it must balance income (premiums) and expenditures (payment of beneficiary claims plus the cost of doing business). Among the criteria for success which any plan must meet, the following key principles, which apply to health insurance plans, are of special interest (Mehr et al. 1976).

- A large group of similar individuals exposed to the same peril must be involved. If individuals are too few or too dissimilar, calculation of probabilities will be undependable, and the difference between loss experienced and loss expected will be great. The plan will fail if the deviation from the expected loss is so large that it cannot be offset by a reasonable addition to the premium.
- The loss produced by the peril must be definable and definite as to its beginning and conclusion so that the coverage may be precisely defined. If mental disorders are covered, precise definitions of the type of disorder, the point of onset, and the form of treatment are necessary, as are reliable prognoses.
- Both the likelihood of occurrence and the likely extent of loss must be calculable. For coverage of mental disorders, reliable data are needed on the incidence of illness, the duration of care, and the costs of care on both a per unit of care and a per case basis. If data on the chance of loss are very unreliable, the degree of accuracy of predicting loss will be low in spite of a large number of plan enrollees. If data on duration and costs of care are not reliable, the degree of accuracy of setting premiums will be compromised.
- The occurrence of loss to each plan enrollee must be accidental or fortuitous; it must be beyond the individual's control.

At the heart of the insurance business is the underwriting function, which includes the selection and classification of risks (i.e., prospective insureds), the fixing of contract terms, and the determination of premiums. Underwriters must make sure that the group insured has the same probability of loss and probable amount of loss as the universe on which premium rates are based. In social insurance (such as Social Security disability), there is no underwriting function as such; instead, the coverage and eligibility provisions of social insurance laws serve a roughly parallel purpose of balancing income and expenditure.

Premium rates are based on calculations of expected loss, which yield estimates containing a degree of uncertainty (underwriting is not an exact science). Risks are classified into groups with about the same expectation of loss. Potential insureds classified as high risks or as incalculable risks make up a group likely to be considered uninsurable at a reasonable, or marketable, premium rate. The remaining risks may be classified into, e.g., medium-risk and low-risk groups and premium rates set accordingly.

Among the factors considered by underwriters are the hazards, or loss-producing propensities, associated with a given exposure. Health insurance losses are particularly subject to the influence of the insured; dishonesty, carelessness, and lack of perspicacity or judgment on the part of the insured are elements of the associated hazard. Insurers refer to this as "moral hazard", thus denoting the intangible loss-producing propensities of the insured per se. (Insurers also recognize categories of physical and legal hazard.)

On the open market, underwriters also weigh and choose the best options for preventing the occurrence of an insurance plan calamity known as "adverse selection"—i.e., that plan is selected by those most likely to claim benefits while individuals less likely to utilize benefits choose another plan. The die may be fatally cast the first time a plan is obliged to raise its premiums: Individuals who perceive themselves at low risk for the covered loss switch out of the plan and leave an even greater proportion of high utilizers. Such a plan will soon become uneconomical and fail. The avoidance of adverse selection is assured in part by the underwriting function and in part by policy provisions which limit coverage or benefits. The latter, referred to as underwriting through the policy, is considered an inferior technique.

Lastly, the premium rate set by underwriters must be adequate, reasonable, and equitable. Adequacy requires that it be sufficient to cover the cost of claims plus the cost of doing business, including a profit sufficient to attract capital into the industry. To be reasonable means to be in line with competitors' rates. Equity from the insurers' point of view (in contrast to the point of view taken in Chapter 5) requires that each insured pay a rate which reflects the probability of occurrence and the probable severity of loss to which he or she is subject.

Practices of Psychiatry

The essence of the feasibility of insurance as a means of financing care for illness is the capacity of physicians to represent their treatments as medically necessary and appropriate. Although psychiatrists are able to comply with this dictum to a considerable extent, the medical model of mental illness breaks down at significant points, and underwriters often find psychiatrists' answers to their questions about the illnesses treated, the treatments utilized, the scope and duration of services insufficient.

Compounding these uncertainties are cultural stereotypes of the psychiatric patient as one who is likely to be seeking care for self-fulfillment purposes or for problems in living rather than for serious, incapacitating illness. The stereotypes are belied by the actual experience of clinical psychiatrists in the United States, according to a recent survey of their opinion on matters concerning insurance. More than 90 percent of the psychiatrists responded that seldom or never do they see patients who are primarily seeking self-improvement. In response to a related question, one comment captured the consensus opinion: "The theory that people seek psychiatric treatment because it's there is baloney. You can't drag most people who need psychiatric treatment into the office" (Psychiatric Viewpoints Report 1983). This is in keeping with the results of the systematic survey of private office practice which found that most patients of psychoanalysts had moderate to severe functional impairment; the nonanalysts' caseload showed a similar range of functional impairment except for a higher proportion of the more severely ill under treatment (Marmor et al. 1975).

Psychiatric services differ significantly from general medical services in that a higher proportion of overall costs is paid by the public sector, chiefly state and local governments. Almost two-thirds of all mental care costs are paid by this sector, compared with less than one-third for all other health care. Public mental institutions and the custodial care associated with them have fixed an ugly image in the public eye. Despite the progress of recent decades, many people still believe that serious mental illness is incurable and its treatment a waste of the public and private resources of society. This view is not unrelated to the fact that much mental illness, especially the most severe pathologies, strikes individuals in the bottom socioeconomic classes (Sharfstein 1978).

Thus, at one extreme, insurers are wary of covering mental disorders because of the large scope for moral hazard: Individuals may bring mental disorder upon themselves, including a perceived need for so-called self-actualization. At the other extreme, insurers fear the potential for supporting thousands of "incurables" languishing in publicly supported custodial care. Persuasive data are needed to dispel these myths; the task still awaits action by the psychiatric profession.

Further, the health insurance industry is a competitive one in which consumer demand is a key factor. Major purchasers of health insurance look at insurers' offerings with an eye to attracting the greatest enrollment of individuals in their group. The features offered in the benefit package must appeal to the ultimate consumer as necessary, sufficient, and reasonably priced. The important role played by consumer demand is spotlighted in these remarks by the senior director of program development for Blue Cross-Blue Shield of Chicago (Raichel 1981):

> Some mental health benefit programs have been reduced by accounts either as one way to reduce overall costs or to find monies for new coverages of greater preference. Benefits for outpatient psychotherapy

> appear particularly vulnerable. We sense that some accounts believe that much of the utilization is for non-essential, high-cost services. . . . These benefits are also viewed as disproportionately expensive given the size of the utilizing population compared to the size of populations using benefits for, as examples, dental or vision care. . . . The decision [to cut back mental benefits] is determined by observations of [employee] preferences expressed by enrollment trends under competing options with varied features and [by] some direct market research.

No matter which way the issues of coverage for mental disorders emerge into concrete problems, they stem from the same roots—the lack of precision and specificity with respect to diagnosis, treatment, and prognosis of illness, and the related absence of an epidemiology of mental disorders.

We have noted that satisfactory resolution of these issues depends in the long run on the discovery of fundamental knowledge. The gradual accretion of data and revelation of fresh perspectives which are part of the discovery process may also yield significant progress. An example may be the third edition of the *Diagnostic and Statistical Manual of Mental Disorders,* a thorough-going effort by the APA to update the core clinical knowledge base as of 1980. Time will tell whether the *DSM-III* will make an impact on insurance issues. To the extent the manual is sufficiently precise to produce measurably greater reliability and validity of diagnoses and clinical courses, and sufficiently consensual to lead into a more definable epidemiology, substantial gains will accrue to the case for better coverage for mental disorders (Sharfstein 1983). Another example may be the monographs currently being developed by the APA Task Force on Psychiatric Treatments (Klerman 1983).

Meanwhile, research findings on other aspects of these issues are at hand and can be marshalled to hold the line against current forces of cost containment, which often use "myth-information" to achieve cuts in psychiatric coverage. The next chapter presents the results of numerous studies which affirm both the stability (hence, the predictability) of the costs of psychiatric care to third-party payers and the effectiveness of those expenditures.

CHAPTER 3

Cost Stability and Cost Effectiveness: The Accumulating Evidence

Special restrictions on third-party payment for psychiatric care have been justified on the grounds that the costs of treatment are uncontrollable and therefore unpredictable. In addition, it is claimed that evidence for the effectiveness of psychiatric treatment is scanty and inconclusive. In this chapter we will review the mounting evidence on both of these issues—evidence which, while perhaps not as conclusive as one would like, compares favorably with that in the rest of medicine.

How Is Cost Determined?

The cost of care for a given illness is the complex outcome of many factors. These include the structure of third-party benefits, unit costs to deliver a service, the number of individuals at risk for the disorder, the price responsiveness of particular treatments, medical definitions of necessity and appropriateness, and the supply of practitioners and institutions that deliver the care. The multiplicity of factors that go into the cost formula results in wide variation in the cost of treating mental disorders under different insurance plans. Variation of cost is true for other medical disorders as well as for psychiatric disorders. The cost of an appendectomy, for example, varies from one geographic region of the United States to another by as much as ten-fold.

Malpractice concerns are another input to professional judgment. The practice of so-called defensive medicine may involve the prescription of costly treatment because of the physician's knowledge of the possibility, however small in statistical terms, of an untoward clinical outcome following the prescription of less costly alternatives.

That the recipient of medical care, the patient, is a poorly informed consumer also affects the cost complex. Indeed, in economic terms, the fee-for-service system creates an inherent conflict of interest for the physician. The physician is a supplier of goods and services who is also able to determine the demand for these goods and services. By virtue of their special knowledge and the authority vested in them by the patient, fee-for-service physicians are empowered to make decisions to use medical services that they themselves provide and then are paid for on a piece-work basis. As George Bernard Shaw wrote in the "Preface on Doctors" to his play *The Doctor's Dilemma:*

> It is not the fault of our doctors that the medical service of the community as presently provided for is a murderous absurdity. That any sane nation having observed that you could provide for the supply of bread by giving bakers a pecuniary interest in baking for you should go on to give a surgeon a pecuniary interest in cutting off your leg is enough to make one despair of political humanity. But that is precisely what we have done. And the more appalling the mutilation the more the mutilator is paid.*

Two factors mitigate this conflict of interest. By far the more important one is the physician's ethical obligation to hold the patient's welfare paramount. The other is the physician's full disclosure of likely consequences to obtain the patient's informed consent to treatment. It is obvious that, given the technical nature of medical treatment and the potency of the doctor-patient relationship, the patient is disposed to accede to professional judgment.

Hence, professional judgment is at the core of the cost formula, and it is here that cost-containment pressures are being brought to bear. Today there is mounting pressure to make cost per se a foremost factor in treatment decisions. Such pressures do not absolve the physician or other provider from the ethical obligation to prescribe care primarily on the basis of the patient's clinical need. Moreover, if a physician goes against his or her clinical judgment to hospitalize a depressed patient because of economic barriers, a suicide attempt could land that individual in the intensive care unit for many days and result in a prolonged hospital stay generating monumental costs to the individual, the family, the third party payer, and society.

Having noted the potentially pernicious effect of current cost-containment pressures, it is necessary to reassert that physicians do weigh, and always have, the financing factor in their judgment process. It is a question of priority, and there is no doubt that the large-scale emergence of third-party payment into the cost complex has changed the weight of the financing factor.

---

*Quoted in The Future of Medical Practice by Arnold S. Relman, *Health Affairs* 2:15-19, 1983.

Indeed, a case can be made that the most salient changes in medical practice since World War II can be traced to the spread of health insurance, now protecting in some degree nearly 90 percent of the population. How? The answer is that third-party financing has created incentives for the introduction of procedures—which are neat, discrete, rational but partial, eminently satisfactory units for the purposes of accounting. The system reimburses resources expended in objective procedures and tests far more readily than those spent in the more artful practices of listening, examining, counseling, and providing verbal interventions with patients. This has been especially noticeable in the last decade in the proliferation of technically sophisticated biomedical procedures.

The spread of reimbursement by third parties has also changed the behavior of patients. With financial barriers to care lowered, patients can virtually ignore the price of care. They become claimants for services to which they feel entitled because they have paid their insurance premiums. Insured against any large out-of-pocket expense, patients often expect doctors to order up a smorgasbord of "already paid-for" diagnostic and treatment procedures. And physicians—aware on the one hand that the costs which the patient will incur are covered by insurance and, on the other hand, desirous of more information about the patient's condition—often comply with the expectation. It is such changed circumstances as these that cause health-care costs to balloon ever higher.

An example in which insurance has affected medical practice is coverage that reimburses only for inpatient care, a limitation that applies to psychiatric more than to other illness. People get a certain kind of care in certain settings depending on whether they have economic protection; the optimal environment is not necessarily the one selected. For example, although a psychiatrist may think that a patient's clinical needs could best be met in an outpatient setting, the physician may recommend hospitalization because only care in that setting is covered by the patient's insurance. Such is the case with Medicare. A survey of clinical psychiatrists in the U.S., asking whether day hospitalization covered by insurance would be a useful alternative to full hospitalization, found that nearly 90 percent of the clinicians agreed (Psychiatric Viewpoints Report 1983). On the other side of this coin are public policy decisions favoring deinstitutionalization, often made so that the care of patients can be shifted from state-supported facilities such as mental hospitals to community settings, where the bulk of support is provided by the federal government through the Social Security system.

The public policy decision to encourage the operation of competitive, or market, forces is an attempt to re-introduce consumer choice and provider cost consciousness into the health-care system. Policy makers must remember, however, that there is always a complex interweaving of clinical and economic concerns in any treatment recommendation. There is also the issue of the allocation of expensive health-care resources across socioeconomic groups, which will be taken up in a later chapter. Again, the shift may occur without regard to clinical needs or the adequacy of community resources (Steering Committee 1981).

RELATIONSHIP OF DEMAND AND COST SHARING

A major source of controversy in the debate about providing third-party payment for psychiatric care, especially outpatient care, is the presumed instability of costs over time. This is based on the idea that the demand for mental care is more responsive to the presence of third-party payers than is general medical care. What is implied is that mental care is more discretionary, or elective, than general medical care and perhaps more subject to excessive utilization when someone else pays the bill.

In fact, definitions of patients (versus clients) and reimbursable providers (M.D.s versus non-M.D.s) are closely related to the issues of demand for care and medical necessity. If demand depends significantly on price, the moral hazard inherent in health insurance increases (Sharfstein 1982). If mental health care is self-actualization or education, the medical and health insurance models are compromised. These possibilities worry the insurance actuary and administrator, and restrictions such as higher copayments and deductibles or limits on number of visits are the tactics they use to protect the viability of plans covering mental disorders.

In an econometric study of private office practice, McGuire concluded that the demand for psychotherapy was about twice as responsive to price as the demand for other physicians' office services (1981). Frank found even greater price responsiveness in a time series and cross-sectional study of the 50 states (1981b). Such reports have bolstered the presumption that the use of outpatient psychiatric care is more responsive to cost sharing than the use of other medical services. However, the most important study to date, recently completed by the Rand Corporation, sheds new light on the question.

THE RAND STUDY

In 1971 the Rand Corporation began a health insurance study that enrolled some 2,700 families, or 7,500 persons, at six sites across the country in 14 different insurance plans having copayments ranging from zero ("free care") to 95 percent. The families were assigned randomly to the different plans; this tactic prevented adverse selection, in which plans are adversely affected by being selected because they offer the best coverage for the medical or mental disorders from which enrollees suffer or for which enrollees expect to be treated.

All plans had a "stop loss" feature, a maximum dollar expenditure (MDE) of $1,000 per family. A 52-visit annual limit was imposed on ambulatory mental health care. It should also be noted that the study population excluded the elderly, military families, those incarcerated in penal or mental institutions, and families with incomes in the top 7 percent nationally. As part of the project, Rand studied ambulatory mental health expenditures under a contract with the National Institute of Mental Health.

The main finding of the first report on the study was that "the percentage response of ambulatory mental health care expense to cost sharing . . . is *roughly* [their emphasis] the same as that for ambulatory medical health care expense" (Wells et al. 1982). Reducing the portion of the cost that the patients paid for outpatient mental health services was found to be accompanied by an increase in use—but that increase was no greater than for other medical care. To the report authors, the findings implied "a similarity in insurance treatment," although other considerations may be introduced in the design of health insurance coverage. Further, it was found that expenditures for mental health care services constituted only about 5 percent of the total health care costs for all insurance plan enrollees.

In an unpublished analysis of the Rand data, Ellis and McGuire argued that the Rand investigators misinterpreted the data (1983). The problem, these economists said, was centered on the influential but disregarded role played by the annual limit on out-of-pocket expenses, or the MDE. The economists thought that one effect of the MDE might make invalid comparisons of use among different plans and thereby "give a misleadingly low estimate of the actual responsiveness to cost-sharing."

Looking at the second year, Wells et al. found that when families had to pay for 95 percent of all their health services (up to the MDE), their outpatient mental care expenses were about half of those of families with free care. They held that this was roughly similar to the general medical expenditures in the 95 percent plan, which were about one-third of the total expenditures in the free plan.

From this they determined essentially that people use extra psychiatric care at about the same rate as extra medical care when they have insurance. But for this to hold true, Ellis and McGuire said, overall expenditures ought to drop steadily as the percentage of costs borne by the individual rises. This did not happen. Wells et al. found, however, that families in a plan with 50 percent coinsurance for both medical and mental benefits used only 13 percent of their benefits for mental care, as did families with free care, far less than those under 95 percent coinsurance.

The economists argued that a family paying nearly all their medical bills by themselves (the 95 percent coinsurance group) was more likely to reach the MDE quickly during a covered year, after which their care was fully covered. They contended that at that point there was little difference between the free care and the 95 percent coinsurance plan and the two should not be compared as they were. Instead, they argued, the effect of cost-sharing would be better assessed by comparing the behavior of consumers with free care to those with 50 percent copayment. And this comparison showed that demand for outpatient mental health care is "highly responsive to cost-sharing" and more responsive than demand for other ambulatory care.

The principal author of the report on the Rand study, the psychiatrist Kenneth B. Wells, acknowledged that in the 50/50 plan the response to medical and mental health insurance was "meaningfully different" from other coinsurance plans. He pointed out, however, that this was a statistical anomaly because a majority of people in the plan resided in Dayton, Ohio, where people tend to visit less expensive general practitioners rather than specialists and thus to spend far less on mental care (Appendix III-G). Moreover, Wells pointed to data from another plan with 50 percent coinsurance for mental care (and 25 percent for medical). He noted that subjects covered by this plan, who were well represented in all non-Dayton sites, responded to the drop in coinsurance of these services at about the same rate as they responded to the decreased cost-sharing for available medical services in the 50 percent coinsurance plan.

"We agree there probably is an MDE effect," Wells commented, adding that Rand will be analyzing its extent. But he said that "such an analysis would not alter the overall impression of the similar response to demand for ambulatory medical and mental health services in the Rand study plans where the upper limit applies to all health services. The probably more important and undisputed conclusion of the study is that even with free care for 52 outpatient psychotherapy sessions, expenses for mental services are only a small proportion—about 5 percent—of total health expenses."

Wells attributed part of the disagreement to the quite different claims experiences of private health insurers. But this high demand for mental services under generous coverage he explained as due to adverse selection. Because families who enrolled in the Rand study were assigned to plans, its conclusions apply only "when insurance coverage for ambulatory mental health services is broadly available to a general population."

Other findings of the Rand study are noteworthy. The researchers found both the use of services by different socioeconomic groups and the choice of type of provider for mental care to be little influenced by the various cost-sharing plans. Nearly equal proportions of enrollees sought care from formal providers (psychiatrists and psychologists) and informal providers (general practitioners and internists). Formal providers cost much more—a median of $280 vs $14 per person. With respect to geographic variation, patients in Seattle and Massachusetts were more likely to see psychiatrists and psychologists, while those in Dayton and South Carolina turned more to general practitioners and internists. The choice of type of provider was influenced by education. The more highly educated enrollees tended to prefer psychiatrists and psychologists (Appendix III-G).

Between 7.1 and 9.6 percent of the population studied used mental benefits; this utilization calculation embraces visits to general practitioners and internists whenever a psychotropic medication or a "mental health reason" was involved in the visit. Only a very small percentage of individuals (0.4) saw clinicians more than 40 times a year and an even smaller number (0.2 percent) reached the annual limit of 52 sessions. Individuals who on the basis of an independent survey had poor mental and physical health were the highest users and tended to seek more services.

In sum, the Rand study is the most ambitious effort to date and deserves to be influential in policy-making forums. Despite the limited applicability of its findings on account of the special features discussed above and the fact that findings reflected changes in demand but not in supply, the Rand study underscores the stability over time of costs for mental care under insurance.

Other Studies of Utilization and Cost

Under contract with the American Psychiatric Association, Frank and McGuire (1983) reviewed more than 40 studies made over the past 25 years on demand and utilization (Appendix VII-C). Not unexpectedly, psychiatric care episodes were found to involve many dimensions that have an impact on costs, such as benefit limitations on inpatient or outpatient care. Indeed, the review pointed up the importance of so-called structural effects, or benefit variables, on utilization patterns. Thus, prepaid group practice plans—most of which have a 20-visit outpatient limit—tended to cluster around the lower end of the utilization experience, while fee-for-service insurance systems experienced utilization two to three times as great.

The review also confirmed that use depends on the demographic characteristics of the patients, especially education, age, and sex, and on the supply of providers, reflecting the all-important geographic factor. The fact that utilization statistics varied widely was no surprise, given all the variables. What was especially interesting, however, was that trends within any single plan clearly indicated that costs were stable and predictable over time.

In another study, supported by the National Institute of Mental Health, the demand elasticity for mental care compared to general health care was considered to be very similar. The investigators concluded that "the elasticity estimates for each mode of mental health care produced by this study are no more divergent than are the various elasticity estimates that have been produced in the literature on health care in general" (Rafferty et al. 1983).

Analysis of one important data base suggests that, within a covered population and within defined geographic areas, after the introduction of a generous benefit or the expansion of a benefit there is a brief increase, then a leveling out of costs over time. This was the case with the Blue Cross-Blue Shield high-option plan for federal employees. In the years 1967-1970, benefits were expanded to a level comparable to general medical benefits, and there were no arbitrary limitations on outpatient visits or days of hospitalization. The stability of costs, after adjustment for inflation, in the decade of 1971-1980 is evident (Graph 3-A, Appendix IV-A). Even if one focuses on coverage of intensive psychotherapy, stability of costs is the rule. A study of intensive psychotherapy utilization by enrollees during 1971-1973 in Washington, D.C., Ohio, California, and the nation as a whole demonstrated the basic stability and predictability of those costs (Sharfstein et al. 1975). Also, only a limited number of enrollees availed themselves of this treatment.

The economist John Krizay has done some studies that also suggest that costs level out over time, or show a "plateau effect." In one (1982), he analyzed the experiences of the two largest participants in the Federal Employees Health Benefits Program, Blue Cross-Blue Shield and Aetna, on a state-by-state basis and translated these data into per capita utilization rates and costs in constant dollars (Appendix III-A). Within each state utilization rates did not change much over the years 1976-1979, and the rank ordering among states by rate of utilization was quite similar for both plans. Nationally, annual benefit costs per covered person under Blue Cross-Blue Shield varied less than $.76 from the mean annual benefit cost, after correcting for inflation. Aetna's experience produced wider variation over the four-year period, but over the last three years the variation was less than $2.50 from the mean annual benefit per covered person. State-by-state experience was also consistent during the four years: States with high utilization rates had those rates over the entire period and those with low utilization rates had low rates over the same period.

Krizay also noted consistency from state to state in the percentage of total enrollees who received psychiatric benefits under these plans. Generally the figure was around 1.5 percent of total enrollment; in only a few states did the percentage of beneficiaries exceed 2 percent of total enrollment. He concluded: "Clearly, availability of insurance financing does not entice an excessive number of people to seek psychiatric treatment."

Another of Krizay's studies (1980) reflected the experience of federal employees enrolled in eight different plans, covering approximately two-thirds of all federal employees, during the period 1973-1978. Looked at separately, each plan showed substantial differences in year-to-year fluctuations in per capita charges, even in constant dollars. But when the total charges per capita of the eight plans were combined, the year-to-year changes flattened out to almost nothing (with the exception of charges recorded for 1975-1976). The standard deviation from the mean annual average per capita cost was only $1.73, or less than 7 percent of the mean. It should be noted, however, that Frank and McGuire doubt that the constancy of psychiatric charges should be interpreted as a leveling-off in demand because other factors were changing during the 1973-1978 period to hold back utilization (1983).

A preliminary review of CHAMPUS utilization data 1980-1983 suggests a similar experience. Two-year data do not constitute a trend, but the experience per capita covered charges of $21.81 in 1980 and $22.83 in 1981 is remarkably similar. Regardless, CHAMPUS utilization measured both by cost per capita and number of users compares favorably with any other known experience where liberal or even moderately restricted coverage is part of the health plan (Frank et al. 1983).

Stability and Predictability—A Comment

Common myths about mental illness include notions about the ubiquity of such illness and the optional or even recreational nature of treatment. If everyone is sick and treatments are fun, then costs can go through the roof when someone else is paying the bill. But the evidence from empirical cost studies is exactly the opposite. Far from being unpredictable and unstable over time, within any given system of third-party payment and geographical area, the demand and costs can be projected with an accuracy similar to that for general medical care. In fact, an actuarial model can be constructed that will predict expected utilization and benefit claims and allow premiums to be computed with a satisfactory degree of confidence (Appendix VII-B).

The issue, then, is not one of breaking the bank, or uncontrollable costs. The issue is accurately predicting expected costs, instituting various accountability mechanisms such as claims and peer review when those expectations are exceeded, and then making choices about the quality and quantity of treatment for the suffering that is mental illness. The extent of psychiatric benefits under third-party payment programs reflects in large part an ethical decision. Willingness to pay the price of treatment, the value of treatment, and the value of the people being treated are all elements in this decision. If we as a society are not willing to pay the price, the mentally ill do not go away. The issue then becomes what we are willing to settle for as options for care as barriers to treatment become insurmountable.

COST BENEFIT AND COST EFFECTIVENESS

The predictability and stability over time of mental treatment costs are a necessary but not sufficient argument for more equitable third-party financing of psychiatric care. The continuing growth of medical care expenditures has made evidence of cost effectiveness essential. Private and public third-party payers are requesting cost-benefit and cost-effectiveness analyses to assist them in reimbursement decisions (Technology and Health Care et al. 1979). The American Medical Association's recent effort to promote cost effectiveness in hospitals and office practices was one response to this request (American Medical Association 1983a).

Further, because consumers rarely know what care they should buy and must rely on providers for guidance, it has always been true that a strictly market approach to allocating health-care resources does not work; a mixed approach has been used. Now there is a call to employ analyses of cost benefit and cost effectiveness in resource-allocation decisions.

Psychiatrists can respond affirmatively to the call for these analyses, which can enhance the climate of trust with regard to the usefulness of psychiatric treatment. Part of the case for cost effectiveness of the overall medical care enterprise is the so-called medical cost offset. As will be seen, the data here document the critical importance of psychiatric care, especially psychotherapy.

SOME DEFINITIONS

Cost-benefit analysis (CBA) is a technique to evaluate the social costs and benefits of different investment strategies. The method attempts to compute all the costs and benefits in monetary terms. Its purpose is to provide input to a decision about the allocation of scarce resources within a given time frame. Hence, on the basis of CBA, programs with the highest ratios of benefits to costs are the prime candidates for potential funding or continuing investment. Theoretically, those with the lowest ratios would not be undertaken.

CBA can be applied to a particular health problem or disease; for example, it could be used to select priorities among treatment programs. In the health arena, however, there are obvious difficulties in measuring all relevant costs and benefits in monetary terms. This is especially true for psychiatric treatment programs, since these programs concern themselves with goals that cannot be expressed in dollars. How can one value in dollars an increased capacity for intimate relationships or relief from psychic pain or a hand-washing ritual? An investigator who recently reviewed the literature on CBA in mental health services emphasized this point in his conclusion that only "restrained" application of the tool was appropriate (Frank 1981a).

In cost-effectiveness analysis (CEA) a less ambitious effort is made, one that may be more consistent with the state of the clinical arts. CEA often uses shorter time horizons; costs are measured in monetary units and effectiveness in "health performance" units. Such an analysis requires groups of comparable patients and criteria for comparable outcomes, usually expressed in nonmonetary terms. Typically, the analysis deals with a fixed objective at minimum cost, or as much of an objective as possible at a fixed cost. One often begins with an estimate of an outcome that is desired for a service or method of treatment, then proceeds to compare the costs of achieving that outcome by various means. An example of this kind of study is May's comparison of the costs and effectiveness of five different methods of treating chronic schizophrenia, which revealed the superiority of neuroleptic drugs in terms of low costs and high clinical effectiveness (1971).

Two Important Cost-Benefit Studies

The most elegantly designed, state-of-the-art study was reported by Stein, Test, and Weisbrod in a three-part series (1980). The first article described a conceptual model for the development of community-based programs for the chronically disabled psychiatric patient and reported the results of a controlled study of a treatment program based on this model. The researchers found that use of the experimental program greatly reduced the need for hospitalization, lengthened community tenure, and enhanced community adjustment. A rigorous cost-benefit analysis, applied to this experiment, was reported in the second article. While the experimental program incurred higher costs than the control program, benefits outvalued costs by about $400 per individual. Other benefits and costs measured in quantitative but not monetary terms showed additional advantages for the experimental program. The third article described the investigators' calculation of social costs to the family and community due to the greater amount of time spent in the community by patients in the experimental program. The conclusion was that benefits to patients in the community were not gained at the expense of others, as has been suggested in the literature. When the experimental program was discontinued, a deterioration in patient gains and a sharp rise in hospitalization followed, suggesting that this kind of community treatment for chronically mentally ill individuals should be on a continuing rather than a time-limited basis.

Reifman and Wyatt (1980) looked at the issue of costs and benefits from a broad societal perspective. The focus was on the impact of the psychoactive medication lithium, approved in 1969, on the costs generated by manic-depressive psychoses. Their conservative estimate of the ten-year savings was $4.2 billion—$2.9 billion in unexpended treatment costs plus a $1.3 billion gain in productivity.

As noted, there are serious methodological difficulties with both CBA and CEA; not even the best studies can eliminate problems with the interpretation of results. This was a major finding of the evaluation of the state of the art by the Office of Technology Assessment of the U.S. Congress, which concluded that such analyses could not serve as "the sole or primary determinant of a health-care decision" (1980). Values other than costs must be taken into account in resource allocation decisions. For example, it may be most cost effective to deliver vocational rehabilitation services to white middle-class, less severely disturbed adolescents, but it is the job-related problems of inner-city youth with serious mental disorder that are of most concern to public policy. Efforts must be made to view cost analyses in a framework that never loses sight of the interests of society, including issues of equity (see Chapter 5).

COST OFFSETS AND THE ROLE OF PSYCHIATRIC CARE

One offshoot of the mind/body Cartesian split in modern society is the distinction that third-party insurers make between "nervous and mental" coverage and general medical coverage. This is a false dichotomy. All physical illnesses have emotional and psychological concomitants and many mentally ill individuals have associated physical disorders.

A corollary of this truth is that psychiatric problems are often presented as physical complaints, while somatic diseases may be initially experienced as emotional symptoms. Patients in the offices of internists and general practitioners often present distress that is largely mental, and a great deal of mental health care is delivered through the general medical care system without being labeled as such (Ford 1983). Restrictions on mental care coverage cannot prevent individuals from obtaining some kind of care, although not necessarily the most appropriate care. What they can prevent is the labeling of mental health care to the third party. Further, there is good evidence that the false dichotomy breeds a false economy in the convention of limiting mental care coverage. Studies show that the provision of specific psychiatric and mental health interventions make it less likely that medical services will be used inappropriately for the alleviation of mental distress.

It is probable that the primary disorder of 15-20 percent of patients in general medical settings is an identifiable psychiatric disorder (Regier et al. 1978). And of the counterpart: Up to 50 percent of psychiatric patients have an identifiable medical disorder (Hall et al. 1982). Mortality rates tend to be higher for psychiatric patients than for the general population.

When psychotherapeutic interventions are used with persons with medical problems, significant cost offsets occur. A quantitative review was made by Mumford et al. of 34 controlled studies of the effects of psychological interventions on recovery of persons who had recently suffered a heart attack or were facing surgery. The data showed these interventions producing large effects in terms of speeding recovery, decreasing requirements for analgesic and sleeping medication, and shortening hospital stays (1982). A review of 11 studies of the effect of psychotherapy on utilization of other medical care showed the average effect to be a reduction in utilization of 20 percent (Jones et al. 1979).

Schlesinger et al. studied utilization of mental and medical services in the Blue Cross-Blue Shield federal employees program, focusing on a group of persons who began outpatient psychotherapy (at least seven visits) following the diagnosis of a chronic medical disease. This group was found to have used 56 percent less medical service during the third year after the diagnosis than a group with the same diseases who received no psychotherapy. The savings in medical utilization following psychotherapy came largely from savings in hospital costs, that is, there were fewer hospital admissions and shorter stays in the psychotherapy group (1983). These findings are particularly impressive because the study used data from the fee-for-service insurance system; most other studies of cost offsets are set in prepaid group practices or health maintenance organizations.

Mumford and her colleagues have lately been able to confirm details of the nature of the association between mental health services and subsequent reductions in the use of other medical services: Reductions occur in inpatient rather than outpatient services, and tend to be larger among persons over age 55 (in press).

The importance of these cost-effectiveness studies for future reimbursement policy decisions must be underscored. A series of cost-effectiveness studies (Duehrssen 1957, 1972) begun in the early 1950s in West Germany was critical in persuading the national health insurance system in that country to include a 250-visit outpatient mental health benefit (lifetime) with a system of prospective approval and peer review.

Reference to this body of work could also help in the funding of subspecialties in psychiatry such as consultation/liaison. One such study (of psychiatric intervention in the postoperative course of elderly female patients requiring surgery for fractured hips) showed that psychiatric consultation and liaison services led to a dollar benefit of almost $200,000 over the cost of the psychiatrist in one year (Levitan et al. 1981).

SHOULD THE BASIS OF REIMBURSEMENT POLICY BE CHANGED?

Because mental treatments are considered to be controversial and because the number of therapies, especially psychotherapies, is often estimated to be in the hundreds (Parloff 1982), some have argued that public policy makers need a standing national group to evaluate the efficacy and safety of mental treatments, especially psychotherapies. It would have authority similar to the Food and Drug Administration's regulatory authority over new drugs and medical devices but could be more scientifically evaluative in focus (London et al. 1982). Other authors have proposed using the criterion of cost as well as the criterion of effectiveness as bases for reimbursement policy (McGuire et al. 1983).

The idea of basing reimbursement decisions on efficacy research is controversial and full of problems. Reimbursement decisions for mental treatments through third-party payers are more restrictive, less rational, and inequitable—but would the proposed cure be worse than the disease? Some feel it would betray the purposes of health insurance, encourage inefficient care, alter a critical research agenda, inhibit innovation, and be an intrusion into clinical practice (Sharfstein et al. 1983a).

Historically, insurance coverage for medical care, introduced in the early years of the Great Depression, was invented to help patients afford the cost of hospital-based care and thus to help hospitals survive in an era of widespread economic distress. No one would argue that third-party reimbursement, public and private, has proven itself an important mechanism to deal with public health and public financing dilemmas. Americans prefer to be protected against catastrophic costs of illness and disability and the expensive care that might be needed. They have this preference not necessarily for purposes of "cure" but for purposes of accessibility to medical resources when in need of care for illness.

Basing reimbursement decisions on proven efficacy or cost effectiveness is perhaps one way to cut back on the high costs of care. Yet, for most medical care, sufficient evidence is not in. The Office of Technology Assessment of the U.S. Congress estimates that only 10 to 20 percent of medical technologies have been proven efficacious through controlled clinical trials (1978). Most medical technologies are "half way" according to Lewis Thomas. That is, they help manage an illness and its impact but do not effect a cure; they prolong life and the need for continued treatment. Nevertheless, reimbursement policy must be delineated even in gray areas where treatments often can be shown to be not harmful but seldom can be proven to be extremely helpful. Third parties pay for medical care of doubtful effectiveness such as antibiotics for viral illnesses, coronary bypass surgery for anginal pain, or multivitamins for fatigue.

For mental treatments generally and psychotherapy in particular there is good evidence—as good as for most medical interventions—on effects, effectiveness, and efficiency. Consider the evidence for psychotherapy: Meta-analysis of 475 controlled studies revealed that the average person treated with psychotherapy exceeded—that is, had more evidence of improvement—than the average control person by approximately .85 standard deviation units across 1,766 outcome variables (Smith et al. 1980). Other studies on the impact of psychological interventions in medical-care situations are summarized elsewhere in this chapter. Current and future research should establish knowledge on the specificity of treatments for certain clearly definable disorders in individuals. Similarly, the need for more good outcome studies grows increasingly evident throughout the health-care arena. In the cautionary terms of the economist Eli Ginzburg addressing medical educators: "If you remain as silent as you have been about the efficiency and equity of [the health-care delivery] system, you will lose your credibility at an appalling rate in years to come" (Ginzberg 1983).

Basing reimbursement policy today on proven efficacy or cost effectiveness would encourage inefficient and poor clinical practice. For one thing, objective units of care—procedures, technologies, drugs—would have an edge in the competition for approval. For another, the information provided by clinicians to third-party payers would be compromised. Third-party payments are made currently on the basis of information provided by the clinician, that is, the patient is a covered individual, the condition a covered diagnosis, the treatments covered procedures. Submission of bills based on an approved therapy list would distort this process. Disguised diagnosis for bills is already common practice (Sharfstein et al. 1980) (Appendix III-E). The corrupting influence of a possibly unenforceable reimbursement policy is a cost itself.

Further, a requirement of proven efficacy or cost effectiveness could lead to the development of a regulatory structure both highly costly and undesirable. There are about 250 recognized forms of psychotherapy. A comprehensive program of research to establish effectiveness and safety would require the testing of these 250 therapies against 150 forms of mental illness and each of the treatments against each other. Even if these 250 forms of treatment were collapsed into 17 generic forms and the 150 disorders collapsed into 50 major categories, 6,800 clinical trials would be required to assess efficacy (Parloff 1982). An expenditure in the billions for this purpose would force a restructuring of national medical priorities. And it would totally derail the agenda of basic research in mental illness, its etiology and pathogenesis Already underfunded, psychiatric research priorities would wither under the pressure for evidence of efficacy or cost effectiveness.

The regulatory agency necessary to develop the protocols and establish reimbursement policy would be an arena of intense interprofessional conflict. Which disciplines would be represented on these boards? How would the threshold of criteria for effectiveness be established? Moreover, pressure for obtaining good results for particular therapies could undermine the objectivity of the research enterprise itself. Such research is time-consuming, costly, complex; an investigator with personal interest in a particular therapy would be tempted to bias experiments in favor of finding an effect. Already evidence of such bias has been found (Smith et al. 1980).

It would not be sensible to postpone, perforce, research questions which must be addressed, particularly specific effects of different approaches to different patients in different settings (Greenspan et al. 1980). Much of medicine is oriented to maintaining patients at current levels of health, that is, keeping the patient from further deterioration. For example, patients with malignant carcinomas may require treatment with the goal of slowing the disease process. In other situations, the best medical practice is to alleviate pain and suffering. Interrupting a natural course of illness or relieving pain are appropriate treatment goals and must appear as such in all efficacy and cost-effectiveness studies.

In sum, it seems wise both to encourage good outcome research and to continue, for the time being, to rely on clinicians for determinations of effectiveness. It is the clinician's judgment of relative effectiveness, given current knowledge of certain treatments for certain illnesses in individuals, that provides the most efficient and effective context for reimbursement. This particular clinical art can be aided by a system of peer review wherein costly, complex, and sophisticated clinical decisions can be reviewed and recommendations made to third parties on a case-by-case basis. Peer review and other means of accountability for third-party financing of psychiatric care are taken up in the next chapter.

CHAPTER 4

The Accountability of Psychiatric Care

Accountability can be defined as the condition of being accountable, liable, or responsible. To account means to furnish a reckoning of money received and paid out, and to give satisfactory reasons for one's actions. Accountability practices—justifying what and how things are done at what costs—are essential to business, for without them no business could succeed. Insurers have often charged that psychiatric care is not accountable in this sense, that its costs are unpredictable because psychiatrists cannot agree on diagnosis or treatment, that psychiatric care is not amenable to review. The major procedures used to assure accountability in the medical field include utilization review, medical audits (medical care evaluation studies), and program evaluation. Utilization review in the form of peer review has become the cornerstone of organized psychiatry's accountability to payers and consumers.

Two factors are behind current cost-containment imperatives; they are inflation of prices in the medical care marketplace and greatly increased per capita utilization of medical services by the U.S. population. Control of utilization—via restricting use to necessary and cost-efficient treatments—has become the focus of cost-containment efforts. What do you do, why, and at what cost are questions being put to all health care providers today. As discussed in Chapter 2, underwriters have always had many questions about what psychiatrists do, why they do it, and what it should cost. Thus, issues of accountability respecting psychiatry are doubly pressing in today's medical care financing environment.

Insurers' questions about the practice of psychiatry reflect their longstanding uncertainty about the nature and extent of mental illness and the effectiveness of various treatments. According to Stan Jones, Vice President for Government Relations, Blue Cross-Blue Shield, the insurance industry would be helped by "reasonably tight definitions of what services are appropriate for what conditions. It seems to be that for 90 percent of all *DSM-III* diagnoses, the appropriate treatment is either individual psychotherapy, or drugs and psychotherapy, or drugs and hospitalization. Surely, greater differentiation about treatments exists. . . . [Further,] it appears to many policy people that any concern that an individual takes to a mental health professional is appropriate for mental health care" (VandenBos 1983).

SOME DEFINITIONS

Insurers routinely monitor utilization for need and appropriateness. To identify use that departs from norms, they use criteria that relate diagnosis to significant patient characteristics; exceptional cases may then be reviewed in detail. Standards have been developed in order to objectify the process of deciding whether or not treatment is appropriate. For example, in a retrospective review of care provided in a hospital, for each condition there would be standards for justification of admission, anticipated length of stay, treatment modalities, discharge plan, and other pertinent aspects.

Peer review is a kind of utilization review in which standards developed by the peer profession are applied in the review process. In medicine, there are peer reviews of medical treatment, education, and investigation; a traditional example is grand rounds, wherein peers discuss a case being treated by one of their number. The differences between insurers' utilization review and medical peer review should be noted. Peer review is intended to improve the quality of care (or education or research) while utilization review is aimed at monitoring necessity and appropriateness of care. Both are relevant in the current environment. Indeed, medical peer review ought not restrict itself to assessments of quality but should also seek to assure, through auditing appropriateness, that incurred costs are justified. By the same token, the concern of insurers' claims review that they pay only for high-quality care might well stimulate greater efforts at mutual consultation with all interested partners of the health insurance contract.

Psychiatric peer review is a process carried out by psychiatrists. It is concerned with utilization review, quality review, continuing education, advocacy with intermediaries for improved care, and cost control. By providing a process for monitoring the utilization, quality, and cost of care, psychiatric peer review aims to maintain professional self-determination and avert monitoring and control by outside agencies (Gibson 1977).

INSURERS' SPECIAL PROBLEMS

Despite insurers' long experience with utilization review, few objective criteria exist for their reviews of mental health benefit utilization for need and appropriateness, particularly for non-institutional care. Hence, review of psychiatric care claims has posed special problems.

Insurers view as inadequate the current level of psychiatry's consensus on diagnoses, appropriate treatments, and prognoses in light of the progress in these areas in other fields of medical care. Insurers have less trouble with surgical procedures, for example, because physical diagnosis is confirmed by laboratory work and the pathology is confirmed by tissue review committees, which serve as a peer review process across the country. Although one might question the cost effectiveness of the number and extent of surgical procedures done in the United States annually, insurance traditionally supports hospitalization and surgical care. The more "definite nature" of surgical procedures and surgical conditions reinforces the propensity of the insurer to finance such care.

Insurers also feel frustrated by psychiatrists' inability to specify ranges of appropriate care and to accept regional normative statistics on average length of stay by diagnosis and age. In response to these special problems, many insurers have opted to control psychiatric benefits by offering only significantly limited benefit packages rather than through their utilization review process.

Confidentiality limits on the payer's access to case data further compound these special problems. The two sides of the confidentiality issue concern payers' need to know for purposes of utilization review and therapists' need to protect the confidentiality of patient disclosures. To what extent does the communication of clinical information from the psychiatrist to the third-party payer compromise the privacy of the doctor-patient relationship? Most psychiatrists insist on strict confidentiality in order for psychotherapy to proceed. If there are many questions about the medical necessity of treatment, its length and intensity, and the qualifications of the provider, how much and how often must this information be provided to the third-party payer? (Sharfstein et al. 1980). When does provision of this information itself interfere with treatment? Such questions are being hotly debated in psychiatry and medicine.

Providers' concerns about the use of diagnostic and treatment information by insurers have led some to report inaccurate information. Findings from two studies of the utilization of mental benefits in the Blue Cross-Blue Shield federal employees program in 1977 suggested that diagnostic information submitted to the carrier on claims forms was inaccurate and of no use for claims or peer review (Sharfstein 1978). The submission of inaccurate information, however, compromises the credibility of psychiatry in the eyes of third-party payers. The practice erodes the confidence of purchasers and insurers of group health benefits in mental health coverages and limits the ability to process claims efficiently and appropriately.

In the current environment of programmatic and fiscal conservatism, there is a clear need for both protection of the patient and efficient use of constrained mental health resources. Mechanisms are needed to assure quality and necessity of care, to allocate the mental health dollar, and to render providers accountable for resources expended. Psychiatric peer review has emerged as the principal mechanism to achieve these objectives.

As previewed in Chapter 1, in 1976 the American Psychiatric Association and CHAMPUS undertook to design and implement an extensive peer review system to monitor the appropriateness of inpatient and outpatient treatment. By 1979 the Health Insurance Association of America was recommending the APA peer review program as a model to other medical societies. The program's success has attracted numerous insurers and third-party administrators; today more than 20 major participants from government and the private insurance industry are involved in it. It may be useful to give a fuller account of the major events of this success story.

A HISTORY OF PSYCHIATRIC PEER REVIEW

Peer review as a tool to promote effective, efficient, and economical health care had its origins in the late 1960s and early 1970s as the sum of money expended on health care, especially public funds, began to rise dramatically. Concerns over the cost of health care through Medicare and Medicaid led Congress to authorize the Professional Standards Review Organization (PSRO) program in 1972. The new law mandated that Medicare and Medicaid pay only for care shown to be medically necessary and provided in the most appropriate settings.

The American Psychiatric Association responded to these events by appointing the Task Force on Peer Review. The subsequent Task Force position paper, approved by the Board of Trustees in December 1972, called for the Association to take positive and effective action to promote the development of psychiatric peer review organizations in each District Branch and at the national level (APA 1974).

At about the same time, the General Accounting Office concluded its audit of CHAMPUS, and the news was not good for providers and consumers of mental health services. The GAO cited the program's liberal mental health benefits as a problem area, and raised questions about CHAMPUS management of the benefits as well as their definitions of such terms as "medically necessary" and "custodial care". The auditors observed that the program was paying for many educational, psychological, and counseling services which did not belong under the rubric of medical treatment (U.S. Senate 1974).

Responsibility for CHAMPUS resides in the Department of Defense, and that agency reacted to the GAO findings by announcing plans to limit severely and arbitrarily its mental health benefits in 1974. It was in response to this turn of events that the Association began difficult, lengthy, and intensive discussions with Defense CHAMPUS managers about the feasibility of substituting peer review for arbitrary limits. In the end, the APA developed a peer review system for CHAMPUS and set up an operational office to manage it, and the proposed limitations were never implemented by Department of Defense.

In 1976 the APA published the *Manual of Psychiatric Peer Review*; this action was coupled with the establishment of a structured, systematic peer review network across the country, with panels of psychiatrists organized in each of the APA's District Branches. These panels now utilize the services of more than 400 psychiatrists who review cases from both national contracts and local insurers. Three psychiatrists review every case, basing their evaluations on guidelines in the manual, which is regularly revised by the APA. In 1982, the APA conducted a total of 5,001 reviews for CHAMPUS and 965 reviews for non-CHAMPUS third-party payers.

Current APA peer review activities are based in part on a Department of Defense collaborative project with the National Institute of Mental Health. The project was SCOPCE-1 (Select Committee on Psychiatric Care and Evaluation). Operating in CHAMPUS, the project demonstrated the potential of peer review as a model process for assuring quality and containing costs (Asher 1981). Elements of the CHAMPUS model for peer review have also been adopted by the American Psychological Association as well as numerous third-party payers.

Psychiatric Peer Review Today

There are indications that peer review activities are meeting their major objectives. With respect to costs, findings to date are encouraging. The mental health share of total CHAMPUS expenditures dropped from 27 percent in 1973 to 16 percent in 1978. An evaluation of SCOPCE-1 concluded that, at a cost of about $250,000, the quality assurance measures applied to residential treatment centers yielded a cost-benefit ratio of 1 to 25; program costs dropped without the intervention of arbitrary benefit cuts. However, a similar evaluation of the second phase of SCOPCE (which focused on psychiatric hospitalization of adults with schizophrenia) found no statistically significant effects on utilization or reimbursement (Sorensen et al. 1980).

According to Alex Rodriguez, Medical Director of CHAMPUS, the peer review service has led to "outright savings" of $4 to $5 million annually since participation began three years ago. These are the savings above the annual cost of peer review to CHAMPUS. Even greater savings may also be accruing through a "sentinel effect." These indirect savings may be 3 to 4 times greater than the direct savings. Rodriguez also noted that the quality of record-keeping and of patient care itself had increased (APA 1983a).

Reports from the private sector also suggest that peer review is working. Aetna, following a double-blind assessment of psychiatrists' claims nationwide, reported substantial lowering of costs accompanied by a rise in quality. No controlled cost analyses of the Aetna system are available, but the program costs in 1981 are said to have been $20,000 and its estimated savings to have been $2.4 million. Similarly, Mutual of Omaha has an estimated savings of between $250,000 and $300,000 during its first year of participation (APA 1983a).

Preliminary reports such as these are encouraging. However, aside from modest expansions of day treatment and outpatient benefits in the Aetna program since institution of a national peer review project three years ago, there is little evidence that effective review of care can work to extend the current limits on the amount of care that can be provided. A common misperception about utilization review activities is that they are designed to limit the amount of care. This is not so. Rather, they are intended to assure that necessary and appropriate care is delivered. Hence, improvements in the process can have little effect on limits on reimbursement. Such limits are set through insurers by state and federal legislatures and policy makers; in the near future they may be set under a more global mechanism such as an all-payer prospective payment system. It remains to be seen whether insurers and health-care policy makers are convinced that effective review of necessary and appropriate care can be carried out; only then may they be willing to extend the limits of care which can be reimbursed.

Two other APA initiatives on accountability deserve mention. One is the *DSM-III* (American Psychiatric Association 1980). As noted in chapter 2, this major work presents a consensually validated system of reliable diagnosis and enhances the ability to estimate numbers of individuals at risk for mental disorders and treatment. The other APA initiative is a coding system for insurance claims reporting, which was developed collaboratively with insurance representatives, including the medical directors of several large companies, to deal with the conflicting needs of insurers and providers with respect to confidentiality (American Psychiatric Association et al. 1982). The coding system lists reportable conditions under six general categories, which are syntheses of diagnosis and degree of impaired function. The coding system promises increased reliability in reported diagnoses and increased third-party confidence in claims information.

To sum up, psychiatric peer review, *DSM-III,* and the coding system are recognized by third-party payers as responsible efforts by the psychiatric community to deal with significant issues of accountability. Although clinical decisions about what treatment a patient needs will continue to be solely the responsibility of psychiatrists, the decision to reimburse psychiatric care will continue to be made by insurers on the basis of such nonmedical factors as coverage eligibility and financial limitations of the contract.

It is not clear at this time whether peer review will meet all the needs of third-party payers. What are the drawbacks of peer review from their viewpoint? Is quality accountability compatible with economic accountability? Can psychiatrists on peer review committees accept contract limitations in spite of their dedication to helping patients? Will inflationary pressures lead to demands for cost containment that override the necessity to make psychiatric care financially accessible through insurance coverage? These questions about accessibility transcend the accountability issue per se and touch on the issue of equity. The next chapter discusses fairness and equity of psychiatric care.

CHAPTER 5

Fairness and Equity for Psychiatric Care

Economic inequality is a fact of life. No subject has generated more public and academic debate in America. One of the most hotly contested questions in the current Congress and Administration is the proper role of government in ameliorating the inequities present in our society. This issue more than any other determines federal regulation of capitalist enterprise, public welfare policies, and public and private third-party health insurance (Page 1983).

Socioeconomic class differences in access to psychiatric care date to the colonial period. Our society's ambivalence toward the "unworthy poor" is reflected throughout the entire history of American psychiatry. The search for a more equitable distribution of mental health services dates from the social reform movements of the first half of the nineteenth century, often called "the moral treatment era" (Bockoven 1972). In the 1840s Dorothea Lynde Dix began her crusade for humane treatment of the mentally ill. It was due to the personal efforts of this undauntable woman that, over the ensuing decades, 30 mental hospitals were founded or expanded in the various states and the District of Columbia; Dix's efforts also helped convince Queen Victoria to set up a Royal Commission to investigate the condition of the insane in Scotland (Braceland 1972). Moral treatment in asylums from the hurley-burley of Jacksonian America was an egalitarian, idealistic approach to psychiatric care which appealed to the public for a few decades before collapsing under the sheer weight of the numbers of the poor, particularly the immigrant poor, with severe, intractable mental illness.

The second half of the nineteenth century is the story of the commitment of large numbers of persons to the state-operated mental hospitals and the overburdening of the public sector beyond any capacity to provide quality services (Rothman 1971). "Economies of scale" of the large state hospital became their chief virtue, as reflected in reports from that time on the expenditures per patient-week in public mental hospitals, which were lower than patient expenditures in private asylums or in general hospitals (Grob 1973).

This was the period of asylum psychiatry, so called because nearly all formal, specialized psychiatric care was delivered in isolation from the mainstream of general medical care, almost entirely in state- and county-supported institutions for the asylum and treatment of the mentally ill. This was also the beginning of our society's public mental health care system (Foley et al. 1983). The segregation of mental from general health care first institutionalized in those days continues to affect the shape of today's public mental health care system—for example, in the segregation of "nervous and mental disorders" insurance coverage from general medical coverage.

In this sociopolitical framework a pattern of care developed in which inadequately funded public institutions largely served the multitudinous poor while well-endowed private institutions served the few rich (Deutsch 1948). This two-class system of mental care mirrored a two-class system of general medical care, but the disparity in levels of funding between mental and general health care probably exacerbated the inequities in the psychiatric care system. A poor patient suffering from "dropsy" on the charity wards of the Pennsylvania Hospital or the Massachusetts General Hospital probably fared better than his or her indigent relation plagued by "moral insanity" and cared for in the state asylum.

PERSISTENCE OF THE TWO-CLASS SYSTEM OF CARE, 1950-1980

Twentieth-century inequities in access to psychiatric services were documented in the classic studies of Faris and Dunham, authors of *Mental Disorders in Urban Areas* (1939), and Hollingshead and Redlich, authors of *Social Class and Mental Illness* (1958). These studies demonstrated that socioeconomic class determines the patterns of mental illness and mental care more strongly than almost any other factor. In the original laboratory for *Social Class and Mental Illness,* south central Connecticut, the state hospital accounted for 95 percent of all public and private inpatient episodes and 66.7 percent of all treatment episodes. Lower-class patients received treatment exclusively through the state facility. There was little outpatient care for the public patient. In general, public patients received mass-produced, assembly-line custodial care while private patients received individualized active treatment.

Wide circulation of the findings of these investigations pricked the conscience of egalitarian America and helped launch an era of sociopolitical, or moral, reform of unprecedented range and scope. The reforms built on the foundation provided by the National Mental Health Act of

1946, which provided grants to the states for developing mental health programs outside the state hospitals. Then, beginning with the Mental Health Study Act of 1955 and peaking with the President's Commission on Mental Health of 1980, a series of congressionally created commissions and presidential task forces overhauled U.S public mental health policy (and practice) top to bottom.

The federal government led the way along several fronts—most dramatically in developing the policies and providing the "seed money" for the program mandated by the Community Mental Health Centers Acts of 1963 and 1965, which created more than 700 community mental health centers. Federal support of psychiatric training led to an increase of 183 percent in the number of psychiatrists between 1955 and 1980 (Appendix II-B). The federal government also provided additional public financing of psychiatric care through Medicaid and Medicare, and expanded psychiatric insurance coverage under the Federal Employees Health Benefits Program and CHAMPUS in order to demonstrate the feasibility and adequacy of third-party financing of psychiatric services (Foley et al. 1983).

As a result of these policies the large state mental hospitals declined greatly in size and scope. As noted in Chapter 1, they accounted for but 9 percent of all treatment episodes in 1977 compared to 50 percent in 1955, the peak year of public asylum psychiatry. Their average yearly census decreased by over 60 percent, although they continued to play an important role in relation to long-term care and, more recently, have become the principal resource for a new population of young, chronic patients who have emerged in the wake of the "deinstitutionalization" policies of the last two decades (Taube et al. 1983). Overall, the psychiatric treatment system expanded four-fold between 1955 and 1977, the greatest expansion occurring in the outpatient sector, from 23 percent to 70 percent of total patient-care episodes (Witkin 1980).

A follow-up in south central Connecticut, entitled "Trends in Mental Health," examined the relationship between social class and treatment in the context of this major shift in psychiatric care of the last quarter century (Mollica et al. 1980). The study revealed that unequal treatment based on socioeconomic class persists: While middle- and working-class patients have achieved financial access to private facilities, especially inpatient units in general hospitals, the poorest patients were pooled in state facilities. Further, the study showed that certain groups of lower-class patients in public outpatient facilities—minorities, the elderly, and persons with chronic schizophrenia—received care involving a low level of intervention and sophistication, such as psychosocial support from nonprofessional therapists. In contrast, outpatients from higher classes received high-intensity treatments such as psychotherapy from psychiatric professionals.

Indeed, as in the 1958 study of Hollingshead and Redlich, there seemed to be an inverse relationship between severity of disorder and intensity (and cost) of treatment; those with the most debilitating diagnoses received the least sophisticated treatments and those with the less debilitating diagnoses received the most sophisticated and costly treatments. Similar studies in other regions (Mayo 1974; Sue 1977; Flaherty et al. 1980) also found evidence of such inequity. Thus, despite the moral vision of John F. Kennedy, "the first President to address himself to Congress on behalf of the mentally ill" (Glasscote et al. 1964), his "bold new approach" of the 1963 Community Mental Health Centers legislation failed to eliminate the two-class system of psychiatric care.

Surely there are many reasons for this phenomenon, ranging from the health-care seeking behavior of patients in the less-favored groups, to the sociocultural barriers to psychiatric treatment, to the lack of financial access for the great majority of the poor. Mollica has asserted that "the psychiatric profession's relation to the lower-class patient appears to remain unchanged" (Mollica 1983). In support of this view he cited numerous studies indicating that lower-class patients are less likely than other patients to be accepted into psychotherapy, are often assigned less experienced therapists, have high rates of dropout, are more commonly treated with drugs, and receive biased psychiatric diagnoses and prognoses. How accurate this is as a characterization is a question requiring further empirical work. The question under discussion here is the extent to which the disparity between general and mental health insurance coverage contributes to the persistence of the two-class system of health care.

EQUITY AND PARITY DEFINED

Equity in health care requires that health services be accessible, available, and utilized by patients according to illness and need, not according to income, insurance coverage, race, geographic locale, sex, age, education, or other characteristics unrelated to clinical need (Goldman et al. 1983). Parity assumes that psychiatric services should be as accessible and available to patients as general medical services. This means that there should be no additional barrier, financial or otherwise, to the utilization of psychiatric services.

Thus defined, parity should lead to increased equity. An important concept, however, is the equitable distribution of the costs of care across all of society, which implies that, once afforded financial access, the poor will use higher-priced and more specialized psychiatric care. This is the issue of distributive equity, examined in detail in the next section.

As documented in Chapter 1, we as a society are a long way from providing for parity of psychiatric care under third-party insurance. Indeed, this disparity is part of a larger ethical problem for all of medical care in the opinion of President Reagan's Commission for the Study of Ethical Problems in Medicine and Biomedical and Behavioral Research; the Commission regarded as an ethical problem the absence of health insurance for more than 20 million persons and the extremely inadequate coverage owned by up to 44 million persons. The Commission report (1983) called on the federal government to assure that all citizens have "equitable access to health care." Although not specifically taking up the inequities present in access and availability of psychiatric care, the report serves as this decade's charter of society's moral obligation to the ill and infirm, including the mentally ill.

A new Robert Wood Johnson Foundation survey (1983) found that more than 28 million Americans reported they had "serious trouble" obtaining medical treatment in 1982. An estimated one million of these people were actually refused treatment for financial reasons, and the hardest hit were the poor and the uninsured. The survey authors found that it was not income, but insurance coverage which determined whether a person received care. Roughly 23 percent of uninsured people, compared to 11 percent of the general public, reported no regular source of medical care. Many of these people had lost their insurance as a consequence of losing their jobs. Individuals with Medicare and Medicaid coverage continued to have access, but individuals who were near-poor and not eligible for Medicare and Medicaid were having the most trouble.

As also documented in Chapter 1, only half of those with insurance have equivalent inpatient coverage, and only 10 percent of those with outpatient coverage have equivalent coverages for psychiatric and general medical care. This implies that approximately 50 percent of those with insurance for inpatient care and 90 percent of those with insurance for outpatient care have poor and inadequate coverage. We can say as a result that the vast majority of Americans face a financial barrier to the securing of adequate psychiatric care, especially when a family confronts serious and chronic mental illness.

The Issue of Distributive Equity

If coverage of psychiatric treatments on a par with other medical services results in the redistribution of resources from the poor to the rich, then parity would not lead to equity. Given the current limited supply of resources for outpatient psychotherapy or for inpatient care, increases in demand produced by decreasing financial barriers may not result in equity. The proposition raises questions about patterns of utilization, need, and demand.

One set of studies should be made to examine the impact of coverage on the duration, quality, and effectiveness of treatment for different socioeconomic classes. A separate set of studies is needed to explore the epidemiologic issues of psychiatric diagnosis and clinical need and the interaction of these differential patterns on socioeconomic, demographic, and geographic variables. And, finally, there is the question of demand, that is, will the relatively more well-off claim greater benefits from providers than the poor even if they do not need the extent and amount of care they demand?

Current evidence points in the opposite direction, however. Data from the 1975 Joint Information Service survey of psychiatrists and their patients in private practice (Marmor et al. 1975) and from the 1980 survey by the Washington Psychiatric Society (Krizay et al. 1980) show that services redistribute toward the poor and near-poor once financial access barriers are overcome. Edwards and colleagues (1979) reviewed data on patterns of psychotherapy utilization and demand and concluded that the poor use ambulatory mental health services in similar proportions to the wealthy once those services prove to be accessible. There is other evidence that third-party payment cutbacks lead to a decrease in access to private care and a shift of patients to the public sector, thereby illuminating the principal cause of the two-class system of care—a two-class system of financing the care (Sharstein et al. in press).

No doubt controversy will continue to swirl about the issue of redistributive equity, especially as a result of cutbacks due to cost-containment efforts by government and industry. Swirl as they may, at some point the momentum will once again favor national health insurance as providing a floor of coverage, or a "right to access," for all Americans, and mental care will be an important part of that proposal. It is interesting to note that the controversy a century ago on public funding for secondary education was quite similar. Those who argued against public education declared that such funds would serve disproportionately the interests of the rich at the expense of the poor. They were proved to be wrong.

STATE MANDATES FOR MENTAL HEALTH INSURANCE

A small number of states have enacted minimum mandates for mental health coverage under all Blue Cross-Blue Shield and commercial insurance plans written within that state. Connecticut was the first, in 1971; ten other states have since passed similar laws and several more are considering doing the same. The insurance industry opposes such mandates, since they put the noncommercial (Blues) and commercial carriers at somewhat of a competitive disadvantage with the self-insurance industry and health maintenance organizations, which are exempt from state regulations. In those states which have the mandates (Appendix I-D), a financial base has been established for inpatient psychiatric care and to a lesser extent for outpatient care as well. These mandates are not without some problems for psychiatry, however (Goldberg 1977).

A recent study by McGuire and Montgomery (1981) compared the experience of states with and without mandates, especially in relation to outpatient care. They found a 10 to 20 percent increase in the use and cost of outpatient mental health services as a result of mandates. The increase stemmed from some structural shifts which, the authors wrote, "do not represent net increases in costs due to mandates, only shifts in the way these costs are finally paid. . . . " The shift was from out-of-pocket and state coffers to the private sector. Clearly, if state policy makers deem it desirable to shift a portion of care from the public clinic and hospital to facilities in the private sector and to distribute more equitably the cost burdens of mental illness, then these mandates are desirable from a societal perspective, or "reasonable state policy."

The investigators also studied the growth in the numbers of mental health practitioners in states with and without mandates. They found that while the growth in the number of psychiatrists was about 7 percent higher in states with mandates than in those without, the corresponding figure for psychologists was much higher—32 percent. Indeed, one impact of mandates, combined with freedom of choice laws (which are prevalent now in 38 states), is the expansion of the market for outpatient and office practice by nonmedical mental health professionals.

Another impact of the mandates in some states has been to clamp a tight regulatory lid on practice. In Massachusetts it has been claimed by some that the mandate effectively maintains psychiatry's status as "the lowest paid medical specialty." Stoddard et al. asserted that the state law had "regulated physicians' fees so that they have scarcely increased, not to mention at the rate of inflation." This was due to the carriers' policy of establishing "physicians' participating agreements" which, under that state law, allowed Blue Shield to restrict payment of physicians and other providers to "profiles" (1983).

Further, the mandates have been used not only to establish floors of insurance coverage but also, by those carriers which have had broader coverages, to cut back to those floors. In effect, floors become ceilings, and those patients who require more extensive care than, say, a $500 outpatient mandate, cannot find such coverage anywhere in the state. Clearly, then, one tradeoff in a more equitable distribution of private insurance benefits across a state is a narrowing of choice when the need is for coverage of more extensive and intensive clinical services. Notwithstanding, McGuire and Montgomery concluded that providing affordable mental care to the largest number of people was the principal benefit of state mandates.

Mandates assure that most state residents have some ability to pay for a minimum amount of mental health care and thereby overcome the widespread prejudice against treatments for mental disorders as reflected in restrictive third-party payments. Mandates mitigate the problem of "adverse selection," and effectively distribute the costs of mental health care to all policy holders within that state, both the good risks and the poor risks.

THE HIGH-COST USERS OF MENTAL CARE: LOSERS IN THE COMPETITIVE GAME

The principal strategy of containing health care costs is to provide for competitive incentives for patients, providers, and third parties in order to maximize the efficiency of psychiatric care. Third-party insurance in the United States is and has always been a competitive enterprise. The most cost-efficient plans with the lowest premiums that can attract the healthiest buyers will thrive in the new, deregulated competitive market (see Chapter 6). However, this approach is in conflict with some of the basic purposes of insurance.

The pooling of resources to protect against the risk of catastrophic illness is a fundamental objective of the insurance idea. Protection against costly inpatient hospitalization is invariably a key element in most health insurance. The high cost of high-technology medicine is another variable which individuals must consider in relation to ability to pay. For psychiatric patients the insurance concept embodied in a catastrophic approach is quite appropriate because small numbers of psychiatric patients account for high costs. But lengthy inpatient care and intensive outpatient treatment are important, valid approaches in psychiatric care today. When the insurance idea moves away from the catastrophic perspective toward a competitive approach, catastrophic coverage is cut first. Since few people are willing to acknowledge the possibility of the catastrophic costs of mental illness in their own family, consumer demand for this coverage is meager. Without it, many patients who are mentally ill will have to turn to the public system for care and support. The equity and fairness goals of third-party coverage are an important focus when considering catastrophic illness and ways to distribute fairly the burden of care. The capacity to treat those mentally ill persons who incur catastrophic costs is clearly at stake in the pro-competitive market.

The benefit structure of the major plans participating in the Federal Employees Health Benefits Program (FEHBP) was recently adjusted to accommodate one notion of catastrophic coverage for mental illness. As can be seen in Appendix IV-B, the coverages, which apply only to inpatient psychiatric care, require an out-of-pocket expense two to four times greater than that required for a physical illness. In addition, the plans have lifetime maximums of $50,000-$75,000. In effect, what was created for federal employees, after an initial out-of-pocket expense, was a "window" of 100 percent coverage up to a lifetime maximum, at which dollar figure all benefits cease. These benefits were provided at no addition to the costs of mental care by means of deductibles and copayments built in to pay for these so-called catastrophic benefits.

Further inequities can be anticipated as access to acute care becomes compromised in order to afford more extended—but definitely not long-term—care in this FEHBP approach. Since the federal program is a bellwether for insurance carriers across the country, such developments must be viewed with some concern. Other developments in the insurance industry and public policy arenas, also affecting the traditional notion of protection from catastrophic costs due to illness, are explored in the next chapter.

CHAPTER 6

Emerging Trends in Health Insurance

The American Psychiatric Association's sponsorship of the work of Louis Reed and his associates resulted in their landmark 1972 publication. As discussed in earlier chapters, the time is ripe to update the data base and appraise the conditions which are today affecting health insurance for psychiatric care. The period between these two APA publications is only 12 years, but one era has ended and another is well underway.

Today America's most urgent health problem is an economic one—the breakneck rate of increase in the cost of providing health care. Health care costs in the United States reached $287 billion in 1981 (Appendix II-C). At 9.8 percent of the Gross National Product, that was a 100-plus percent increase over 1971, when health care costs were 4 percent of GNP. Projections are that these costs will reach $500 billion in 1987, a 75 percent increase over 1981, and $1 trillion in 1997, a 350 percent increase over 1981 costs.

Perhaps half of the trouble with health care costs can be attributed to population growth and greater per capita utilization of health goods and services. The other half springs from spiralling, uncontrolled price inflation.

For the last 20 years inflation in medical care costs has grown faster than the overall Consumer Price Index. For the 12-month period ending October 31, 1982, medical costs rose 11.1 percent, or more than twice the 5.1 percent rise in the CPI for the same period. Economists project this trend to continue through the year 2000. Many have hypothesized that marketplace forces could push costs above the level that U.S. society may willingly bear (Cockrell 1983).

These cost and inflation concerns have eclipsed concerns about access and launched a new era in which market forces have freer rein. Procompetition and deregulation are favored catchwords today, useful in spurring major changes in patterns of health care reimbursement and delivery. The impact of the new market forces on the financing and treatment of mental illness is broadly discernible. Before describing the emergent trends, however, it is useful to examine the current perception of markets vs. regulation as the superior means of resource allocation. A basic distinction between these approaches can be stated simply: Under the market approach, producers' prices determine how much, by what method, and for whom goods and services are produced; in the regulatory approach, government makes these decisions.

In the U.S. health care system a mix of the two operates, but the market approach is dominant. The old era's semi-regulated market mechanisms are judged to have failed for three principal reasons. First, because health insurance insulates consumers from out-of-pocket costs, coverage stimulates use. Further, health insurance tends to promote the use of more expensive providers, in part because the insurance preferentially covers some of the more expensive forms of care (e.g., inpatient vs. outpatient) and in part because higher price is usually associated with higher quality. The market approach fails so long as cost fails to ration use of health care by inducing consumers to seek lower-cost alternatives. The shade of "moral hazard" is recognizable here.

The second reason is the unique character of medical care as a commodity—that is, the nature of the doctor-patient relationship. Bluntly stated, the doctor acts as agent for the consumer in deciding how many of what kinds of services will be used. Not only does the doctor-agent incur no costs by doing so, he or she actually generates income in the process. Classic conflict-of-interest is at play.

The third principal "anti-market" feature is retrospective reimbursement. For example, hospitals are paid their audited costs irrespective of levels of utilization; in effect, they are free to develop services whether or not anyone uses them. Losses which occur because of low utilization can be made up through cost-based reimbursement. Hence, hospitals are protected from the normal market pressures of economic competition and survival of the fittest.

In sum, it is widely perceived that market mechanisms, as constituted, were not competent to control the use and cost of health care services. Solutions suggested to effect quick, decisive braking of costs focus on cost containment and selective deregulation. Thus, even now we are seeing reimbursement for health care services switching from retrospective to prospective payment, from third-party reimbursement to negotiated contracts. It is predicted that 90 percent of health care services in 1990 will be delivered through contract arrangements between providers and third-party payers and their intermediaries; 90 percent of hospitals will be part of systems, 25 percent of hospital revenues will be derived from non-therapeutic services, and 40 percent of physicians will be employed by health-care organizations (Modern Health Care 1983). Loosening restraints on competition and emphasis on price rather than quality competition are other aspects of proposed solutions. The trends now emergent in the health insurance field are described below; their deep and far-reaching effects on mentally ill patients and the psychiatric provider community are explored in the final chapter of this book.

The Elements of Cost Containment

Cost management is the overriding concern of major purchasers and funders of health insurance in both public and private sectors. Purchasers are now keenly involved in decisions about which benefits, how much, at what costs. For example, concern over their share of the nation's bill for health care has altered the traditional role of employers as more or less passive purchasers (Appendix III-F). Their outlays constitute about one-half of the nation's annual $300 billion bill for health care (U.S. Chamber of Commerce 1982).

Trends of cost management appear in the growing visibility of coalitions of business and legislative support of new alternate delivery systems such as preferred provider organizations. Other activities indicative of the new reality are listed below:

- modifications of benefit plans to encourage "cost efficiency";
- extensive development of data systems;
- efforts to strengthen utilization review;
- offering more "cafeteria benefit" plans;
- supporting "wellness" programs;
- greater use of self-insurance;
- experimenting with "consumer choice" systems; and
- supporting deregulation, although on a selective basis.*

These activities are affecting such factors as funds allocated, benefits offered, program eligibility, philosophy and scope of coverage, and reimbursement mechanisms.

Funds allocated to health care were significantly reduced by the federal Omnibus Budget Reconciliation Act of 1981, which cut Medicaid outlays through 1984. Additional reductions for 1985 and beyond have been proposed. The Medicare program recently experienced a 3 percent reduction, realized through cutting costs of program administration. Future cuts are expected, as are benefit design changes such as freezing reasonable charge limits for physician services (U.S. House of Representatives 1983). In the private sector, psychiatric benefits have been

*U.S. Chamber of Commerce 1978a, 1978b.

reduced in numerous programs in the last few years (American Psychiatric Association 1983b); especially notable are the recent major cuts made in the FEHBP.

Eligibility standards are being re-appraised. Purchasers in the private sector have made no changes as yet, but changes in eligibility standards of public insurance programs have reduced access to health care for millions of persons unable to afford private insurance (Robert Wood Johnson Foundation 1983). Recent reviews of policy changes in state Medicaid programs reveal that eligibility cutbacks and new restrictions on covered services are in force, and numerous reimbursement reforms are underway (Iglehardt 1983; National Governors Association 1982).

Changes in the philosophy of coverage, as well as reductions in the extent and scope of coverage, are evident. Competition for premium dollars has sharpened—e.g., offering more popular benefits, such as dental and vision care, and trimming less popular ones such as psychiatric care. A key perception is that the market for health insurance has matured and there is little new business to be written. Moreover, it is widely believed that the competition among carriers intensifies in marketplaces where self-insurance also competes.

The extent and scope of coverage are being affected by the movement to redirect health insurance from first-dollar coverage to more traditional catastrophic approaches. Plans are being offered which shift initial costs to the individual insured in an attempt to force the potential consumer to consider cost in making a choice about utilization of services. The consumer-choice approach may also be extended in an attempt to influence provider behavior. For example, consumers may be able to choose among competing carriers for one or another standard coverage package, or choose among competing health maintenance organizations, which can vary coverages and prices, or choose among physicians and hospitals offering competing charge schedules. Plan benefit designs are also being altered to emphasize cost effectiveness—e.g., by promoting care in outpatient treatment settings and by using the results of efficacy research as criteria for approving those kinds of treatment which will be reimbursed.

Regardless of stated coverage, reimbursement methodology is shifting as evidenced by public and private third-party payers' rapid adoption of prospective payment as the basis of compensation for hospital care (Appendix II-D). It is now generally accepted that retrospective payment mechanisms in large part caused the dramatic, persistent increases in hospital care costs that began in the mid-1960s (Appendix II-C). Prospective rate setting—in which rates of hospital compensation are determined at the beginning of a specified period before the provision of specified services—is seen as a sorely needed cost-containment incentive.

All prospective rate-setting systems claim cost containment as a primary objective. For example, state rate-setting laws typically assign an agency the job of assuring that hospital rates reflect "the costs of efficient production of services," or "the economy-wide inflation rate," or that costs are "reasonable." To judge the reasonableness of rates, rate-setting systems may focus on per unit costs, or aggregate hospital costs, or aggregate system costs. In general, the systems and responsible agencies recognize the need to conserve hospitals' ability to provide quality care and to remain financially viable.

Several prospective payment systems are now in operation or being planned (Appendix II-D). In the public sector, Congress enacted legislation in 1983 to this end for hospital care under the Medicare program, and also provided incentives for states to adopt similar procedures for Medicaid programs. Free-standing psychiatric hospitals and psychiatric units in general hospitals are currently exempt, but their exemption will be reviewed in 1985 (Public Law 98-21). This national experiment in "diagnostic-related groupings," or DRG payment methodology, for hospital care is being carried out even as developmental work is underway to extend prospective payment methods to outpatient and long-term care as well. At the state government level, a majority of states now have prospective payment systems for at least one payer. In the private sector, many third-party payers—commercial, Blue Cross-Blue Shield, self-insureds—have adopted or have similar systems under development. The private plans will likely apply to both hospital and physician care (Prospective Payment Guide 1983).

"Pro-Competitive" Strategies

A variety of so-called pro-competitive strategies have evolved, all designed to improve the performance of the health care market by increasing the strength of selected competitive forces. The strategies are employed differentially with various groups to achieve desired effects. They may be categorized as follows.

- Increased cost sharing and multiple plan competition. This strategy increases deductibles, coinsurance, and copayments to heighten consumers' awareness of cost. Further, subscribers are annually offered choices among plans by their purchasing agent (private or public employer). This strategy has attracted great interest and has been incorporated into several legislative proposals introduced in recent sessions of Congress. The current Administration's proposal for Medicare vouchers is one variation of it.
- Alternatives to fee-for-service arrangements. Development of alternate delivery systems (ADS)—e.g., prepaid medical groups and prospective payment organizations—has been encouraged because such

arrangements put providers at financial risk, thereby creating incentives for increasing efficiency in services delivery. Health maintenance organizations, HMOs (Appendix VI), are a familiar example of an ADS which has been around since the late nineteenth century. Historically occupying a very modest place in the market, current expectations are for an HMO growth spurt of 15-25 percent annually (Punch et al. 1984).

• Reduction of practice and reimbursement constraints. Organized medicine and other provider groups are advantageously placed to influence the market for health services. While some actions are directed to assuring minimum standards of quality, others may be directed to advancing the economic interests of the profession. These contraints are under increasing scrutiny (National Center for Health Services Research 1982). Recent developments in the pro-competitive area are typified by a new California law enabling the establishment of preferred provider organizations (PPO) designed to introduce price competition among hospitals and physicians. A PPO contracts with hospitals and providers to serve employees of companies that agree to give their workers financial incentives to use the PPO's services. In return for this increased business, the PPO gives the employer a discount on the cost of services and provides the employer with utilization data. The law authorizes both government and private insurance companies to negotiate prepaid contracts as a tool to contain costs. Although negotiated contracting is not a new method per se, its use in the current context of excess hospital beds and an over-supply of health care providers portends vast changes in the financing and organization of health care services (American Medical Association 1983b).

Regarding efforts to reduce constraints on competition, recently enacted legislation in the District of Columbia is instructive. In most states prevailing medical practice laws were developed with major input from state, county, and local medical societies; as a result, they often contain provisions favorable to the interests of these groups. Federal laws have nullified some of the anti-competitive provisions of state medical practice acts—e.g., those applying to the development of HMOs. D.C. legislators recently enacted a law with the same pro-competitive effect.

The D.C. health facility licensing law (Act 5-77, 1983) provides that hospitals, when evaluating applications for hospital privileges, may not discriminate against five groups of non-physicians: clinical psychologists, podiatrists, nurse midwives, nurse anesthetists, and nurse practitioners. The law's supporters claim that it will cut costs by encouraging substitution of labor and collaboration among professions with different skills. The most significant cost reduction that may result from collaborative practice is substitution of physician services. It remains to be seen whether other states will follow D.C.'s lead and look for ways to nullify professional constraints on competition. Consumer activism and antitrust law suits brought by non-physicians against physicians may eventually push other states to pass laws that open up the hospital privilege process. Certainly state legislatures are becoming increasingly knowledgeable about the application of antitrust laws in health care (Tibbitts et al. 1984).

Licensure and third-party reimbursement practices constitute another area where constraints on competition are being examined with an eye to elimination. As deregulation takes hold—i.e., fewer regulatory barriers to market entry—the debate intensifies over which professionals may perform psychotherapy independently, for example, and what practices may be defined as psychotherapy. The perception is that licensure and certification are only partially justified on the traditional basis of public protection; other motivations are seen to relate to economic issues.

State freedom-of-choice (FOC) laws and state laws mandating insurance coverage for psychiatric care are further complications. FOC laws amend state insurance codes to require that carriers provide reimbursement for services rendered, usually by a psychologist or social worker, if the contract covers services within the authorized scope of practice of such professionals as defined by the state's licensure laws. Psychologists have led the way in promoting FOC legislation in 31 states. Seven states have FOC laws favoring social workers as well.

FOC laws promote competition, but they cut another way as well. It is not difficult to understand insurers' reluctance to expand definitions of reimbursable providers of psychiatric care, for the potential number which might be included is significantly larger than the 30,000 practicing psychiatrists now included. Negative reaction was expressed by one major insurer as follows: "Therapists have been quick to put pressure on insurance companies when they don't like what we are doing. Mainly, psychologists are the beneficiaries of these FOC laws, but, increasingly, battles are being fought by social workers and marriage and family therapists. Some insurance companies are fighting back hard. We just don't consider their services as medically necessary." Experience bears out that, where FOC laws are in force, utilization of psychiatric services often increases. In consequence, according to one insurance official, "We are now seeing some new group customers shying away from mental health coverage. . . . They are waiting to see what their state will require in minimum benefits and freedom of choice laws" (Psychotherapy Finances 1981).

Clearly, the trends rapidly emerging in the field of health insurance for psychiatric care should command the attention of the psychiatric profession and individual psychiatrists. An affirmative action agenda is outlined in the concluding chapter.

CHAPTER 7

Agenda for 1984 and Beyond

The emerging trends in health insurance entail profound changes in the assumptions and premises of the insurance model for the financing of medical care. They challenge the psychiatric community to develop effective strategies not only in response to but in pro-active anticipation of their impact. The challenges include and go beyond advocacy of better levels of insurance coverage. How well the profession responds—how adaptable psychiatric practice is—this will determine not only whether expansion of coverages is possible, but also whether even the prevailing discriminatory coverages will be maintained without further deterioration. A keener awareness of economic issues is key for both the leadership of the profession and the individual practitioner.

In the near-term, for example, pressures to link reimbursement to efficacy will increase because of payers' strong interest in basing cost-control mechanisms on proven efficacy. Treatments with high demonstrated efficacy would be reimbursed by public and private third-party payers, while less efficacious treatments would not. Since outcome studies are seldom conclusive and rely on statistical analyses of large groups of patients, this could be a particularly problematic area for psychiatric treatment. The profession and practitioners must move now to meet this challenge. Psychiatry must also anticipate 5 and 10 years into the future and begin now to develop an agenda of cost-effectiveness studies, perhaps similar to the West German studies of the early 1950s which led to a major expansion of psychotherapy coverage in that country a decade later (Sharfstein 1978). If in the United States an FDA-like agency is formed to determine which treatments and at what level reimbursement will be made, such studies could be pivotal in the allocation of resources (London et al. 1982). The dangers and pitfalls of such an agency are discussed in Chapter 3.

Much of psychiatric care calls for passivity on the part of physicians. Persuasion, not passivity, is needed in the sphere of politics. Increased lobbying, marketing, and educational efforts are required in public and private arenas for continued development of treatment opportunities. This includes matters of reimbursement as well as matters of accreditation and quality control.

Increasing consumer advocacy is also important. Articulate groups of patients and ex-patients, families and friends, such as the National Alliance for the Mentally Ill, must be valued and supported. Service and support opportunities for the mentally retarded enlarged dramatically in response to political pressure from parents and friends of the mentally retarded. The mentally ill require similar opportunities. Necessary but insufficient is patient advocacy by providers of care, for the self-serving nature of provider advocacy undermines its credibility. The families and non-provider friends of patients can be the most politically effective advocates for psychiatric treatment and care.

If but one lesson must be learned about current assumptions it is that the funds for health care are finite and diminishing, and priorities for their use are rapidly being established. An important issue for medical care and psychiatry is that a large segment of the indigent community who need care will have reduced access to treatment. If they are to have access to the private sector, individuals require financial support. New coverage mechanisms must be developed combining both public and private funding to pay for needed care in and out of the hospital. Opportunities include the management of public institutions by private hospitals through contractual mechanisms, and the packaging and offering of services in a totally different manner, such as by capitation.

Prospective payment methodologies will increasingly guide the allocation of limited health care resources. The change from retrospective to prospective payment will alter the way all medical services are organized, managed, and delivered. The implications for the way psychiatry is practiced are significant. Predetermined, fixed levels of expenditure may be inappropriate for psychiatric patients, for whom there is considerable variability in the course of illness and the necessity of treatment, in the need for continued care, and in the extent or prevalence of catastrophic conditions. Of further relevance to psychiatric practice is that prospective payment will increasingly be based on diagnostic assessment; improvements in diagnostic methodology will be closely linked to reimbursement opportunities.

In planning for prospective financing it is helpful to conceptualize the main tasks of psychiatric practice and to rank them in order of necessity when one is confronted with a finite and modest budget. Similar thinking took place in the era when it was anticipated that national health insurance would be enacted into law and access to health care would grow (Astrachan et al. 1976). Although the respective goals are very different (cost-containment vs. increased access), prospective payment schemes will alter psychiatric practice as fundamentally as would the advent of national health insurance.

Four major task areas in psychiatry were identified by Astrachan and colleagues—medical, reparative, social control, and humanistic. These task areas will be differentially influenced by prospective payment agendas. It is psychiatry's medical tasks that have priority, with emphasis on accurate diagnosis and skilled treatment. Reparative tasks, which include habilitating and rehabilitating the person with chronic illness and defects, will suffer in the era of economic retrenchment. For large numbers of noninstitutionalized individuals these reparative tasks are crucial, but the prospectively determined health insurance dollar will be a very limited source of funding. Sheltered workshops, supervised residential settings, training in socialization and other skills will need to be funded from other sources, particularly from vocational rehabilitation and social welfare agencies. Social control tasks and humanistic tasks are even less likely to receive funding from health coffers.

The pressures for these changes in the methods of payment are coming from the payer community, which includes business, labor, government, and coalitions of consumers. These groups are also calling for higher levels of scrutiny of mental illness treatment and payments. Thus, increased accountability through peer review and documentation of cost effectiveness are other important elements in an overall strategy for the 1980s.

Quality of Care vis-à-vis Cost Containment

A key question is whether economic considerations (especially cost containment) and quality of care considerations are compatible. The pressure for increased utilization and peer review continues whether or not such activities are successful from a cost-containment perspective. Increased willingness by providers to cooperate with payers and regulators in the development of criteria for treatments and direct participation of these providers in the review mechanisms are essential rather then merely desirable. This is true throughout the medical care enterprise, but is especially true for psychiatry. The payer community focuses on the longer length of stay for psychiatric patients and remains uncertain about the nature of mental illness and the clinical treatment process and the consequences of inadequate treatment. Continued leadership in utilization and peer review is critical. If accountability systems remain under the purview of the professionals who deliver the care, psychiatrists will be positioned to emphasize the quality of care issue and to make known the consequences of poor quality and inadequate care.

A mindless, bureaucratic approach to cost containment spurred by pressures from payers can result in changes in treatment patterns toward less intensive treatments and treatment settings or no treatment at all. If costs are fixed in advance, a shift from more costly modalities such as inpatient care to less costly ones such as outpatient care becomes a careful, individual clinical consideration, and the development of innovative treatment programming requires skilled, creative clinical leadership. But if third-party coverage only pays for short-term acute care, the clinical needs of a large number of psychiatric patients will not be met unless they can afford such care out-of-pocket. Longer term hospital alternatives for seriously disturbed adolescents and intensive psychotherapy and psychoanalysis for a variety of disabling disorders will not be covered in such an approach. A basic ethical question is raised as quality long-term care remains available only to those who can afford it. This is not true for general medical care because most of the more intensive and costly treatments are made available through third-party financing.

It is important that a perspective of flexible programming be maintained, for it offers alternatives of combining various intensities of treatment based on clinical need and individual assessment. Again, it is psychiatry which can provide the leadership in justifying higher quality and more intensive care, both inpatient and outpatient. Consumers are not often in the best position to select a health package to suit their needs; this is particularly true for psychiatric care.

Another trend looming ahead involves the spread of the new computer-based technology and sophisticated management information systems, which will monitor care and patterns of care with a thoroughness and timeliness unknown in the past. This monitoring will include the amount and sources of payments for patients and will enable providers to evaluate and possibly change and target clinical programs to particular patient groups, thereby, it can be hoped, assuring financial viability for these programs and for the kind of clinical practice which can take individual needs into account. This includes the possible redesign of the mix of inpatient, day treatment, and outpatient care, varying lengths of stay in hospital and day hospital programs, and varying intensity of outpatient therapy.

In brief, efficiency, effectiveness, accountability, and quality must prevail over ideology, traditionalism, and the status quo. As financing mechanisms are reconceptualized, clinical paradigms must adapt.

A telling example involves development of new alternative delivery systems (ADS) such as preferred provider organizations as well as increased promotion of older ADS such as health maintenance organizations and individual practice associations. A key feature of these ADS is the primary care network, or triage which includes control over access to specialty care. How can or should psychiatry relate to these new systems?

This is a particularly active concern in California right now, where the capacity of psychiatrists to promote a "gatekeeper" function, in addition to their consultant role, to the high-cost users of medical care is an important element. Blue Cross of California has begun to provide some details about its "Prudent Buyer Plan." This is an example of uncreative thinking and retrenchment. Blue Cross intends to limit psychiatrists participating as providers to a maximum fee of $50 per visit. The insurer will pay 50 percent of this amount and the patient will pay the other 50 percent. Fifty visits per year, whether inpatient or outpatient, are allowed under this plan. There are several inpatient options included in the Prudent Buyer Plan. One contains no psychiatric coverage; others range from payment of 50 percent of costs, with a $5,000 per year limit, to payment of 80 percent of costs with a 30-day limit. In contrast, inpatient services for other medical care are reimbursed at 80-100 percent of costs and physician payments are tied to an "allowable fee schedule" which has no patient copayment.

This proposal and others in the same vein simply avoid dealing with the difficulties of striking a balance between cost management and access by psychiatric patients to quality care. In the absence of strong leadership and advocacy, cost-containment imperatives combined with long-standing discriminatory approaches to psychiatric patients could lead to a major catastrophe for these patients.

Position of the American Psychiatric Association

The principal purpose of the American Psychiatric Association's publication of the work of Reed and associates in 1972 was to establish a data base confirming the stability and predictability of utilization and the relatively modest cost of psychiatric care paid for by health insurance and other third-party sources. To review again the conditions which prompted this line of thought, the health insurance industry was growing at a rapid pace, increasingly paying for out-of-hospital as well as inpatient care. In 1965, with the passage of Medicare and Medicaid, U.S. society as a whole undertook to assure the provision of needed medical services to all citizens. Thus, the medical care market was also expanding dramatically. For psychiatric patients to receive their fair share of this expansion, efforts on a number of fronts were required. Federal start-up funds were critical, but it was intended that eventually the primary financial support for psychiatric service, as for other health service, would come through health insurance and other third-party payments. There was general recognition that psychiatric patients had a greater chance of receiving high quality care if that care were paid for in the same way as most other medical care in the country was paid for—by insurance.

Now, however, some 20 years later, we are in a time of appraising anew our assumptions about the organization and financing of medical care. New ideas are being tested and new approaches introduced. The diagnosis-related groupings system under Medicare is the first phase of an elaborate experiment in prospective payment and competition. It will have far-reaching effects on treatment opportunities for the mentally ill. This book, in the tradition of the 1972 book, attempts to analyze contemporary and anticipate future conditions by putting together the strongest data that make the case for medically necessary and comprehensive psychiatric treatments, and by discerning the impact of the new economic imperatives of pro-competitive approaches and privately regulated systems.

The principal policy objective of the American Psychiatric Association was established more than 30 years ago, when the first component to consider health insurance issues was formed. Simply stated, the objective is to ensure that psychiatric patients are not treated differently from other medically ill patients in regard to insurance coverage. Third-party funding, supporting medically necessary treatment, must extend fully to the psychiatric patient. If not, a basic egalitarian goal is compromised and the two-tiered system of care for mental illness is perpetuated; this system is especially harmful for those with long-term mental illness and its associated catastrophic costs. A public asylum system for the many and a private office system for the few, never in keeping with our society's humanitarian and egalitarian principles, is no more acceptable today than in the past.

Psychiatrists and their friends must increase their efforts to educate the broad spectrum of American society, and especially the decision makers, on the necessity and effectiveness of treatments for mental illness, a problem that affects significant numbers of citizens in every walk of life. Influencing the public, the large purchasers of health care, and those who establish public policy is indeed a complex and difficult task. This book has made a start by directing attention to the features of the new medical markets and the importance of accountability through strengthened peer review; support of consumer involvement and continued research on cost effectiveness and outcome have also been cited as instrumental activities.

Indeed, we are on the threshold of a substantial gain in our understanding of the overall social and economic benefits of psychiatric treatments to the high-cost user of medical care, the socially disabled, and the economically unproductive. Increased investment in analyzing and defining the economics of psychiatric care and the milieu in which decisions about coverage are made will pay off in better, more rational allocation of resources for the psychiatric patient.

The Agenda Topics

A core research agenda which will produce this dividend will contain the following four topics.

- Cost and utilization. More data must be developed to demonstrate convincingly that the costs of insurance coverage for psychiatric illness are predictable and affordable. Also needed is continued effort to resolve definitively the questions of whether and if so, in what manner coverage per se increases the demand for psychiatric treatment and prompts unnecessary utilization.
- Offset effect. The direct and indirect effects on overall medical care costs of providing psychiatric services require further documentation. More rigorous estimates of both the offset effect on utilization of other medical services and the cost impact of untreated illness on the U.S. workforce and society at large are in order.
- Quality assurance and cost accountability. Further development and analysis of balanced approaches are needed to facilitate the framing of rational, cost-effective policies to control utilization of psychiatric treatment. The agenda here includes development of a variety of structural and administrative mechanisms to satisfy the needs of patients, clinicians, and third-party payers. These range from benefit design choices which permit appropriate care and simultaneously provide realistic disincentives for unnecessary utilization to appropriate and meaningful criteria for standard claims and utilization review activities which allow both payers and providers to assure quality, develop standards, and manage costs.
- Consumer and purchaser data. There is a need for continued development of a knowledge base on consumer and purchaser preferences, especially with regard to the perceived weaknesses and strengths of psychiatric coverage. The public willingness to pay for coverage is an essential underpinning to any insurance program. Competent strategy development in the 1980s will require continued refinement of our understanding as to why these groups do or do not demand better coverage for psychiatric care; simultaneously, we must marshal the evidence needed to educate these groups.

An indispensable element of this research agenda is expanded investment in the basic research enterprise, that is, studies on the causes and cures of mental illness. Biological and psychological research must become synergistic and forge a synthesis of knowledge capable of producing practical improvements in the treatment of serious mental disorder. A synthesis of brain and mind sciences will also serve to expose the irrational mind/body dichotomy as portrayed by third-party carriers in distinguishing so-called "nervous and mental disorders" from general medical disorders. This false dichotomy perpetuates the financial discrimination which undermines quality care.

It is the role of a profession to emphasize quality issues. In addition, the promotion of accessibility, accountability, and efficiency are consistent with the ethical obligations of the professional. The authors wish to conclude by underscoring the nature of and need for professional leadership. We hope that our appraisal of the current and emerging conditions affecting psychiatry will support that leadership function.

Appendices

V. CHAMPUS 167

VI. Health Maintenance Organizations: Utilization and Coverage of Mental Health Services 180

VII. Evaluation and Prediction Models 188

I. Who Has What Kind of Coverage in the Private Sector?

The studies and data in this section of the appendices show that coverage for treatment of mental illness is extensive but it is often more restricted than coverage for physical illnesses. Trend data from 1972 show an increase in both number of plans covering mental illness and the restrictions placed on that coverage.

About half the states mandate some type of coverage for mental illness under private insurance plans.

Narrative And Selected Tables From: Health Insurance Coverage For Treatment Of Mental Illness Of Full-Time Employees Of Medium And Large Size Establishments In The Private Sector

Prepared for APA, April 1983
by John Krizay and Health Data Associates

MENTAL HEALTH COVERAGE IN THE PRIVATE SECTOR

Summary and Highlights

Health insurance coverage for treatment of mental illness in 1981 was extensive; all but a tiny fraction (1 percent) of all full-time employees in medium and large size establishments had, at least, hospital coverage. Nearly 60 percent of these had inpatient coverage equal to inpatient coverage for other illnesses, although this fact, alone, does not suggest that such coverage was "good" or, even "adequate."

Outpatient coverage is likewise widespread, at least insofar as coverage of psychiatrists' services is concerned. Approximately 90 percent of all participants were covered for some outpatient treatment by psychiatrists. However, there is some evidence to suggest that while most private sector employees have covered access to outpatient psychiatric services, such coverage may often be quite restricted. For example, over half of the participants were covered by plans requiring 50 percent co-payment while nearly two-thirds—including some of those with 50 percent co-payment requirements—are covered by plans with specific dollar maximums.

Clinical psychologists do not fare as well as M.D.s in this survey. Less than 40 percent of participants had coverage that paid for the services of clinical psychologists in 1981. Coverage of psychologists ranged widely from a low of just over 20 percent of full-time blue collar workers in retail trade to 70 percent of blue collar workers in the mining industry. Even in the mining industry, it should be noted, psychologists are not covered as independent providers.

Coverage of treatment in special institutions established to deal with mental illness was even less extensive than coverage of clinical psychologists. Other than the transportation and communications industry, such coverage was provided, generally, to less than a third of the participants. Those employed, in finance, insurance, and real estate, in particular, had few participants so covered, and less than 10 percent of blue collar workers in the construction industry were provided coverage of treatment in specialized facilities.

The presentation of various forms of coverage by industrial sector is designed to help pinpoint deficiencies in extent or availability of coverage. For example, the tables presenting equal inpatient coverage by funding media show that Blue Cross seems far more reluctant to provide equal coverage of hospital care than the commercial carriers. Other highlights of the numerical presentations are:

- Ninety-two percent of all participants have some outpatient coverage; 89.4 percent have outpatient physician coverage, but only 39.7 percent have coverage of clinical psychologists. Eight percent have no outpatient coverage.
- Fifty-eight percent of all participants have hospital care that is the same as for other illnesses. Commercial carriers cover the overwhelming share of those with equal hospital coverage.
- Three times as many participants in plans insured by commercial carriers have equal hospital coverage as those with coverage more restricted than for other illnesses. Less than one-half as many participants in Blue Cross have equal hospital coverage.
- Ten percent have outpatient coverage that is the same as for other illnesses. (Table 2)
- Fifty-four percent have outpatient coverage subject to 50 percent co-payment; 62 percent subject to separate dollar maximums.
- Fewer blue collar workers have equal inpatient coverage or any coverage for outpatient treatment by psychiatrists or clinical psychologists, or treatment for alcohol abuse. (Tables 3, 6–8)
- Among industry sectors, the construction industry has a greater percentage of participants with equal hospital coverage than other sectors, and runs a close second to the wholesale trade industry in coverage of outpatient physician services and outpatient hospital coverage.

Table 1
PERCENT DISTRIBUTION OF PARTICIPANTS IN SURVEY
(By Occupational Group and Industrial Sector)

		White Collar		Blue Collar
Industry	All Full-Time Participants	Professional/ Administrative	Technical/ Clerical	Production
Mining	2.1%	1.4%	0.9%	3.0%
Construction	1.7	1.7	1.2	2.0
Manufacturing	58.1	51.4	32.6	72.7
Transportation/ communication	12.4	13.3	14.0	11.3
Wholesale trade	4.2	5.3	5.0	3.4
Retail trade	8.7	6.6	14.7	6.9
Finance, insurance real estate	10.0	13.7	27.0	0.4
Services	2.8	6.6	4.6	0.3

Table 2
PERCENT OF FULL-TIME PARTICIPANTS WITH *SOME* COVERAGE FOR THE TREATMENT OF MENTAL ILLNESS—1981
(By Occupational Group and by Various Services)

		White Collar		Blue Collar
	All Full-Time Participants	Professional/ Administrative	Technical/ Clerical	Production
Inpatient	99.0%	100.0%	99.0%	99.0%
Outpatient	93.0	94.0	94.0	92.0
Alcohol	37.9	42.6	37.9	35.8
Special Psychiatric Institution	21.3	22.7	23.2	19.9
Outpatient Hosp.	90.0	92.2	91.6	88.4
Outpatient M.D.	89.4	90.9	91.0	88.0
Clinical Psych.	39.7	44.8	41.5	36.5

Table 3
PERCENT OF PARTICIPANTS WITH HOSPITAL COVERAGE FOR MENTAL ILLNESS EQUAL TO COVERAGE FOR OTHER ILLNESSES—PRIVATE SECTOR, 1981
(By Occupational Group and Industrial Sector)

Industry	All Full-Time Participants	White Collar: Professional/ Administrative	White Collar: Technical/ Clerical	Blue Collar: Production
Mining	31.0%	64.4%	80.8%	16.7%
Construction	73.7	78.0	78.1	71.0
Manufacturing	60.1	66.3	63.5	57.5
Transportation/ communications	52.3	52.2	47.7	55.2
Wholesale trade	63.9	65.3	61.3	64.6
Retail trade	62.7	64.1	61.1	63.7
Finance, insurance, real estate	61.7	63.2	61.7	37.4
Services	62.5	63.2	61.1	57.0
Total	**59.0**	**63.2**	**61.1**	**57.0**

Table 4
PERCENT OF PARTICIPANTS WITH HOSPITAL COVERAGE FOR MENTAL ILLNESS EQUAL TO COVERAGE FOR OTHER ILLNESSES—PRIVATE SECTOR, 1981
(By Occupational Group and Funding Media)

	Participants w/Equal Coverage	Self Insured	Blue Cross	Commercial	HMO
White Collar:					
Professional/ Administrative	63.5%	11.5%	18.5%	69.7%	0.3%
Technical/Clerical	61.1	13.6	15.9	70.1	0.4
Blue Collar:					
Production	57.0	23.2	16.9	59.6	0.3

Table 5
PERCENT OF FULL-TIME PARTICIPANTS WITH COVERAGE FOR MENTAL ILLNESS SUBJECT TO LIMITS SEPARATE FROM COVERAGE OF OTHER ILLNESSES
(By Occupational Group)

		White Collar		Blue Collar
	All Full-Time Participants	Professional/ Administrative	Technical/ Clerical	Production
Separate inpatient limits:				
By # of days	30%	26%	28%	33%
By $ maximum	15	14	16	15
Separate Outpatient* limits:				
By # visits	21	20	23	20
By $ maximum	62	64	63	61
50% co-pay**	54	57	56	51

*Includes multiple restrictions.
**Applies to Major Medical only.

Table 6
PERCENT OF PARTICIPANTS WITH COVERAGE FOR TREATMENT OF MENTAL ILLNESS BY M.D.s IN OUTPATIENT SETTINGS—1981

		White Collar		Blue Collar
Industry	All Full-Time Participants	Professional/ Administrative	Technical/ Clerical	Production
Mining	87.6%	93.0%	81.7%	87.4%
Construction	94.1	94.9	92.0	94.5
Manufacturing	89.1	91.5	90.2	88.2
Transportation/ communication	87.4	86.2	88.7	87.3
Wholesale trade	95.6	97.0	96.2	94.3
Retail trade	88.4	89.2	91.9	84.5
Finance, insurance, real estate	92.4	92.7	92.2	96.8
Services	87.0	87.2	88.7	74.4
Total	89.4	90.0	91.0	88.1

Table 7
PERCENT OF PARTICIPANTS WITH COVERAGE FOR TREATMENT OF MENTAL ILLNESS BY CLINICAL PSYCHOLOGISTS—1981

		White Collar		Blue Collar
Industry	**All Full-Time Participants**	**Professional/ Administrative**	**Technical/ Clerical**	**Production**
Mining	63.2%	43.7%	37.2%	70.9%
Construction	24.3	27.1	16.9	25.3
Manufacturing	40.1	46.2	47.5	36.7
Transportation/ communication	43.7	50.0	42.9	40.8
Wholesale trade	39.0	54.1	42.4	26.4
Retail trade	32.1	38.0	39.4	22.3
Finance, insurance, real estate	37.6	39.7	37.0	29.1
Services	36.2	38.4	34.7	26.9
Total	39.7	44.8	41.5	36.5

Table 8
ALCOHOL ABUSE TREATMENT
(By Occupational Group)

		White Collar		Blue Collar
	All Full-Time Participants	**Professional/ Administrative**	**Technical/ Clerical**	**Production**
% w/alcohol coverage	37.9%	42.6%	37.9%	35.8%
% w/alcohol and M.D. but *not* clinical psychologist	15.6	19.2	17.0	13.5
% w/alcohol and M.D. *and* clinical psychologist	19.6	21.9	19.4	18.7

Survey Scope: Background And Methodology

This analysis is derived from data gathered by the Bureau of Labor Statistics, U.S. Department of Labor in connection with its 1981 "Level of Benefits" study which surveyed medium and large sized establishments in the private sector. Included were 270 pages of questions concerning health insurance coverage. Global results of the survey were published by the BLS in August 1982. The remaining material, including most of the information gathered regarding mental health coverage and all data referring to the eight different industrial categories surveyed, BLS left in raw form.

The BLS survey covered full-time, private sector employees working in medium and large-sized firms. The minimum size of an establishment ranged from 50 to 250 workers depending on the industry as follows:

Mining	250
Construction	250
Manufacturing:	
Chemical, petroleum, electrical and non-electrical machinery, equipment and supplies, transportation equipment, and instruments	100
All others	250
Transportation and communication:	
Railroad, local transit, deep sea transportation, air, communication, electrical, gas, and sanitary services	100
All others	250
Wholesale trade	100
Retail trade	250
Finance, insurance, real estate	100
Services:	
Accounting, bookkeeping	50
All others	100

The sample consisted of 1505 establishments divided into eight major industry divisions listed above. Some 24 million full-time employees are included within the scope of the survey. The sample frame was stratified, first, by broad industry group based on total employment in the establishment. The sample size was allocated to each stratum (defined by industry and size) proportional to the total employment of all sampling frame establishments in the stratum (e.g., a stratum containing 1 percent of total employment within the survey scope was allocated 1 percent of the sample). Thus, the probability of any unit being selected in the sample is proportionate to its size. *Within each stratum,* a random sample was selected. Data was collected by field representatives between January and July 1981. The average reference period for data collection is March 1981.

Hay-Huggins Health Care Plans Surveys: Noncash Compensation Comparison

SUMMARY

Employers are expanding efforts to control medical claim costs and to promote employee health. Forty-seven percent cover pre-admission testing expenses. Fifteen percent of participants are considering increasing plan deductibles, in addition to 7 percent who have already done so. Twenty-four percent have, and 21 percent are considering, health promotion programs. Thirty-eight percent provide home health care coverage, and 30 percent have an alcohol-and-drug assistance program.

Some level of psychiatric care is provided in 94 percent of all plans and BLS data shows that 59 percent of all workers with inhospital mental health coverage have the same coverage as for other illnesses. (See BLS data, Appendix IA for additional coverage comparisons.)

As expected, more firms, 50 percent, now offer HMO options as alternatives to their standard plans. Where a choice exists enrollment in HMOs is generally low (under 10 percent). Also, 42 percent of respondents found administering HMO options an administrative hassle. Seventy-four percent indicated HMO premiums were higher than the alternative insured plan.

Regarding plan financing, larger employers are continuing to substitute minimum premium or self-insurance arrangements in place of fully insured coverage. Fifty-seven percent now use minimum premium or self-insurance for some or all medical coverages, in contrast to 37 percent in the 1978 survey.

As health care costs continue to rise (64 percent reported claim increases of 15 percent or more), most employers are increasing plan maximums and switching from plans paying scheduled amounts to those paying a portion of reasonable and customary charges. Seventy-eight of the supplemental major medical plans now have maximums of $250,000 or more. Although a strong case could be made for doing so, few firms have increased their major medical deductibles. As a result, claims administrators are paying part or all of the many smaller claims that originally were not intended to be picked up by the plan.

Another area of activity in medical plans is the inclusion of a "catastrophic" feature under major medical coverage. Sixty-eight percent of the plans now provide a dollar limit to the employee's share of coinsurance, generally $500 to $2,000 of out-of-pocket expenses.

The prevalence of dental plans continues to increase dramatically. In 1976, 34 percent of the survey participants had plans. In 1980, 59 percent had plans. Now 69 percent of the more than 800 survey participants provide the coverage. Dental is fully employer-paid for employee coverage in 79 percent of the plans and for dependent coverage in 52 percent. On average, monthly premiums run about $7 for each employee and $11 for each dependent unit. Most plans (77 percent) have deductibles and reimburse portions of reasonable and customary charges.

Preventive care tends to receive the most generous coverage, and major expenses like dentures and orthodontics are covered the least generously.

Vision care coverage is gradually becoming more common. Ten percent of the participants have plans, up from 4 percent in 1977.

AUTHOR'S NOTE

Although the Hay-Huggins Noncash Compensation Comparison for years 1972 through 1982 does not provide a continuous sample, it is possible to trace a crude trend in psychiatric benefits offered in the private sector plans surveyed. The number of survey respondents as well as the extent of data gathered increased per year and the individual participants varied from year to year. However, the percentage changes were large enough to confidently state the direction of change if not the magnitude of change.

The percentage of participating plans that included coverage of any kind for outpatient psychiatric benefits increased dramatically between 1972-1983 but during that same time period the percentage of plans covering those benefits at 50 percent or less also dramatically increased. Coverage of outpatient psychiatric treatment seems to be similar in the industrial firms and in the financial-service firms which participate. This is not true of inhospital coverage. Industrial firms were more likely to have the same inhospital coverage for mental and nervous disorders as for other illness than were financial-service firms. While inhospital coverage has remained less discriminated against than coverage of outpatient treatment, there has been a sizable decrease in the number of plans which cover inhospital psychiatric care on the same basis as other illnesses.

1983—Industrial and Financial Services

4. In-Hospital Psychiatric Care Coverage

Of the 582 companies which provide under base plan in-hospital psychiatric care, 534 (92 percent) provide doctors' services coverage under their basic plan while three plans (1 percent) have no coverage.

Table 9
BASIS OF ROOM AND BOARD COVERAGE FOR IN-HOSPITAL PSYCHIATRIC CARE UNDER BASIC PLAN—1983

	Industrial		Fin./Svc.		Total	
	No.	%	No.	%	No.	%
Same as for other confinements	226	65	86	45	312	58
Same coverage with separate maximum	119	35	103	54	222	41
Total plans	345	100	189	100	534	100

Of the 222 plans that provide the same coverage maximum, 49 percent of the plans have a 30 day limit, 14 percent have a 59-74 day limit, 19 percent have a 31-49 day limit and 17 percent have a 120 day limit. Of the 582 companies which provide in-hospital doctor expenses, 445 (76 percent) provide coverage under their basic plan.

Table 10
COVERAGE OF IN-HOSPITAL DOCTOR EXPENSES RELATED TO PSYCHIATRIC CARE UNDER BASIC PLAN—1983

	Industrial		Fin./Svc.		Total	
	No.	%	No.	%	No.	%
Same as for other hospital confinements	229	80	99	63	328	74
Same coverage with separate maximum	59	20	58	37	117	16
Total plans	228	100	157	100	445	100

For the 117 companies that have separate maximums for in-hospital psychiatric care, 103 express their maximum in number of visits, as the following table illustrates.

Table 11
MAXIMUM NUMBER OF VISITS FOR IN-HOSPITAL PSYCHIATRIC CARE IF SEPARATE MAXIMUM UNDER BASIC PLAN—1983

	Industrial		Fin./Svc.		Total	
	No.	%	No.	%	No.	%
30	2	4	4	8	6	6
30	2	41	27	56	49	47
31-59	4	7	9	18	13	13
60-119	17	31	7	14	24	23
120	8	15	7	14	24	23
120	1	2	1	2	2	2
Total	54	100	49	100	103	100

Sixty-two companies expressed their maximum as dollar limits.

Table 12
TREATMENT OF OUTPATIENT PSYCHIATRIC CARE—1983

	Industrial		Fin./Svc.		Total	
	No.	%	No.	%	No.	%
Subject to plan deductible	443	89	243	88	686	89
Subject to separate deductible	15	3	3	1	18	2
Not subject to deductible	13	3	10	4	23	3
Not covered	26	5	18	7	44	6
Total	497	100	274	100	771	100
No response	42		38		80	
Total major medical plans	539		312		851	

Seventy-one percent of the plans with out-patient psychiatric coverage are subject to coinsurance other than the overall major medical coinsurance, as shown in the following table.

Table 13
EMPLOYER COINSURANCE FACTOR FOR OUTPATIENT PSYCHIATRIC CARE COVERAGE

	Industrial		**Fin./Svc.**		**Total**	
Percent	**No.**	**%**	**No.**	**%**	**No.**	**%**
50	—	—	2	1	2	0
50	325	81	164	76	489	79
60-70	44	11	30	14	74	12
71-89	13	3	10	5	23	4
90-100	12	3	7	3	19	3
Other	12	3	7	3	19	3
Total plans with separate coinsurance	404	100	216	100	620	100

Forty-four percent of the plans have a dollar limit on eligible charges for each visit under outpatient psychiatric care.

Table 14
MAXIMUM ELIGIBLE DOCTOR'S FEE PER VISIT
(Before Application of Coinsurance)

	Industrial		**Fin./Svc.**		**Total**	
Amount in Dollars	**No.**	**%**	**No.**	**%**	**No.**	**%**
10	5	3	6	7	11	4
11-19	9	5	4	4	13	5
20	38	21	22	25	60	22
21-29	26	14	13	14	39	14
30	30	17	7	8	37	14
31-49	37	20	15	17	52	19
50	21	12	12	13	33	12
50	15	8	8	9	23	8
Varies	1	0	3	3	4	2
Total	182	100	90	100	272	100

Most plans have no limit on the maximum number of visits, as shown below.

Table 15
PREVALENCE OF A MAXIMUM NUMBER OF VISITS FOR OUT-PATIENT PSYCHIATRIC CARE

	Industrial		Fin./Svc.		Total	
	No.	%	No.	%	No.	%
Maximum per year	103	24	64	28	167	25
No maximum	325	76	169	72	494	75
Total	428	100	233	100	661	100
No response	43		23		66	
Total plans	471		256		727	

Table 16
MAXIMUM NUMBER OF VISITS PER YEAR FOR OUTPATIENT PSYCHIATRIC CARE

	Industrial		Fin./Svc.		Total	
Visits	No.	%	No.	%	No.	%
30	9	9	7	12	16	10
40-50	66	64	36	54	102	61
51-74	20	19	19	30	39	23
91-100	4	4	1	2	5	3
120	4	4	1	2	5	3
Total	103	100	64	100	167	100

Forty-one percent of the plans covering out-patient psychiatric expenses have no dollar maximum other than that in the overall major medical plan. Ten percent have a maximum for out-patient psychiatric expenses, combined with in-patient expenses. The remaining 49 percent of the plans have separate dollar maximums for outpatient care, either as a maximum per year or as a maximum per lifetime.

Table 17
SEPARATE DOLLAR MAXIMUM PER YEAR ONLY FOR OUT-PATIENT PSYCHIATRIC CARE

	Industrial		Fin./Svc.		Total	
Amount in Dollars	**No.**	**%**	**No.**	**%**	**No.**	**%**
500	3	2	1	1	4	2
500	37	22	15	21	52	21
501-599	—	—	2	3	2	1
600-750	15	9	5	7	20	8
751-999	1	—	—	—	1	—
1000	54	31	21	30	75	30
1040-1800	27	16	14	19	41	17
2000-2500	20	12	6	8	26	11
3000-4999	6	3	3	4	9	4
5000	3	2	1	1	4	2
5000	6	3	4	6	10	4
Total	172	100	72	100	244	100

Table 18
SEPARATE DOLLAR MAXIMUMS PER LIFETIME ONLY FOR OUT-PATIENT PSYCHIATRIC CARE

	Industrial		Fin./Svc.		Total	
Amount in Dollars	**No.**	**%**	**No.**	**%**	**No.**	**%**
3000	1	2	4	9	5	5
5000	3	5	2	4	5	5
7000-10,000	18	29	11	24	29	24
15,000-20,000	1	2	—	—	1	1
20,000-30,000	25	40	16	35	41	38
40,000	—	—	2	4	5	5
50,000	9	14	6	13	15	14
50,000-100,000	3	5	2	4	5	5
100,000	3	5	3	7	6	6
Total	63	100	46	100	109	100

Of the plans that have a combined maximum of per year and lifetime—31 Industrials and 25 Financial/Service—the most common per year maximum is $1000. The lifetime maximums reported were in the $10,000 to $50,000 range.

Table 19
PREVALENCE AND ELIGIBILITY FOR RETIREE MEDICAL COVERAGE

	Industrial		**Fin./Svc.**		**Total**	
	No.	**%**	**No.**	**%**	**No.**	**%**
Early retirees	46	9	14	4	60	7
Normal retirees	11	2	17	5	28	3
Both	373	70	215	70	588	70
No retiree coverage	103	19	66	21	169	20
Total	533	100	312	100	845	100
No response	6		3		9	
Total Plans	539		315		854	

Table 20
OUTPATIENT PSYCHIATRIC COVERAGE

	Any kind of outpatient coverage			**Coverage of 50% or less**		
	Total	**Industry**	**Fin./Svc.**	**Total**	**Industry**	**Fin./Svc.**
1972		unknown (N/R)		52	—	—
1973		not reported		48	49	46
1974		not reported		59	—	—
1975	74	combined		34	combined	
1976	84	82	87	61	60	63
1977	87	86	87	59	60	58
1978	77	76	78	41	41	41
1979	92	92	93	76	80	62
1980	91	90	94	77	80	79
1981	92	92	92	80	82	76
1982	92	93	91	78	82	74
1983	94	95	93	74	77	72

Table 21
INHOSPITAL PSYCHIATRIC COVERAGE
(Same as for other illnesses)

	Total	Industry		Fin./Svc.
1972	77		combined	
1973	80	83		76
1974	82		combined	
1975	*65*		combined	
1976	63		combined	
1977	65	69		58
1978	66	72		55
1979	58	64		46
1980	59	64		50
1981	57	62		46
1982	54	60		43
1983	58	65		45

Source: Hay-Huggins Non-Cash Compensation Comparison

Table 22

Insurance Coverage for Mental Illness in 300 Private Sector Health Plans: United States, 1983

	Total All Plans	Type of Plan Basic/MM	Type of Plan CMM	Source of Benefit Insured	Source of Benefit Self Insured	Source of Benefit BC/BS	Source of Benefit Comb.	Size of Case[1] (# of Employees) Sm.	Size of Case[1] (# of Employees) Med.	Size of Case[1] (# of Employees) Lge.
Total Plans in Category	300	156	144	149	84	27	30	65	48	187
Percent of Programs with:										
• Inpatient and Outpatient coverage same as for other conditions.	6%	6%	6%	9%	4%	7%	3%	2%	8%	8%
• Inpatient coverage same as other conditions; reduced coverage for Outpatient.	59%	51%	67%	62%	73%	19%	47%	55%	58%	60%
• Reduced coverage for both Inpatient and Outpatient.	31%	38%	24%	27%	19%	70%	46%	42%	27%	29%
	100%[2]									
	(Column entries above are percentages expressed in relation to category total)									
	(Column entries below are percentages expressed in relation to total number of employees)									
Percent of Employees with:										
• Inpatient and Outpatient coverage same as for other conditions.	6%	4%	2%	2%	3%	.1%	.3%	0%	.2%	.6%
• Inpatient coverage same as other conditions; reduced coverage for Outpatient.	44%	21%	23%	21%	21%	1%	3%	.1%	1%	42%
• Reduced coverage for both Inpatient and Outpatient.	46%	30%	16%	9%	2%	23%	8%	.4%	.8%	45%
	100%[2]	100%		100%				100%		

[1] "Small" plans cover fewer than 5,000 employees, "Medium" plans cover 5,000-10,000 employees, and "Large" plans cover 10,000 or more employees.

[2] Column totals in all cases will not add to 100% due to 3% of all plans, 4% of all employees which have the *same* coverage on an outpatient basis but reduced coverage for inpatient care.

Source: Muszynski et al; Ins. Coverage of Mental Health in 300 Plans, 1983.

Table 23
PRIVATE HEALTH INSURANCE COVERAGE OF MENTAL ILLNESS/MANDATORY COVERAGE (AS OF 11/83)

STATE	TYPE OF CONTRACT	TREATMENT SETTING	ALLOWABLE DAYS	ALLOWABLE DOLLARS	TREATMENT PROVIDER	OTHER PROVISIONS
Arkansas 1979 Ark. Acts. Act 803 (H.B. 936)	Individual and group plans	Outpatient	Not specified	Not specified	Licensed outpatient psychiatric centers	
Colorado Rev. Stat. 10-80116	Group	Inpatient	45 days per year; year: minimum	Not specified	Not specified	Two days partial hospitalization = one day inpatient care;
		Partial hospitalization (hospital, psychiatric hosp.)	90 days per year; minimum	Not specified	Not specified	Use of mental health benefits reduces alcohol benefit days;
		Outpatient: (major medical) comprehensive health corporations, hospitals, community mental health centers, mental health clinics	Not specified	$1,000 per year: minimum	Direct supervision of physician or psychologist	Copayment requirement may go to 50%. Deductible requirement same as other illnesses; Benefits payable to state institutions
Connecticut Gen. Stat. 38-174d	Group hospital or medical services corporations	Inpatient: public or private hospital	60 days per year: minimum	Not specified	Not specified	
Gen. Stat. 38-373	Individual and group comprehensive (optional contracts)	Outpatient: (major medical)	Not specified	50% copayment required $1,000 per year: maximum	Not specified	
		Outpatient	Not specified	$1,000 per year: maximum	Physician, nurses	Mental conditions defined by insurance commissioner; Additional medical social services benefits

STATE	TYPE OF CONTRACT	TREATMENT SETTING	ALLOWABLE DAYS	ALLOWABLE DOLLARS	TREATMENT PROVIDER	OTHER PROVISIONS
Maryland Ann. Code art. 48A, 470E, 477E, 354D	Individual, group, all nonprofit health corporations	Inpatient: hospital	30 days per year: minimum	Not specified	Not specified	Benefits only for acute mental illness which professional practitioners judge subject to short term therapy
		Outpatient: (major medical)	Not specified	50% minimum of benefits for other illnesses (usual deductibles)		
Massachusetts Gen. Laws 175:47B, 176:8A, 176B:4A, 176G:4	All general health insurance, employees health & welfare funds, nonprofit hospital corporations, medical service corporations & HMOs	Inpatient: public or private mental hospital	60 days per year: minimum	Not specified	Diagnosis or treatment by psychotherapist or psychologist	Mental or nervous conditions as described by Amerian Psychiatric Association;
		Outpatient: comprehensive health service organization, licensed hospital, state approved mental health or day care centers	Not specified	$500 per year: minimum		Inpatient benefits in general hospital same as other illness
Minnesota Stat. Ann. 62A.151	Group, nonprofit health corporations, HMOs	Licensed residential treatment facility	Same as other inpatient hospital, medical coverage	Same as other inpatient hospital, medical coverage		Applies only to emotionally handicapped children as defined by public welfare commissioner
Sta. Ann 62A.152	Group, nonprofit health corporations	Outpatient: licensed hospital, approved community mental health center or clinic	Not specified	90% of first $600 per year: minimum	In approved facility or by psychologist or psychiatrist	Required only if policy provides inpatient benefits for mental illness

STATE	TYPE OF CONTRACT	TREATMENT SETTING	ALLOWABLE DAYS	ALLOWABLE DOLLARS	TREATMENT PROVIDER	OTHER PROVISIONS
New Hampshire Rev. Stat. Ann. 415:18-a 420-5-a	Group contracts for medical or hospital expenses, group medical service corporations					
	Non-major medical policies	Inpatient: licensed general hospital or psychiatric hospital, public mental hospital	Same as other illnesses	Same as other illnesses		
		Outpatient: psychiatrist or psychologist Public mental hospital	15 hours per year: minimum	Same ratio of benefits to fees for psychiatric care as for physician care		
		Community mental health center		Same benefit ratio to charges for mental health care as for physician care		
	Major medical policies	Inpatient	Not specified	$3,000 per year; minimum with lifetime maximum of $10,000	Psychiatrist, psychologist	
		Outpatient	Not specified			
		Partial hospitalization (licensed general or mental hospital, community mental health center, office of psychologist or psychiatrist	Not specified			

STATE	TYPE OF CONTRACT	TREATMENT SETTING	ALLOWABLE DAYS	ALLOWABLE DOLLARS	TREATMENT PROVIDER	OTHER PROVISIONS
Rev. Stat. Ann. 419:5-a	Hospital service corporations	Same benefits as above except that: benefits for mental disorders under nonmajor medical policies are the same as for other diseases. Direct charges by psychiatrists or psychologists may be excluded from reimbursement.				
North Dakota Cent. Code ch. 26-39	Group, nonprofit hospital or medical service corporations	Licensed	70 days per year; minimum	Not specified	Not specified	One inpatient benefit day = two days partial hospitalization: Inclusive of alcohol and drug abuse benefits.
		Partial hospitalization	140 days per year; minimum			
		Combination	Combination			
Ohio Rev. Code 1737.28, 1738.24, 3923.28, 3923.30	Group, medical care corporations, health care corporations, hospital service associations, government employes or self-insured.	Outpatient: office, home, hospital, community mental health facility approved by state or JCAH.	Not specified	$500 per year: minimum subject to reasonable co-insurance and deductible.	By or under supervision of physician or psychologist	Note: Only requires outpatient mental health benefits in contracts covering mental or emotional illness; Individual may be limited to $500 total under all contracts; Facility utilization and peer review required; Four year sunset clause; Records required for premium determination.
Virginia Code 38.1-348.7	Individual, group, all nonprofit health corporations.	Inpatient: general or mental hospital.	30 days per year.	Same as other illnesses.	Not specified	Includes different inpatient alcohol and drug abuse benefits under mental disorders which are void if optional alcohol & drug abuse benefits chosen.

STATE	TYPE OF CONTRACT	TREATMENT SETTING	ALLOWABLE DAYS	ALLOWABLE DOLLARS	TREATMENT PROVIDER	OTHER PROVISIONS
Wisconsin Stat. 632.89	Group	Inpatient: hospital	30 days per year: minimum	Not specified	By or under supervision or referral of physician.	Includes family interview; Part of alcohol, drug abuse and mental illness package.
		Outpatient: partial hospitalization, licensed outpatient facility, hospital (if other outpatient benefits covered).				
California Ins. Code 10125, 10127 11512.5	Group, self-insured, certain nonprofit hospital service plans	Terms as agreed upon in contract	Terms as agreed upon in contract	Terms as agreed upon in contract	Terms as agreed upon in contract	1373, Health & Safety Code, health service plans may permit or exclude such benefits
Florida Stat. 627.668	Group	Inpatient	30 days per year: minimum	Not specified	Not specified	Mental disorders as defined by American Psychiatric Association
		Outpatient	Not specified	$500 per year: maximum 50% co-insurance	Appropriate mental health professional	Option incurs additional premium
Illinois P.A. 79-1514, 1976 Ill. Laws	Group accident & health; hospital and medical & health service corporations	Not specified	Not specified	50% copayment; lesser of $10,000 or 25% of lifetime limit per year: maximum	Physician or clinical psychologist	

STATE	TYPE OF CONTRACT	TREATMENT SETTING	ALLOWABLE DAYS	ALLOWABLE DOLLARS	TREATMENT PROVIDER	OTHER PROVISIONS
Kansas Stat. Ann. 40-2, 105	Group	Inpatient: licensed medical care facility, licensed community mental health center or clinic, psychiatric hospital	30 days per year: minimum	Not specified	Not specified	Must be refused in writing to avoid option Inclusive of alcohol or drug abuse benefits
		Outpatient	Not specified	100% of first $100 or 80% of next $500 per year: minimum	Physician or psychologist	
Louisiana Rev. Stat. 22:213.2	Group	Same as other illnesses	Same as other illnesses	Same as other illnesses	Physician: prescribed by psychiatrist; psychologist or licensed social worker in consultation w/physician	Maximum 12 months waiting period for mental illness benefits
Maine 1979 Me. Laws, ch. 419 (L.D. 1390)	Group policies	Outpatient	Not specified	Not specified	Mental health centers	Covers outpatient community mental health services
Maryland Ann. Code art. 48A, 477M, 354J	Group, nonprofit health corporations	Partial hospitalization—hospital, psychiatric day care center, community mental health center	30 days per year: minimum	Not specified	Medically directed psychiatric care	Option available for appropriate premium

STATE	TYPE OF CONTRACT	TREATMENT SETTING	ALLOWABLE DAYS	ALLOWABLE DOLLARS	TREATMENT PROVIDER	OTHER PROVISIONS
New York 1977 N.Y. Laws ch. 984.893	Group, hospital service corporations or health service corporations	Inpatient: hospital	30 days per year: minimum	Not specified	By certified facility or by psychiatrist or psychologist	Mental disorder defined by insurance policy: Subject to co-insurance and deductible set by superintendent of insurance: Optional social worker benefits
		Outpatient: certified by state	Not specified	$700 per year: minimum		
Oregon Rev. Stat. 743.558	Group	Inpatient: hospital	30 days per year: minimum	Not specified	Not specified	
		Outpatient: (major medical)	Not specified	50% up to $500 per year; usual deductible		
Vermont Stat. Ann. ch. 107, 4089	Group	Inpatient: general hospital, public or private mental hospital, community mental health center	45 day equivalent per year: minimum	Not specified	Not specified	Available for additional premium: Insurance company may require utilization review for payment;
		Outpatient: general hospital, public or private mental hospital, licensed mental health facility	Not specified	100% of first 5 visits; 80% thereafter or $500 per year: limit	In approved facility or by licensed mental health professional	Mental disorder defined as mental condition in diagnostic categories of international classification of disease as revised
Virginia Code 38.1.-348.7	Group, all nonprofit health corporations	Outpatient	Same as other illness	50% co-insurance & $1,000 per year: minimum	By hospital, mental health center, physician or psychologist	Alcohol & drug abuse included unless other specified option is chosen

STATE	TYPE OF CONTRACT	TREATMENT SETTING	ALLOWABLE DAYS	ALLOWABLE DOLLARS	TREATMENT PROVIDER	OTHER PROVISIONS
West Virginia Code 33-15-4a. 33-16-3a	Individual, group	Inpatient		Not specified	Not specified	Must be refused in writing
		Public or private mental hospital:	45 consecutive days per year: minimum			Mental condition defined by American Psychiatric Association
		General hospital	Same as other illnesses			Also covers 50 sessions per year w/psychologist or psychotherapist (supervised employee of mental health center)
		Outpatient: comprehensive health organizations, licensed hospital, approved mental health clinic	Not specified	50% up to $500 per year		
Georgia 56-2447 (S. 105-Laws '80)	Individual, group, nonprofit health corporations	Inpatient: hospital	Coverage for treatment of mental disorders to be same as other physical illness	Not specified	Not specified	The optional endorsement required to be made available shall not contain any exclusions, reductions, or other limitations as to coverages, deductibles, or coinsurance provisions which apply to the treatment of mental disorders unless such provisions apply generally to other similar benefits provided or paid for under the accident and sickness insurance benefit plan, policy, or contract.

STATE	TYPE OF CONTRACT	TREATMENT SETTING	ALLOWABLE DAYS	ALLOWABLE DOLLARS	TREATMENT PROVIDER	OTHER PROVISIONS
		Outpatient	Need not call outpatient for more than 40 visits per policy year	Not specified	Not specified	
Missouri 376381	Group, health sources corporation, HMO	Inpatient: hospital Residential Treatment Center	May be limited to 30 days	Not specified	RTC, if prescribed by physician specializing in treatment of mental illness	
		Outpatient: Residential Treatment	Not specified	Not less than 50% UCR to max. of $1,500 in benefit period; shall also offer 50% UCR for 20 psychotherapy visits	Physician or psychologist unless rejected by policy holder	Recognized mental illness as defined by American Psychiatric Association
Montana 3-22-701	Group, health service corporations	Inpatient: hospital	May be limited to 30 days per year	See below	Not specified	
		Outpatient	Not specified	$1,000 per benefit period; and maximum lifetime benefits to $10,000 or 25% of lifetime policy limit, whichever is less		30 outpatient visits per year with deductible and co-insurance not less favorable than illness generally.

STATE	TYPE OF CONTRACT	TREATMENT SETTING	ALLOWABLE DAYS	ALLOWABLE DOLLARS	TREATMENT PROVIDER	OTHER PROVISIONS
Tennessee 56-7-1004	Group hospital, medical or major medical	Inpatient	Not specified	Not specified	If contract provides inpatient benefits, shall include CMHCs with inpatient care facilities	
		Outpatient: CMHCs	Not specified	Not specified		

II. Changes in Delivery of Mental Health

Tables and charts in Appendix Section II show the dramatic transfer of patient care episodes from inpatient care, especially state and county mental hospitals, to outpatient psychiatric services. These changes were noted between 1955 and 1977. During this same period, the number of psychiatrists per 100,000 population more than doubled while the number of psychologists and social workers more than tripled. Some of this growth was due to an increased demand resulting from the closure of "warehousing" institutions.

The federal mental health dollar has been primarily going to Community Mental Health Clinics (CMHC) budgets while state and third-party dollars primarily support institutions. The local mental health dollar is fairly evenly divided among expenditures for community, county, CMHC, and institutions. CMHC, institutions and other community programs derive the largest percentage of their revenues from state sources.

Table 24

Number and Percent Distribution of Mental Health Facilities—by Type of Facility: United States, Selected Years 1970-1980

Type of Facility	1970	1972	1974	1976	1978	1980
	Number of Mental Health Facilities					
All facilities	3,005	3,187	3,315	3,480	3,738	3,727
State and county mental hospitals	310	321	320	303	297	280
Private psychiatric hospitals	150	156	180	182	188	184
Non-Federal general hospitals with separate psychiatric services	797	770	796	870	923	923[1]
V.A. psychiatric services[2]	115	119	119	126	136	136[1]
Federally funded community mental health centers	196	287	391	517	555	691[1]
Residential treatment centers for emotionally disturbed children	261	344	340	331	375	368
Freestanding psychiatric outpatient clinics	1,109	1,123	1,092	1,076	1,160	1,053
All other facilities[3]	67	67	77	75	104	92
	Percent Distribution of Mental Health Facilities					
All facilities	100.0	100.0	100.0	100.0	100.0	100.0
State and county mental hospitals	10.3	10.1	9.7	8.7	8.0	7.5
Private psychiatric hospitals	5.0	4.9	5.4	5.2	5.0	4.9
Non-Federal general hospitals with separate psychiatric services	26.5	24.2	24.0	25.0	24.7	24.8[1]
V.A. psychiatric services[2]	3.8	3.7	3.6	3.6	3.6	3.6[1]
Federally funded community mental health centers	6.5	9.0	11.8	14.9	14.9	18.5[1]
Residential treatment centers for emotionally disturbed children	8.7	10.8	10.3	9.5	10.0	9.9
Freestanding psychiatric outpatient clinics	36.9	35.2	32.9	30.9	31.0	28.3
All other facilities[3]	2.3	2.1	2.3	2.2	2.8	2.5

[1] Since January 1980 data are *not* available for V.A. psychiatric services, separate psychiatric services of non-Federal general hospitals, and federally funded community mental health centers (CMHCs), data are shown for February 1981 for CMHCs and for January 1978 for V.A. psychiatric services and separate psychiatric services of non-Federal general hospitals.

[2] Includes V.A. neuropsychiatric hospitals, V.A. general hospitals with separate psychiatric settings, and V.A. freestanding psychiatric outpatient clinics.

[3] Includes freestanding psychiatric day/night facilities and other multiservice mental health facilities with an inpatient setting which are not elsewhere classified.

Note: Information on facilities in Puerto Rico, Virgin Islands, Guam, and other U.S. Territories are excluded. Data are given at a point in time in January of a particular year.

Table 25

Mental Health Care Settings: The Changing Scene 1955-1977

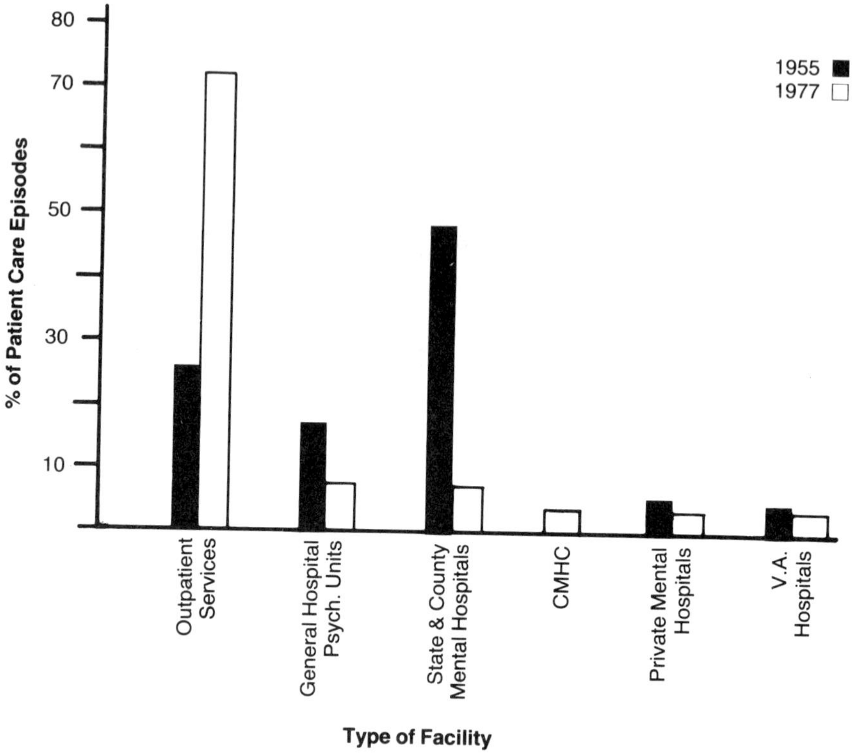

By % of Patient Care Episodes

Type of Facility:	1955	1977
Outpatient Psychiatric Services	23%	72%
General Hospital Inpatient Psychiatric Units	16	9
State & County Mental Hospitals	49	9
Community Mental Health Centers	0	4
Private Mental Hospitals	7	3
V.A. Hospitals	5	3

Source: Division of Biometry, NIMH

Table 26

Growth in Number and Rate of Mental Health Professionals: United States, 1955-1980

Group of Professionals	1955	1980	Change
Psychiatrists[1]			
Number	10,600	30,023	183% more
Rate per 100,000 population[2]	6.4	13.7	114% more
Psychologists[3]			
Number	13,500	56,933	322% more
Rate per 100,000 population[2]	8.1	25.9	220% more
Social Workers[4]			
Number	20,000	83,000	315% more
Rate per 100,000 population[2]	12.1	37.8	212% more

[1] Data until 1960 included American Psychiatric Association membership plus filled psychiatric residency positions. 1960-1980 data also included nonmembers of APA who reported their specialty as psychiatry to the American Medical Association. Approximately 10% of all psychiatrists in 1980 were child psychiatrists.

[2] Source for civilian population of the United States: U.S. Bureau of the Census: *Current Population Reports,* Series P-25, numbers 802 and 888.

[3] Data based on membership in the American Psychological Association. Until 1980, 37% of all psychologists were in clinical counseling or guidance psychology. In 1980 between 26,000 and 28,000 (52%) were licensed or certified health science provider psychologists.

[4] Data based on membership in the National Association of Social Workers. Approximately 20% to 25% of all social workers were in mental health practice. In 1980, 11,000 were on the register of "certified clinical social workers."

Table 27

National Health Expenditures and Percent of Gross National Product (In billions of dollars): United States, Selected Years 1950-1981

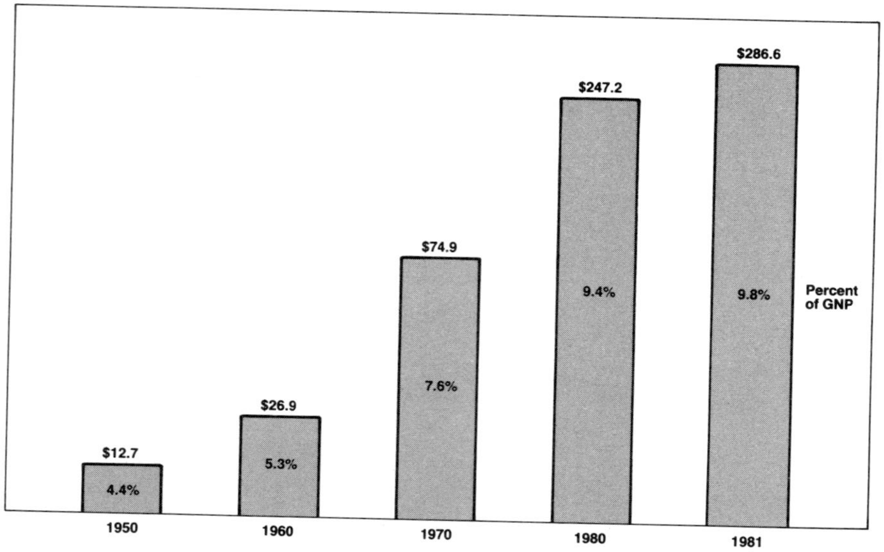

Note: The Gross National Product (GNP) is defined as the market value of goods and services produced by labor and property supplied by U.S. residents before deduction of depreciation charges and other allowances for business and institutional consumption of fixed capital goods.

Source: American College of Surgeons, Socio-Economic Factbook for Surgery 1982, Surgical Practice Dept., 1982.

Table 28
WHERE THE 1979 MENTAL HEALTH DOLLAR CAME FROM: SUMMARY CHART OF EXPENDITURES GROUPED BY CATEGORY

Budget Category	Sources*								
	Federal		**State**		**Local**		**Third-Party**		**Total**
CMHC	87,853	(29.48)	115,178	(38.68)	33,822	(11.35)	61,090	(202.50)	100%
Other community programs	14,261	(7.54)	143,544	(75.92)	14,710	(7.78)	16,548	(8.75)	100%
Institutions	—	—	573,330	(71.27)	33,603	(4.18)	187,294	(23.28)	100%

*In thousands of dollars and (percentages)

Source: Financing Mental Health: Patterns of Funding and the Analysis of Costs and Benefits in Services Delivery at the State and Federal Levels, Robert R. Rich and Neal M. Goldsmith, School of Urban and Public Affairs, Carnegie-Mellon University, Pittsburgh, PA 15213

This table represents financial data gathered by the Mental Health Policy research project (NIMH Grant No. 30792) over a three-year period from 1979 to the present from state sources (fiscal analysts, legislators, Governor's offices, etc.) and NIMH Biometry Division.

This table represents financial data gathered by the Mental Health Policy research project (NIMH Grant No. 30792) over a three-year period from 1979 to the present from state sources (fiscal analysts, legislators, Governor's offices, etc.) and NIMH Biometry Division.

Table 29

Where the Federal MH Dollar Goes—1975*
Summary Pie Chart of Expenditures Grouped by Department

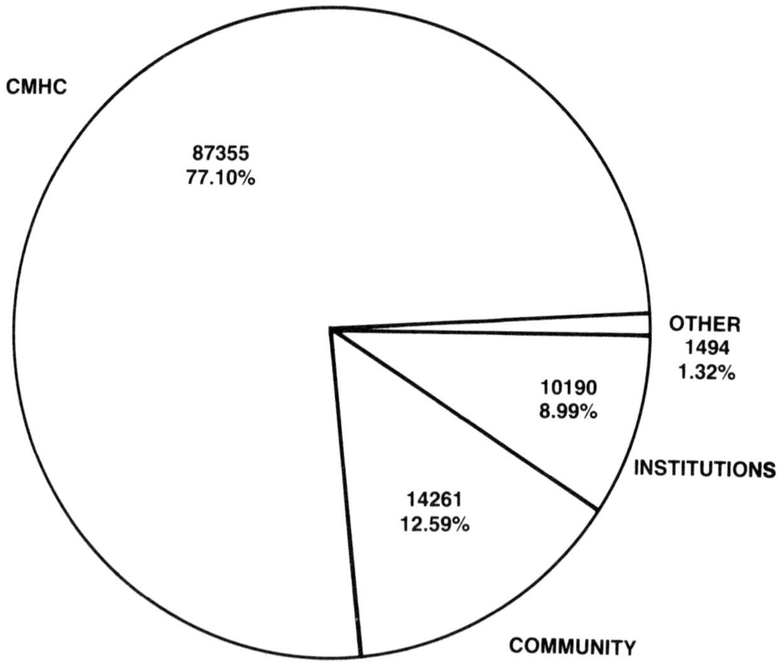

*In Thousands of Dollars and Percentages

This table represents financial data gathered by the Mental Health Policy research project (NIMH Grant No. 30792) over a three-year period from 1979 to the present from state sources (fiscal analysts, legislators, Governor's offices, etc.) and NIMH Biometry Division.

Table 30

Where the Third Party MH Dollar Goes—1979*
Summary Pie Chart of Expenditures Grouped by Department

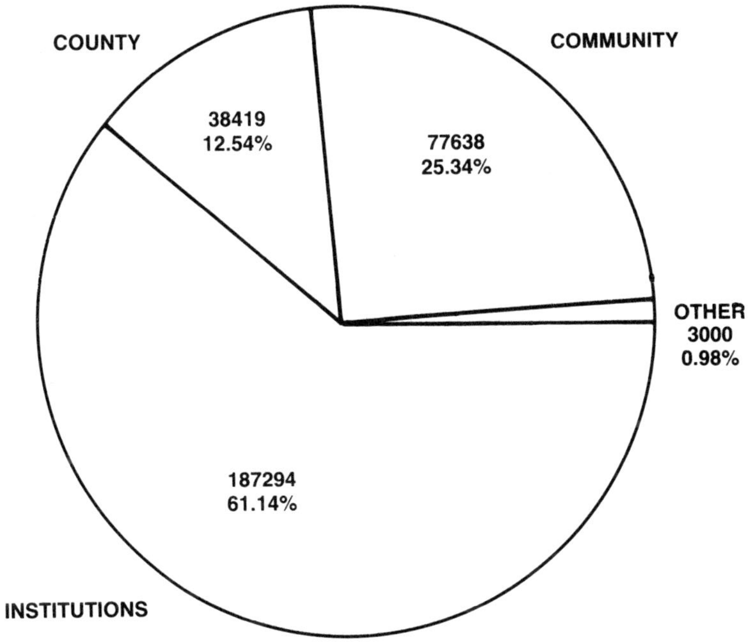

*In Thousands of Dollars and Percentages

This table represents financial data gathered by the Mental Health Policy research project (NIMH Grant No. 30792) over a three-year period from 1979 to the present from state sources (fiscal analysts, legislators, Governor's offices, etc.) and NIMH Biometry Division.

Table 31

Where the State MH Dollar Goes—1979*
Summary Pie Chart of Expenditures Grouped by Department

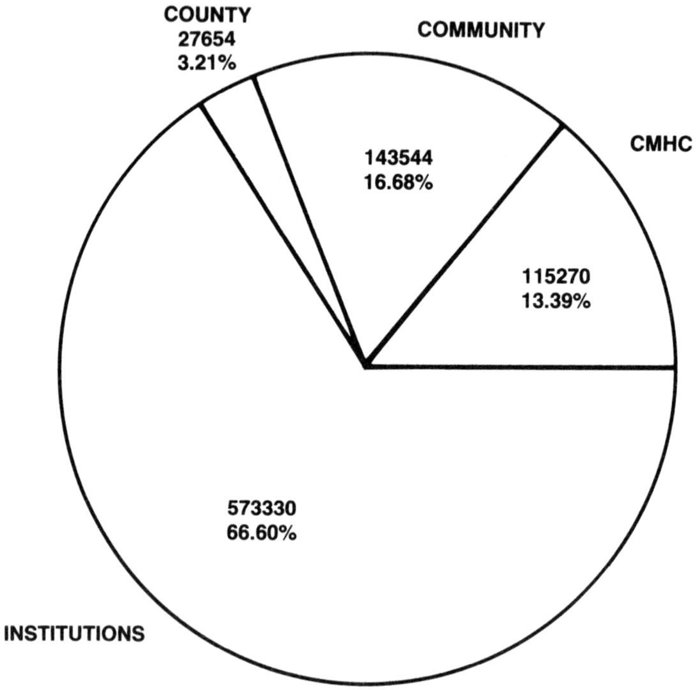

*In Thousands of Dollars and Percentages

This table represents financial data gathered by the Mental Health Policy research project (NIMH Grant No. 30792) over a three-year period from 1979 to the present from state sources (fiscal analysts, legislators, Governor's offices, etc.) and NIMH Biometry Division.

Table 32

Where the Local MH Dollar Goes—1979*
Summary Pie Chart of Expenditures Grouped by Department

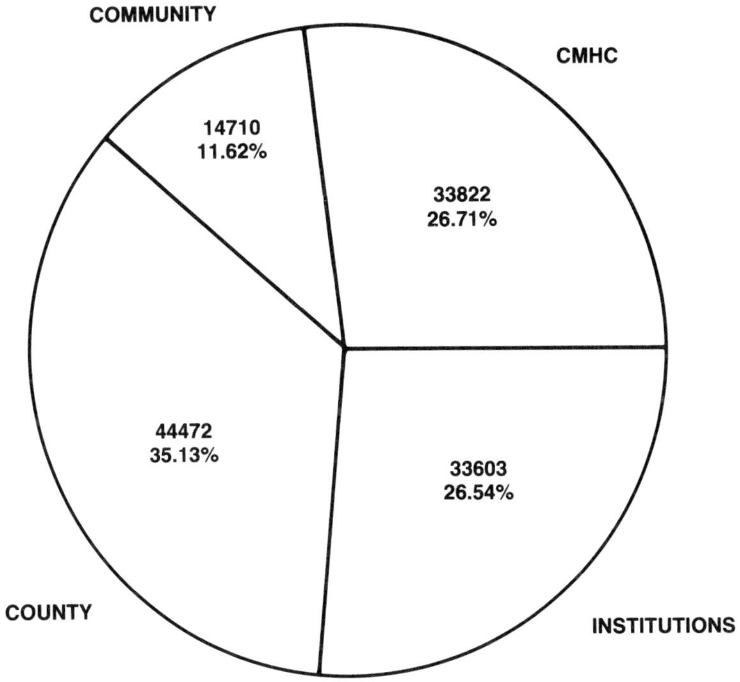

*In Thousands of Dollars and Percentages

Current Developments In Prospective Reimbursement Systems For Financing Hospital Care

EXCERPTS FROM:
AN INFORMATION PAPER

Prepared For Use By The
Special Committee On Aging
United States Senate

October 1983

U.S. Government Printing Office
Washington: 1983

Executive Summary

State ratesetting programs have, at least in some cases, been effective in reducing the rate of growth in hospital expenditures. For example, the national growth in average annual per capita hospital costs between 1976 and 1980 was 13.8 percent per year. In contrast, seven States with mandatory ratesetting programs had an average annual per capita increase of 10.5 percent—a 25-percent reduction in the rate of increase.

These States and their annual average rates of increase in per capita hospital costs between 1976 and 1980 include: Connecticut, 11.2 percent; Maryland, 13.2 percent; Massachusetts, 11.4 percent; New Jersey, 11.8 percent; New York, 9.1 percent; Washington, 10.9 percent; Wisconsin, 12.5 percent.

A majority of States now have prospective payment systems for at least one payer in operation. Using such devices as revenue caps, rate and budget review, DRG's, price competition, and primary care networks, State governments are actively seeking reasonable and affordable prices for hospital care.

The trend toward prospective payment systems includes a variety of new and creative State and local programs developed, and in some cases implemented over the last year.

A primary example of a prospective payment strategy is the recent Federal decision to introduce fixed dollar rates for different types of diagnostic related groups (DRG's) in the medicare program. But the price constraint imposed on medicare costs will not, alone, resolve the overall problem of hospital cost increases.

With only medicare reimbursement under a fixed-price prospective system, hospitals may shift the medicare revenue costs that exceed their other payers. This possibility is significantly reduced in many States by new and important approaches to the full containment of hospital costs. Because of immediate fiscal pressures, an increasing number of States are operating and developing payment systems that seek to establish a fixed purchase price for hospital services. This paper presents a framework for understanding the many different State prospective systems now in operation.

Prospective Payment Mechanisms

At the heart of each alternative prospective payment system is the mechanism for determining the actual dollars to be spent for hospital services. At a minimum, attention must be given to the following components: (a) Determination of the unit of payment; (b) scope of revenue subject to the prospective system; (c) establishing the rate; and (d) reviewing and modifying established rule.

(A) Determination of the Unit of Payment

Prospective payments are made on the basis of hospital cost performance as measured by specific units of payment, which may include the total hospital budget, separate department budgets, direct medical and indirect administrative costs, actuarially defined costs per subpopulation, type of diagnosis, length of stay, average per diem costs, and units of service produced. Different units of payment can produce different kinds of hospital responses in order to keep costs below the prospective payment rates. For example, prospective systems that control a hospital's total revenues, rather than establish per diem or per case payment rates, create less incentive for the hospital to try to circumvent the cost-control system by increasing admissions or lengths of stay. Payment units based on per case, per diem, or specific services are all open to circumvention by increases in volume. In addition, if such units are used, extensive utilization controls may be necessary in order to insure that only the needed quantity of care is provided. The use of total revenue caps or capitated reimbursement strategies may motivate hospitals to reduce the quantity (admissions and patient days) and the unit costs of services (through changes in case mix or reductions in scope of service).

(B) Scope of Revenue Subject to the Prospective System

Much of the discussion about prospective payment systems focuses on the scope of the revenues subject to the incentives contained in such systems. As a general rule, all-payer systems that prospectively determine all hospital revenue will have a more significant impact on hospital expenditures than single or partial payer programs, because the greater proportion of hospital revenue controlled, the more the cost-containment potential of the prospective system is increased. A common fear expressed about such unilateral payment systems is that a centralized regulatory environment may be created that may not recognize the legitimate fiscal needs of hospitals for meeting future contingencies such as the purchase price of new technology, increased demands by physicians, and requests to create new community "outreach" programs.

(C) Establishing the Rate

One of the basic components of a prospective reimbursement programs is the method used for establishing the actual rate to be paid for hospital care.

Although there are a variety of practical methods currently used, four general methods can be identified. *Direct negotiation* typically involves direct contact between the ratesetting organization and either individual hospitals or their collective representatives. In general, hospitals present their financial requirements and ratesetters challenge these needs on the basis of designated target rates. Bargaining over payment amounts often provides the opportunity for the ratesetters to consider the circumstances and requirements of individual facilities.

The negotiation approach can require extensive administrative effort when applied to large numbers of institutions or to widely diverse hospital facilities. The relative skills of the respective ratesetters, rather than clear objective factors, can also play a major role in determining the actual prices paid.

The *bidding approach* involves the solicitation of bids from hospitals prior to the payment period. The purchasers of services select the lowest bid or establish criteria for evaluating the submitted bids. Although the bidding approach reflects market-based assumptions, since price competition among hospitals may be weak in a given market, securing meaningful cost-containing bids in this manner may be impractical. This is particularly true if hospitals are unwilling to participate or compete with each other by offering different price and service packages.

Under the *budget review and approval* approach, the rate-determining authority or agency periodically examines the budgets and schedules of individual hospitals and establishes rates according to guidelines prescribed by the authority. The frequency and extent of the review determines the influence this approach may have on hospital costs. The success of the budget review approach typically depends on the extent of good data, technical resources, and the expertise of the budget reviewers in evaluating hospital costs, operations, and accounting procedures.

Setting rates through the *application of a formula* is an approach that varies widely from simple techniques to quite sophisticated methods. One common application of this approach is the calculation of appropriate payment levels for a given hospital based on a projection of the historically averaged costs of care for patients likely to be served by that institution. For example, by determining the "average cost per patient" for the prior year and trending it forward to the coming year with adjustments for such variables as case mix, potential demand, changes in actuarially defined population characteristics, and inflation, estimates of expected costs can be developed. The DRG methodology in the medicare program uses a formula that fixes future prices for different types of medical diagnoses based on an adjusted estimate of the expected costs for each separate diagnostic group.

Another way of using a formula for determining prices is to place each individual hospital into a "peer group" of similar facilities based on a set of key differentiating variables. In this approach, each hospital in a given group is assumed to share common fiscal requirements with all other hospitals in the same group. After calculating an aggregate measure of costs for each group for the prior year and adjusting it to reflect probable changes, the same prospective rate is applied to each hospital in each separate group.

These four approaches to setting prospective rates are not mutually exclusive. Many of the programs currently in place combine elements from each of the methods. For example, formulae are often found with budget review and approval approaches that set overall financial ceilings, and direct negotiation is often a part of the bidding approach.

Several different techniques are used to review and modify prospective hospital payment rates. Some involve an examination of the internal cost history and past trends within a single hospital. Others involve comparative examinations of groups of similarly situated hospitals. Such reviews may be based on an examination of the use of cost screens or statistical analyses, the examination of specific operating procedures, financial data, or the simultaneous review of budget and costs reports.

Other guidelines are used to evaluate proposed increases or to modify previously established rates, such as imposition of legislatively determined ceilings or variable rates of increase based on external economic factors (e.g., consumer or market-basket indices) and internal factors (e.g., case mix, bed size, etc.).

MEDICAID HOSPITAL REIMBURSEMENT

(As of July 1983)

		Alternative Payment Systems				
		Medicaid Only				
STATE	Medicare Principles	Prosp. rate setting	Rate of increase control	Other	Multiple Payer	Expected Changes in 1984
Alabama		X[1]				
Alaska	X					
Arizona				X[4]		
Arkansas	X					
California				X[5]		
Colorado			X[1]			
Connecticut	X					
Delaware	X					
Florida	X		X[1]			
Georgia		X[2]				
Hawaii	X					
Idaho			X[3]			
Illinois		X[1]				
Indiana	X					
Iowa		X[1]				
Kansas	X					
Kentucky			X[1]			
Louisiana	X					
Maine	X					X[12]
Maryland					X[6]	
Massachusetts					X[4]	
Michigan			X[1]			
Minnesota	X					
Mississippi		X[1]				
Missouri		X[1]				
Montana	X					
Nebraska		X[1]				
Nevada	X					
New Hampshire	X					
New Jersey					X[8]	
New Mexico	X					
New York					X[9]	
North Carolina		X[1]				
North Dakota	X					
Ohio	X					
Oklahoma		X[1]				
Oregon	X					
Pennsylvania	X					X[13]
Rhode Island					X[10]	
South Carolina	X					
South Dakota	X					
Tennessee	X					
Texas	X					
Utah			X[2]			X[14]
Vermont	X					
Virginia		X[1]				
Washington					X	
West Virginia	X					X[15]
Wisconsin			X[2]			X[16]
Wyoming	X					
District of Columbia	X					
TOTAL	26	10	7	2	6	

1. Per diem
2. Per discharge
3. Per admission
4. Negotiation/Per discharge
5. Negotiation/Per diem
6. Budget/Rate review and approval (all payer system)
7. Budget/Revenue limits (all payer system)
8. Budget/Rate review and Approval/Rate per case (all payer)
9. Prospective cap on revenues (all payer system)
10. Negotiated "Maxi-Cap"—statewide percentage revenue limit increase
11. Budget/Rate review and approval
12. In 1983 Maine established a Health Care Finance Commission empowered to implement a mandatory, all payer prospective rate setting program. The law authorizes the Commission to seek a waiver for Medicare participation in the system.
13. Pennsylvania is considering implementing a prospective reimbursement system for Medicaid only, based upon diagnosis related groups.
14. Utah is considering adopting a DRG methodology to its alternative payment system for Medicaid.
15. In 1983 West Virginia created a Health Care Cost Review Authority to implement a mandatory, all payer rate setting program by mid-1984. A waiver for Medicare participation has not been granted as yet.
16. In 1983 Wisconsin modified its program by creating a mandatory all payer rate-setting program to be administered by a three member commission. The program is to be fully implemented by January 1, 1985. The law specifically prohibits the commission from using a case-mix methodology, such as DRGs, until January 1, 1987.

Source: Intergovernmental Health Policy and Office of Reimbursement Policy, Health Care Financing Administration, DHHB.

III. Utilization Studies

The experience of large groups shows that about 2 percent of the group utilize mental health benefits and only about 16 percent of these account for more than one-half of all psychiatric benefits paid. Within small groups, however, utilization rates vary widely and are not easily predicted. Utilization varies geographically as does length of stay. This geographic variation appears to be consistent over time.

One variable that hinders accurate utilization analyses is the prevalence of error in diagnoses reporting on insurance forms. A couple of studies address the problem and its primary cause—fear about confidentiality.

Tables from Federal Employees' Experiences as a Guide to the Cost of Insuring Psychiatric Services in the Various States

By John Krizay, M.A.
American Journal of Psychiatry 139:7, July 1982

The two largest plans in the Federal Employees Health Benefits Program—Blue Cross and Blue Shield and Aetna—have reported benefit payments and the number of people who have used psychiatric services on a state-by-state basis for two decades. The author translates this experience into per capita utilization rates in constant dollar terms and compares the benefit costs of the two plans over a 4-year period (1976-1979). Within each state, utilization rates did not change much over the 4 years, and the rank ordering among states by rate of utilization was quite similar for both plans. The author believes that the consistency noted can be useful in estimating costs of psychiatric coverage at the state level. (Am J Psychiatry 139:866-871, 1982)

Table 33
1979 DATA ON FEDERAL EMPLOYEES' ENROLLMENT IN AND UTILIZATION OF PSYCHIATRIC SERVICES THROUGH BLUE CROSS AND BLUE SHIELD (BC/BS) AND AETNA, BY STATE

State	Federal Employees in State		Number of People Covered		Percent of People Covered Who Received Benefits		Benefits per Covered Person		Rank Order of Benefits	
	N[a]	%	BC/BS	Aetna	BC/BS	Aetna	BC/BS	Aetna	BC/BS	Aetna
Alabama	59.9	1.6	117,873	20,728	1.4	1.5	$17.26	$10.57	20	36
Alaska	15.3	3.7	12,962	12,855	1.7	1.2	10.26	6.15	43	46
Arizona	34.5	1.5	51,900	19,266	1.6	1.4	16.40	11.83	24	31
Arkansas	18.4	0.9	29,818	10,380	1.2	1.5	13.46	8.67	32	41
California	290.1	1.3	256,349	155,015	1.9	1.8	34.83	16.67	4	15
Colorado	47.9	1.8	78,119	12,936	1.8	2.3	30.65	17.77	6	11
Connecticut	21.0	0.7	17,339	3,492	2.6	2.1	45.39	24.96	2	2
Delaware	5.0	0.9	11,436	938	1.5	0.7	16.72	24.20	22	4
District of Columbia, Maryland, Virginia	483.0	4.8	1,092,059	141,564	2.7	2.6	47.42	24.86	1	3
Florida	79.3	0.9	125,426	49,532	1.6	1.7	17.78	15.22	18	20
Georgia	75.9	1.5	144,329	27,674	1.7	2.0	28.08	20.16	7	5
Hawaii	25.0	2.8	2,115	3,883	1.8	2.0	17.07	13.88	21	24
Idaho	10.5	1.2	8,148	5,703	1.2	1.1	7.08	4.78	47	48
Illinois	101.7	0.9	178,470	29,707	1.1	1.1	20.08	13.82	14	25
Indiana	40.2	0.7	74,302	10,846	1.0	1.0	11.62	9.35	38	40
Iowa	19.0	0.7	37,454	5,950	1.0	1.0	10.74	11.85	40	30
Kansas	22.6	1.0	39,654	6,042	2.6	2.0	39.60	29.73	3	1
Kentucky	34.3	1.0	61,422	9,157	1.2	1.5	13.68	11.36	31	33
Louisiana	31.4	0.8	53,616	14,313	1.2	1.4	13.03	16.10	35	16
Maine	9.2	0.8	22,851	3,563	1.3	1.0	10.29	6.27	42	45
Maryland[b]										
Massachusetts	57.8	1.0	154,705	7,564	2.0	2.3	32.26	19.05	5	8
Michigan	53.4	0.6	87,457	9,462	1.3	1.4	16.35	11.91	25	29
Minnesota	29.4	0.7	29,226	8,052	1.6	1.3	18.38	15.27	16	19
Mississippi	26.8	1.1	42,955	8,365	1.1	1.2	10.19	9.88	44	37
Missouri	65.0	1.3	110,694	19,122	1.4	1.4	23.89	15.60	10	18

Table 33 (continued)
1979 DATA ON FEDERAL EMPLOYEES' ENROLLMENT IN AND UTILIZATION OF PSYCHIATRIC SERVICES THROUGH BLUE CROSS AND BLUE SHIELD (BC/BS) AND AETNA, BY STATE

Montana	12.4	1.6	11,456	7,148	1.2	1.2	10.84	5.51	39	47
Nebraska	15.4	1.0	24,710	5,412	1.2	1.3	12.89	17.76	37	12
Nevada	9.2	1.4	6,423	9,758	1.7	0.9	14.87	7.58	30	43
New Hampshire and Vermont	19.1	1.4	26,578	5,890	1.3	1.4	8.26	12.14	46	27
New Jersey	68.6	0.9	119,607	14,767	1.6	1.4	22.60	18.04	12	10
New Mexico	26.5	2.2	40,506	14,069	1.2	1.5	16.29	12.12	26	28
New York	166.2	0.9	210,948	25,647	1.3	1.6	22.96	18.69	11	9
North Carolina	41.8	0.8	62,324	12,630	1.3	1.9	13.04	10.91	34	35
North Dakota	8.3	1.3	16,101	1,335	1.0	1.0	13.36	7.59	33	42
Ohio	89.4	0.8	157,620	21,855	1.3	1.6	20.16	16.02	15	17
Oklahoma	46.8	1.9	86,372	32,198	1.5	1.9	16.25	19.06	27	7
Oregon	26.8	1.1	23,876	15,195	1.1	1.3	12.17	11.82	28	32
Pennsylvania	128.0	1.1	202,849	21,602	1.6	1.4	25.74	17.66	9	13
Rhode Island	9.4	1.0	27,388	667	0.9	1.5	16.64	4.54	23	49
South Carolina	31.4	1.1	69,524	9,079	1.1	1.9	10.49	15.00	41	21
South Dakota	9.9	1.4	13,811	3,493	0.6	0.9	4.80	7.21	50	44
Tennessee	68.0	1.6	60,439	11,879	1.9	1.7	18.03	14.31	17	23
Texas	148.0	1.1	306,740	62,551	1.5	1.8	22.56	19.71	13	6
Utah	34.6	2.6	68,060	5,439	1.3	1.5	15.02	13.11	29	26
Vermont[c]										
Virginia[b]										
Washington	58.9	1.6	31,587	30,122	1.9	1.4	17.32	9.82	19	39
West Virginia	15.7	0.8	27,256	5,249	0.9	1.1	9.00	11.23	45	34
Wisconsin	26.2	0.6	33,224	6,371	1.6	1.6	12.92	16.80	36	14
Wyoming	6.4	1.5	9,229	2,576	0.9	1.0	5.42	9.84	49	38
Overseas	129.1		25,739	17,549	0.4	0.3	6.09	3.26	48	50
Total	2,852.0	1.3	4,503,818	940,960	1.8	1.7	$27.55	$16.39		

[a]Expressed in thousands.
[b]See data for District of Columbia, Maryland, and Virginia.
[c]See data for New Hampshire and Vermont.

Table 34
1979 BY STATE, CONVERTED TO 1981 PRICES

State	Mean Benefit per Covered Person		Range of Benefits per Covered Person			
			BC/BS		Aetna	
	BC/BS	Aetna	Low	High	Low	High
Alabama	$25.44	$18.25	$21.46	$27.76	$13.14	$24.29
Alaska	13.51	10.74	11.49	16.66	7.62	15.69
Arizona	21.97	15.76	20.40	23.44	12.97	17.53
Arkansas	11.82	13.48	9.38	16.74	10.78	16.45
California	37.94	22.25	34.17	43.32	20.73	24.12
Colorado	27.34	24.40	33.04	33.31	21.20	30.21
Connecticut	56.29	51.48	52.54	59.35	31.04	73.00
Delaware[a]	18.87	16.21	12.85	22.67	8.43	30.09
District of Columbia, Maryland, Virginia	58.52	34.80	57.22	59.82	30.16	42.80
Florida	22.00	20.74	21.19	22.40	19.56	23.56
Georgia	30.73	24.60	28.70	34.93	19.32	31.53
Hawaii[b]	28.00	15.38	16.63	41.89	8.10	20.45
Idaho	9.89	6.67	8.81	12.18	3.88	11.12
Illinois	23.14	17.73	19.81	25.87	15.49	20.32
Indiana	14.63	15.45	13.95	15.10	11.63	22.61
Iowa[a]	15.34	16.86	13.18	18.33	12.88	23.59
Kansas	44.81	33.05	38.88	50.29	28.94	36.98
Kentucky[a]	21.81	18.14	17.01	25.68	14.13	26.52
Louisiana[a]	18.07	19.93	16.21	30.68	17.67	21.56
Maine[b]	10.97	20.17	7.52	13.41	7.80	37.98
Maryland[c]						
Massachusetts	37.83	20.93	34.30	39.56	17.25	23.69
Michigan	19.85	15.38	18.51	20.75	14.37	17.90
Minnesota[a]	17.45	19.47	7.52	22.86	16.17	24.65
Mississippi	12.57	15.81	12.21	12.98	12.29	20.86
Missouri	29.54	20.03	26.96	32.31	18.05	24.14
Montana	9.73	6.71	6.71	13.48	4.97	7.86
Nebraska	17.36	18.25	16.03	18.39	15.68	22.09
Nevada	16.72	9.39	12.76	20.89	8.12	10.86
New Hampshire and Vermont[a]	13.26	14.42	10.27	17.28	7.17	19.47

Table 34 (continued)
1979 BY STATE, CONVERTED TO 1981 PRICES

State	Mean Benefit per Covered Person		Range of Benefits per Covered Person			
			BC/BS		Aetna	
	BC/BS	Aetna	Low	High	Low	High
New Jersey[a]	26.13	17.45	14.02	28.11	14.50	22.43
New Mexico[a]	23.70	15.96	20.26	25.39	13.17	21.90
New York[e]	30.99	20.47	27.18	36.83	16.04	23.25
North Carolina	16.60	15.33	15.73	17.35	11.89	19.43
North Dakota[b]	15.94	21.50	12.26	18.59	9.44	45.10
Ohio	24.17	20.76	21.99	25.95	19.44	22.51
Oklahoma	20.94	22.59	18.08	23.82	18.37	27.18
Oregon	15.06	12.34	14.84	15.24	10.59	14.70
Pennsylvania	30.73	19.30	27.61	33.73	17.16	21.96
Rhode Island[b]	22.04	11.17	20.49	23.86	5.65	18.77
South Carolina[b]	11.78	16.93	9.87	13.05	11.47	22.23
South Dakota	5.02	12.20	4.09	5.97	8.97	14.80
Tennessee	22.36	21.90	20.79	24.03	18.09	26.73
Texas	31.24	26.06	28.06	33.25	21.92	29.66
Utah[a]	19.78	15.89	18.66	21.83	10.90	18.35
Vermont[d]						
Virginia[c]						
Washington	18.37	11.05	16.00	19.48	9.70	12.29
West Virginia[c]	11.06	12.38	10.20	12.28	8.20	18.32
Wisconsin	14.10	22.04	12.33	16.07	17.82	25.47
Wyoming[c]	8.17	13.57	5.79	11.49	5.98	21.34
Overseas	6.31	6.88	5.28	7.57	4.15	11.27
Total	$33.56	$21.68	$33.05	$34.26	$19.90	$24.53

[a]Benefit costs in these states were consistent in 3 of the 4 years. Revised figures dropping off the "unusual" year are available from the author on request.
[b]No consistent pattern was found (the high range is probably the safest predictor).
[c]See data for District of Columbia, Maryland, and Virginia.
[d]See data for New Hampshire and Vermont.
[e]Pattern was consistent in only 2 of the 4 years (the mean is probably a good long-term predictor).

Table 35
GEOGRAPHIC COMPARISON OF OUTPATIENT CHARGES FOR MENTAL DISORDERS (BLUE CROSS/BLUE SHIELD FEHB HIGH OPTION SUPPLEMENTAL BENEFITS)

	Wash., D.C., Metropolitan Area				Ohio				California			
	Utilizers (N=21,589)		Amount Covered (Total=$32,963,910)		Utilizers (N=8,084)		Amount Covered (Total=$1,588,210)		Utilizers (N=4,259)		Amount Covered (Total=$4,287,887)	
Expenditure (dollars)	N	Percent	Dollars	Percent	N	Percent	Dollars	Percent	N	Percent	Dollars	Percent
0-999	14,112	65.4	4,647,202	14.1	7,785	85.7	444,258	28.0	3,236	76.0	1,035,709	24.2
1,000-1,999	3,023	14.0	4,324,554	13.1	148	8.1	206,124	13.0	502	11.8	708,324	16.5
2,000-3,999	2,315	10.7	6,524,801	19.8	81	3.9	221,334	13.9	301	7.1	844,849	19.7
4,000-5,999	906	4.2	4,373,944	13.3	14	0.7	69,974	4.4	98	2.3	472,704	11.0
6,000-9,999	732	3.4	5,689,906	17.3	26	1.2	205,150	12.9	78	1.8	597,409	13.9
10,000-14,999	294	1.4	3,574,409	10.9	20	1.0	258.785	16.3	28	0.7	339,556	7.9
15,000-19,999	157	0.7	2,712,711	8.2	7	0.3	113,508	7.1	14	0.3	242,196	5.6
Over 20,000	50	0.2	1,115,383	3.4	3	0.1	69,081	4.3	2	0.0	47,140	1.1

Source: "Insuring Intensive Psychotherapy" by Sharfstein and Hagnas, AJP 132:12, Dec. 75.

OTA Study of Variation in Hospital Length of Stay

A 1980 case study by the Office of Technology Assessment focused on hospital lengths of stay (LOS) and their relation to health outcomes. As the search for health care cost containment intensifies, regional differences in cost per capita, LOS, admissions per 1000 and even the distribution of diagnosis, assume greater research importance.

The OTA study found high LOS concentration in the North East and low LOS more prevalent in the West (Table 37). Mental disorders deviated from the general trend by having longer average LOS in the North Central region than in the North East region and shorter average LOS in the South than in the West (Table 38). Using LOS for schizophrenia diagnoses for regional medicaid utilization comparisons, OTA found the highest LOS in the North East and the lowest in the West (Table 40). Distribution of mental disorders was also found higher in the North East (6.3 percent of all health conditions) and lowest in the South (3.3 percent) Table 39.

OTA concludes that, although regional differences clearly exist, too little is known about the economic benefits of decreased LOS and, more importantly, the possible negative effects on patient health. Research on the economics of health care develops more and more questions but the questions help define parameters for future research.

EXCERPTS FROM:

Health Technology Case Study 24: *Variations in Hospital Length of Stay: Their Relationship to Health Outcomes* (Washington, D.C.: U.S. Congress, Office of Technology Assessment, OTA-HCS-23, August 1983).

In general, average length of stay (LOS) in short-term, non-Federal hospitals has been falling since 1968 in the United States. Figure 1 shows the trends in LOS since 1965, the year in which the Medicare and Medicaid laws were passed, for the United States as a whole and for each of four age groups. The increase in LOS that followed the enactment of the Federal health insurance legislation and continued through 1968 in both the U.S. average and the elderly is the only dramatic departure from an otherwise virtually unbroken decreasing trend. The early years of the Medicare program also witnessed a rapid rise in the proportion of hospitalized patients that were elderly. While this proportion has risen continuously from 16 percent in 1965 to 26 percent in 1980, fully 40 percent of the increase took place between 1965 and 1968 (130). Since 1968 all age groups have shown decreasing lengths of stay; the elderly have decreased by 25 percent, the older adult group by 18 percent, the young adult group by 15 percent, children by 12 percent, and the combined U.S. average by 14 percent.

Given this pervasive downward trend in LOS, the stability of the geographic differences in LOS over time is remarkable.

Table 36

Age Specific Trends in Hospital Length of Stay

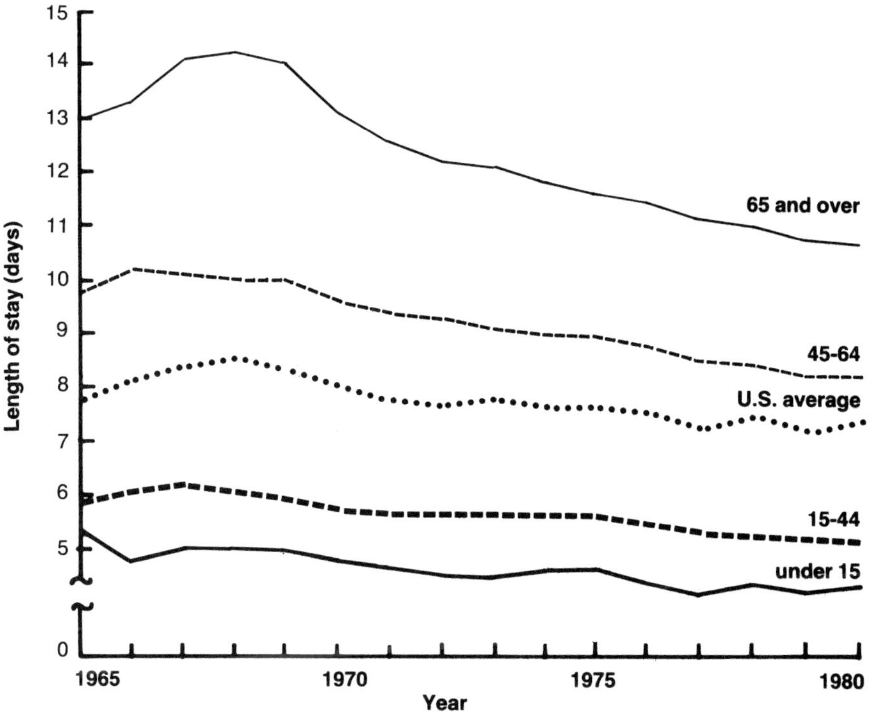

SOURCE: *Vital and Health Statistics,* series 13, Nos. 2, 10, 14, 17, 19, 23, 26, 31, 41, 48, 55, 60 64 (Washington, D.C.: National Center for Health Statistics 1967-82

Table 37

Regional Differences in Hospital Length of Stay: Trends Over Time

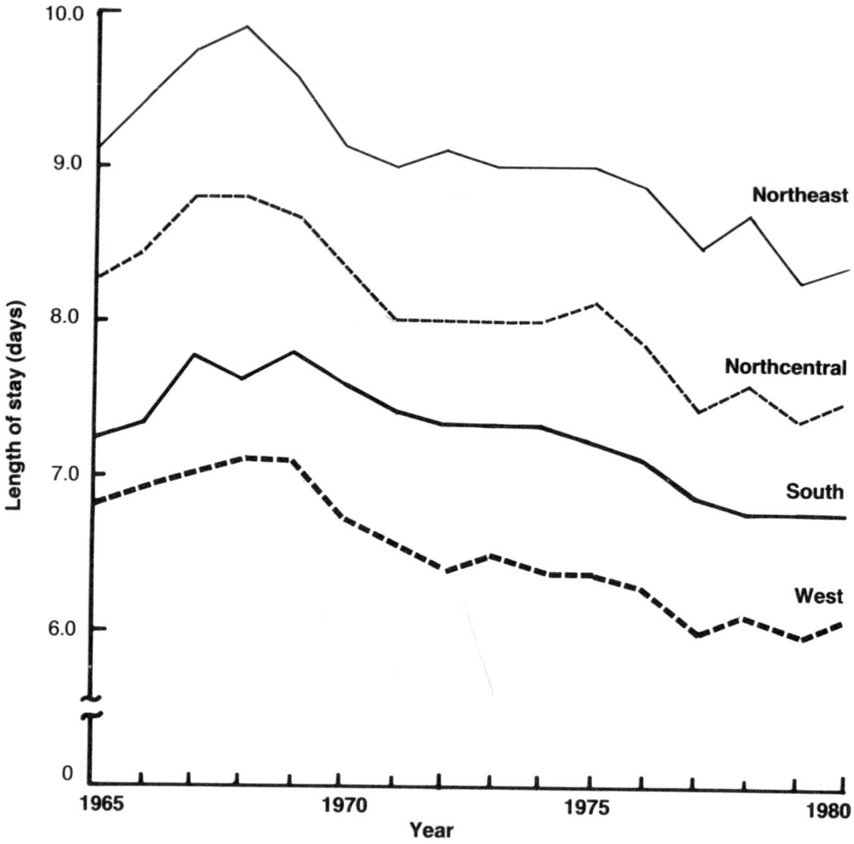

SOURCE: *Vital and Health Statistics,* series 13, Nos. 2, 10, 14, 17, 19, 23, 26, 31, 41, 48, 55, 60 64 (Washington, D.C.: National Center for Health Statistics. 1967-82).

Table 38
DIAGNOSIS-SPECIFIC LENGTH OF STAY BY REGION: 1980

Condition	LOS in days				
	U.S.	NE	NC	S	W
1. Mental disorders	11.6	11.6	13.4	9.8	10.7
2. Neoplasms	10.5	12.0	10.7	10.1	8.5
3. Circulatory disorders	10.0	12.4	10.2	9.2	8.1
4. Endocrine, nutritional, metabolic, and immunity disorders	9.6	11.8	9.7	8.9	7.7
5. Perinatal disorders	8.7	8.1	9.5	9.0	7.3
6. Musculoskeletal diseases	8.3	9.8	8.9	8.1	6.5
7. Skin diseases	8.0	9.5	7.8	7.4	7.8
8. Injury and poisoning	7.7	9.5	7.8	7.3	6.6
9. Hematologic disorders	7.2	8.8	6.9	6.8	6.0
10. Gastrointestinal diseases	7.0	7.9	7.2	6.6	6.2
11. Infectious and parasitic diseases	6.9	7.7	7.3	6.6	6.1
12. Congenital anomalies	6.6	6.8	7.5	6.0	5.9
13. Respiratory diseases	6.3	7.6	5.9	6.3	5.4
14. Genitourinary disorders	5.6	5.7	5.8	5.6	5.0
15. Diseases of the nervous system	5.4	6.3	5.5	5.4	4.5
16. Symptoms, signs, and ill-defined conditions	4.5	5.0	4.6	4.6	3.7
17. Supplementary classification (85% newborn deliveries)	3.7	4.3	4.1	3.4	3.0
18. Complications of pregnancy and childbirth	2.5	2.2	2.6	2.7	2.3
All conditions	7.3	8.5	7.5	6.8	6.1

Key: NE = North East, NC = North Central, S = South, W = West.

SOURCE: *Vital and Health Statistics*, series 13, No. 64, DHHS publication No. (PHS) 82-1725 (Washington, D.C.: National Center for Health Statistics, 1982).

Table 39
DISTRIBUTION OF CASES BY DIAGNOSIS BY REGION: 1980

Condition	Region (percent of cases)				
	U.S.	NE	NC	S	W
1. Mental disorders	4.5	6.3	4.9	3.3	3.9
2. Neoplasms	6.5	8.0	6.6	5.5	6.7
3. Circulatory disorders	13.6	14.5	13.1	13.6	13.2
4. Endocrine, nutritional, metabolic, and immunity disorders	3.0	3.0	3.1	3.1	2.7
5. Perinatal disorders	0.2	0.2	0.3	0.2	0.3
6. Musculoskeletal diseases	5.9	4.6	6.6	5.7	7.0
7. Skin diseases	1.6	1.7	1.6	1.6	1.4
8. Injury and poisoning	9.5	8.4	9.3	9.3	11.8
9. Hematologic disorders	0.9	1.0	0.9	0.9	0.7
10. Gastrointestinal diseases	12.3	12.1	12.1	13.4	10.5
11. Infectious and parasitic diseases	1.7	1.7	1.6	1.9	1.6
12. Congenital anomalies	0.9	0.9	1.0	0.8	0.9
13. Respiratory diseases	9.1	8.1	9.2	10.1	8.2
14. Genitourinary disorders	9.5	9.4	9.2	10.4	8.3
15. Diseases of the nervous system	4.7	4.4	5.4	4.0	5.1
16. Symptoms, signs, and ill-defined conditions	1.7	1.3	1.7	2.0	1.6
17. Supplementary classification (85% newborn deliveries)	11.7	10.9	11.0	11.8	13.5
18. Complications of pregnancy and childbirth	2.7	3.4	2.5	2.4	2.6
All conditions	100.0	99.9	100.1	100.0	100.0

Key: NE = North East, NC = North Central, S = South, W = West.

SOURCE: *Vital and Health Statistics*, series 13, No. 64, DHHS publication No. (PHS) 82-1725 (Washington, D.C.: National Center for Health Statistics, 1982).

Table 40
HIGHEST AND LOWEST DHHS REGIONS FOR MEDICAID LENGTH OF STAY IN 1980 BY DIAGNOSIS RELATED GROUP (DRG)

Description and number of DRG	Number of cases	Highest region	LOS (days)	Lowest region	LOS (days)
1. Normal Mature Newborn (318)	357,633	II[a]	5.2	IX	3.3
2. Normal Delivery (278)	208,641	V	3.3	IX	2.2
3. Complicated Delivery (281)	159,092	V	3.8	IX	2.8
4. Functional Intestinal Disorder (206)	58,990	II	5.5	X	3.6
5. Schizophrenia (89)	44,206	II	20.5	IX	11.5
6. Seizures, syncope, chest pain, or epistaxis with secondary diagnosis (323)	30,236	II	7.3	X	4.0
7. Electrolyte disorder (333)	27,016	II	9.2	X	5.2
8. Urinary symptoms (328)	20,860	II	7.2	X	4.3
9. Fracture with major operation, including hip athroplasty (348)	16,792	II	18.9	IX	12.0
10. Diabetes (75)	15,276	II	12.0	X	6.8
11. Congestive heart failure (132)	15,996	II	11.6	X	6.7
12. Ischemic heart disease without operation (124)	12,095	II	8.5	X	4.8
13. Acute Myocardial Infarction (121)	11,578	II	14.4	X	9.8
14. Pneumonia over age 30 (167)	11,066	II	12.0	X	7.8
15. Emphysema without operation (176)	10,941	III	14.4	X	6.9

[a]Region II = New York, New Jersey; Region III = Pennsylvania, Delaware, West Virginia, Virginia, District of Columbia, Maryland; Region V = Illinois, Indiana, Ohio, Wisconsin, Michigan, Minnesota; Region IX = California, Nevada, Arizona, Hawaii; Region X = Washington, Oregon, Idaho, Alaska.

SOURCE: *PSRO Data Reporting and Analysis System* (Baltimore, Md.: Health Standards and Quality Bureau, 1982).

The Mental and Nervous Disorder Utilization and Cost Survey: An Analysis of Insurance for Mental Disorders

By O.B. Towery, M.D., Steven S. Sharfstein, M.D., and Irving D. Goldberg, M.P.H.

Am J Psychiatry 137:9, September 1980

The Mental and Nervous Disorder Utilization and Cost Survey in Washington, D.C., has yielded useful information about outpatient utilization within an insurance plan with broad mental health coverage, as well as evidence that a comprehensive benefit with a low deductible and copayment can be offered and reasonably utilized. From the results of this survey and a substudy of claims made during 1977, the authors conclude that psychiatric diagnostic information submitted on insurance claim forms may often be inaccurate, primarily because of providers' concerns about confidentiality; such information is of little use for peer review or claims review. The authors state that caution must be exercised in generalizing from the experience under this plan to speculate about outpatient utilization which might result from broad coverage on a national level.

The Mental and Nervous Disorder Utilization and Cost Survey (MANDUCS) is a statistical aggregation of all outpatient claims in one year for patients in the Washington, D.C., area who are covered by the Government-Wide Service Benefit Plan, usually referred to as the Blue Cross and Blue Shield Federal Employee Program (FEP). It represents the first large-scale survey of primarily office-based private practice using insurance claims forms.

Findings

Tables 41-45 present some of the major findings from the MANDUC survey. During the 1977 calendar year there were approximately 758,771 participants in the Washington, D.C., area Blue Cross and Blue Shield FEP. As can be seen from Table 41, mental disorder claims were submitted during 1977 for 15,484 individuals (2 percent of the enrolled population), for a total of 506,451 outpatient visits. The total charges for these visits were $20,115,309, for an average of $1,299.10 per individual and $40.00 per visit. The cost of outpatient psychotherapy per enrollee was approximately $26.50 per year.

As can be seen in Table 41, most patients were seen by psychiatrists, followed by psychologists and psychiatric social workers. Only a small proportion of patients were seen by psychiatric nurses and non-psychiatric physicians. The proportion of visits claimed by each type of provider was similar, with psychiatrists making claims for 69.6 percent of the visits, psychologists 18.4 percent, social workers 11.6 percent, psychiatric nurses 0.3 percent, and nonpsychiatric physicians 0.2 percent.

Table 42 presents data on the percent of individuals with paid claims who made a specified number of visits to the indicated type of provider. Similarly, Table 43 presents data on the percent of all visits to that provider type accounted for by those individuals. Table 43 shows that approximately one-half of all visits paid for were those of individuals who made 60 visits or less, and Table 1 reveals that these individuals represented 84 percent of all subjects in the study. Stated conversely, nearly one-half of all visits paid for were the 16 percent of individuals who made 60 visits or more in 1977. This situation, in which a small number of recipients use a large portion of services, is comparable to other medical benefits, especially those in the "catastrophic" category. In Table 44 we see that these individuals accounted for more than one-half of all money claimed for the 1977 outpatient mental benefit.

It can be seen from Table 43 that psychiatrists tended to have more claims for individuals with a large number of visits in 1977 than did the other types of providers. Although about 60 percent of the visits claimed by both the psychologists and social workers were for individuals with 50 visits or less, only about 40 percent of the visits claimed by psychiatrists were for such individuals. It is possible that some of this difference is attributable to the great number of psychoanalysts in the area.

For discussion purposes we have included in Table 45 the distribution of diagnostic categories that were recorded on the claims which were paid. Although these data are valid from the standpoint that they represent what was submitted on the insurance claims, we do not believe that they accurately reflect actual practice in the area. A substudy conducted by the Washington Psychiatric Society provided evidence that providers have submitted less "severe" diagnoses (i.e., more diagnoses of neurosis and transient situational adjustment reaction) because of legitimate concerns about confidentiality. For the substudy, area psychiatrists were asked to anonymously submit aggregate data on the numbers of FEP patients they saw in 1977 and their diagnoses, with no identifying patient information.

Diagnoses seen in the Washington Psychiatric Society study were much more evenly distributed across diagnostic categories than those in the MANDUC survey, and the distribution more closely resembles that found in other studies of private-practice psychiatry, such as the Joint Information Service study of 1975 (1). Because of this finding, we feel that tabulations such as numbers of visits and dollars claimed based on each diagnostic category are of little value for peer and claims review purposes unless mechanisms can be developed to collect these data separately from personal identifying information. We have therefore omitted these data from our presentation.

Discussion

There is a paucity of knowledge about the utilization of outpatient mental health services in the private sector. Nonetheless, health insurers and others must make difficult decisions related to the types of services and service providers, as well as length and intensity of treatment, that should be covered. The MANDUCS data can be very informative when used alongside data from other studies of different populations in different treatment settings. However, we would like to caution about the extent to which these data can be used as a basis for speculation about the degree of utilization nationwide if the entire population were covered by an outpatient nervous and mental benefit as comprehensive as the Blue Cross and Blue Shield FEP. The Washington area is in many ways not typical of the rest of the country. There is a very dense concentration of mental health providers in the Washington area, probably as dense as or denser than any other area in the country. In general, the insured population is more highly educated and of a higher socioeconomic class than is found in most areas. Employment and other demographic characteristics of the insured, such as average age and family size, no doubt also affect the utilization patterns in this area.

Given these considerations, it is probably safe to conclude that utilization under the FEP represents the most intensive utilization that might occur under such a comprehensive mental health benefit. Certainly the utilization is greater than has been reported in other studies of outpatient psychiatric practice (2).

A final issue that merits discussion relates to any attempt to analyze utilization patterns of a health insurance benefit based on the data submitted on the claims form. This is the question of the accuracy of the data that are submitted.

The most questionable item submitted on FEP mental and nervous disorder insurance claims is the diagnosis. Even though many have questioned the usefulness of a DSM-II diagnosis in determining the appropriate length and intensity of psychotherapy, insurers have generally insisted that a DSM-II diagnosis be submitted as part of the routine claims procedure. The one hypothesis was that fears about confidentiality might lead providers to submit diagnoses perceived to be less severe because of the social stigma and negative connotations of many diagnoses.

If these diagnoses are inaccurate, we feel that it is probably due to providers' concerns about confidentiality. Such diagnostic information is of little use for peer review or claims review unless mechanisms are developed to collect it without personal identifying data. Such a system, developed by the Washington Psychiatric Society, has been described elsewhere (3).

References

(1) Marmor J, Scheidemandel P, Kanno C: Psychiatrists and Their Patients: A National Study of Private Office Practice, Washington, DC. Joint Information Service of the American Psychiatric Association and the National Association of Mental Health, 1975.

(2) Reed LS: Coverage and Utilization of Care for Mental Conditions Under Health Insurance—Various Studies, 1973-74. Washington, DC, American Psychiatric Association, 1975.

(3) Sharfstein SS, Towery OB, Milowe ID: Accuracy of diagnostic information submitted to an insurance company. Am J Psychiatry 137:70-73, 1980.

TABLE 41
MANDUC SURVEY DATA ON THE UTILIZATION AND COST OF OUTPATIENT SERVICES FOR MENTAL DISORDERS FOR 15,484 INDIVIDUALS IN 1977, BY TYPE OF PROVIDER

Measures of Utilization and Cost	Board-Eligible Psychiatrists	Clinical Psychologists	Psychiatric Social Workers	Psychiatric Nurses	Nonpsychiatric Physicians	All Providers
Individuals						
Number	11,232	3,760	2,459	126	91	15,484[a]
Percent	72.5	24.3	15.9	0.8	0.6	100[a]
Total visits	352,303	93,155	58,713	1,376	904	506,451
Average number of visits per individual	31.4	24.8	23.9	10.9	9.9	32.7
Median number of visits per individual	15.9	15.4	14.7	6.8	6.2	19.5
Total dollars claimed	14,788,492	3,504,803	1,760,327	27,861	33,826	20,115,309
Percent of total dollars claimed	73.5	17.4	8.8	0.1	0.2	100
Average dollars per individual claimed	1,317	932	716	221	372	1,299
Average dollars per visit claimed	42	38	30	20	37	40

[a]Not a row sum because some individuals were seen by more than one type of provider.

Table 42
MANDUC SURVEY DATA ON THE CUMULATIVE PERCENT OF 15,484 INDIVIDUALS WITH A SPECIFIED NUMBER OF VISITS TO VARIOUS TYPES OF PROVIDERS IN 1977

Number of Visits	Percent of Individuals					
	Board-Eligible Psychiatrists	Clinical Psychologists	Psychiatric Social Workers	Psychiatric Nurses	Nonpsychiatric Physicians	All Providers
1-5	24.7	21.9	20.0	42.9	44.0	17.0
1-10	39.0	37.2	37.1	66.7	72.5	31.5
1-20	55.9	57.8	60.3	87.3	86.8	50.8
1-30	66.2	70.9	75.1	92.1	92.3	63.4
1-40	74.9	80.3	84.3	96.8	96.7	73.4
1-50	80.5	87.4	89.0	98.4	97.8	80.2
1-60	83.9	90.5	91.5	98.4	100.0	84.0
1-80	89.6	95.1	95.4	99.2	100.0	90.2
1-100	93.5	98.1	98.0	100.0	100.0	94.2
1-150	97.4	99.7	99.3	100.0	100.0	97.8
1-200	99.5	99.9	99.7	100.0	100.0	99.6
1-200+	100.0	100.0	100.0	100.0	100.0	100.0

Table 43
MANDUC SURVEY DATA ON CUMULATIVE PERCENT OF VISITS ACCOUNTED FOR BY 15,484 INDIVIDUALS WITH A SPECIFIED NUMBER OF VISITS TO VARIOUS TYPES OF PROVIDERS IN 1977

	Percent of Visits					
Number of Visits	**Board-Eligible Psychiatrists**	**Clinical Psychologists**	**Psychiatric Social Workers**	**Psychiatric Nurses**	**Nonpsychiatric Physicians**	**All Providers**
1-5	2.0	2.6	2.4	11.3	12.7	1.6
1-10	5.6	7.4	8.1	29.4	35.0	5.1
1-20	13.7	20.0	22.7	56.2	55.6	14.0
1-30	21.9	33.3	38.3	66.4	68.8	23.7
1-40	31.8	46.7	51.9	82.8	84.0	34.5
1-50	39.8	59.5	60.6	89.2	88.5	43.8
1-60	45.8	66.3	66.4	89.2	100.0	50.3
1-80	58.6	79.5	77.7	93.8	100.0	63.5
1-100	69.6	90.4	87.5	100.0	100.0	74.6
1-150	85.0	97.7	93.8	100.0	100.0	88.1
1-200	96.4	99.5	97.0	100.0	100.0	97.0
1-200+	100.0	100.0	100.0	100.0	100.0	100.0

Table 44
MANDUC SURVEY DATA ON THE CUMULATIVE PERCENT OF DOLLARS CLAIMED BY 15,484 INDIVIDUALS WITH A SPECIFIED NUMBER OF VISITS TO VARIOUS TYPES OF PROVIDERS IN 1977

	Percent of Dollars Claimed					
Number of Visits	Board-Eligible Psychiatrists	Clinical Psychologists	Psychiatric Social Workers	Psychiatric Nurses	Nonpsychiatric Physicians	All Providers
1-5	2.1	3.5	2.5	12.4	13.7	1.7
1-10	5.8	8.5	8.3	29.9	36.2	5.4
1-20	14.0	21.5	23.1	57.3	57.1	14.4
1-30	22.3	34.6	38.8	67.9	68.3	23.9
1-40	31.9	48.3	52.1	86.3	82.6	34.4
1-50	39.9	60.7	60.9	93.3	88.1	43.6
1-60	45.6	67.4	66.7	93.3	100.0	49.9
1-80	58.3	80.2	77.7	96.1	100.0	62.7
1-100	68.6	90.6	87.4	100.0	100.0	73.3
1-150	84.3	97.7	93.8	100.0	100.0	87.3
1-200	96.3	89.5	97.1	100.0	100.0	96.9
1-200+	100.0	100.0	100.0	100.0	100.0	100.0

Table 45
MANDUC SURVEY DATA ON THE NUMBER AND PERCENT OF 15,484 INDIVIDUALS WITH A SPECIFIED DIAGNOSIS OF MENTAL DISORDER ON CLAIMS BY ALL PROVIDERS IN 1977

	Individuals with Diagnosis	
DSM-II Diagnosis	Number[a]	Percent
Schizophrenia	821	5.3
Affective disorders	474	3.1
Psychotic organic brain syndrome	32	0.2
Neuroses	12,742	82.3
Personality disorders	1,585	10.2
Alcoholism	145	0.9
Drug dependence	17	0.1
Psychophysiologic disorders	182	1.2
Transient situational disorders	1,892	12.2
Nonpsychotic organic brain syndrome	36	0.2
Mental retardation	11	0.1
All other diagnoses	858	5.5

[a]Numbers total more than 15,484 because some individuals received more than one diagnosis.

Accuracy of Diagnostic Information Submitted to an Insurance Company

By Steven S. Sharfstein, M.D., O.B. Towery, M.D., and Irvin D. Milowe, M.D.

Findings from two studies of the utilization of the mental health benefit under the Washington, D.C., area Blue Cross and Blue Shield Federal Employees Program suggest that diagnostic information submitted to insurance companies on claims forms is often inaccurate and therefore of little use for claims or peer review. The authors conclude that inaccurate information is submitted primarily because of legitimate concerns about patient confidentiality. They urge that special claims and peer review procedures be developed to assure confidentiality of sensitive clinical information. A pilot project developed by the Washington Psychiatry Society and Blue Cross and Blue Shield is offered as an example of the kinds of systems that need to be devised.

Since the beginning of the MANDUC survey, there was concern that many of the data collected on the claims forms would be inaccurate. A new form that was developed in the national offices of Blue Cross and Blue Shield, the Mental Health Report Form, was sent about the same time as the MANDUC survey began to the local plans that administer the FEP. This form asked for a diagnosis, symptoms, and an estimate of degree of impairment; the identifying information attached to it included name, address, and insurance membership numbers.

Both providers and patients strongly objected to the form because they feared breaches of confidential information. After one year of use Blue Cross and Blue Shield withdrew the form and substituted a requirement for an augmented itemized bill, which included the patient's name, age, beginning date of treatment, type of treatment, and diagnosis. Although serious questions were raised about the validity of the symptom and degree of impairment information formerly collected, these became less relevant once the form was no longer in use. However, questions about the accuracy of the diagnosis submitted with the itemized bill persisted.

In an effort to assess the accuracy of the diagnoses submitted to Blue Cross and Blue Shield, the Washington Psychiatric Society sent a letter to all members asking them to complete anonymously an enclosed form to indicate the numbers, ages, and diagnoses of patients seen in 1977 under the FEP. Letters were sent to approximately 1,000 members, and 305 forms were returned; 23 members indicated that they had seen no FEP patients in 1977, and 4 forms were filled out incorrectly, leaving 278 forms to be tabulated.

Findings

The WPS reported age and diagnoses for 6,604 patients, over half of the number of patients recorded in the MANDUC survey (N = 11,232). There was a remarkable similarity in the age groupings in the two studies; to some extent this indicates that the WPS study is indeed representative of patients seen under the FEP. The striking differences between the two studies are seen when diagnostic categories are compared (Table 46). In the MANDUC survey 84.3 percent of the outpatients received a diagnosis of neurosis, and in the WPS study only 28.4 percent received this diagnosis. There were 10.6 percent of patients with a psychotic diagnosis (schizophrenia, psychotic organic brain syndrome, or major affective disorder) and 9.5 percent with a personality disorder diagnosis in the MANDUC survey, as opposed to 24.7 percent and 20.8 percent, respectively, in the WPS study. In general the diagnoses seen in the WPS study are more evenly distributed than those in the MANDUC survey, which are skewed toward the diagnosis of neurosis.

Discussion

Two sets of inconsistent study results about a given population suggest that one or the other or both are inaccurate. Certainly diagnostic data from both studies can be no more accurate than current diagnostic terminology permits. The appropriateness of *DSM-II* diagnoses for categorizing the many types of problems that lead individuals to seek psychotherapy is open to question. Our point is not that the *DSM-II* categories are without function or validity but rather that at times one diagnosis might be selected for lack of a better choice. To the extent that this occurs, diagnostic information from both studies is inaccurate.

It is possible that the WPS forms returned do not represent a random sample of patients or that those completing the form recorded inaccurate diagnoses. Each provider may have encountered problems in constructing his past year's experience with FEP patients, or some providers may want to create a picture that they are dealing with more severely disturbed patients than would appear from the MANDUC survey. Most psychiatrists in the Washington area are aware that continuation of the present Blue Cross and Blue Shield FEP psychiatric benefit has been questioned in the past; it may be that many of the respondents to the WPS study felt their practices might be threatened if it appeared as though the benefit was not being utilized by those with more severe disorders.

In this light, it is useful to compare the results of other studies of private practice psychiatry with the present studies. In a national study of private practice psychiatry conducted by Marmor and associates (1), 45 percent of patients seen were given a diagnosis of neurosis, 18 percent a diagnosis of psychosis (schizophrenia, major affective disorder, and organic brain syndrome), and 18.1 percent a diagnosis of personality disorder. In a 1977 study of private psychiatrists conducted by Langsley (2) in central California, 31 percent of patients were given a diagnosis of neurosis, 27 percent psychosis (affective disorder and schizophrenia), and 9 percent personality disorder. Finally, in a 1975-1976 survey by the National Center for Health Statistics, psychiatrists sampled indicated that 42 percent of patients seen were given a diagnosis of neurosis, 15.9 percent psychosis (schizophrenia and affective disorder), and 13.5 percent personality disorder (3).

Clearly, the data from the WPS study more closely resemble the diagnostic percentages found in these three studies, with less than half the patients receiving a diagnosis of neurosis and substantial numbers receiving diagnoses in the psychosis and personality disorder categories. Although the evidence is not conclusive, we feel that the MANDUCS data deviate from the patterns in the other four studies largely because the information for each patient in the MANDUC survey was not anonymous.

Many insurance companies allege that they have an elaborate, "foolproof" system for maintaining the confidentiality of claims data. This is little consolation to the clinician charged with the weighty responsibility of assuring that no potentially damaging information about his patient is released. The information needed to evaluate the security procedures of each insurance company's claims department is usually not readily available, and the legal question of who can and cannot have access to any set of data is usually very complex and subject to change over time. The relative lack of control that the clinician has over such information after it has left his office adds greatly to the uncertainty.

Because of the social stigma and often pejorative connotations attached to certain psychiatric diagnoses, many clinicians are concerned that writing down a diagnosis which the patient may see can have adverse effects on the therapeutic process. Insurance companies have a legitimate stake in the fiscal accountability of their program, and they are increasingly concerned about quality assurance. One solution is to develop peer review and claims review procedures that make it possible to review cases with no one person having access to both patient-identifying data and sensitive clinical information. A system recently developed jointly by the Insurance Coordinating Committee of the Washington Psychiatric Society and representatives of Blue Cross and Blue Shield enables peer review of selected cases in an anonymous fashion by utilizing an assigned number for each case. The collection of identifiable clinical data by the insurer is still possible; in fact, a diagnosis is still required. This system does, however, offer an approach that minimizes infringements on confidentiality. It enables the insurer and peer reviewers to review cases and make decisions based on information much more relevant and valid than the submitted diagnosis. Potentially, such a system allows for an accountability process that requires only the name, date, type of treatment, and charge on the claims forms.

It is clear from the MANDUC survey that a diagnosis submitted directly to an insurance carrier with no provision for anonymity will not reassure practitioners on the confidentiality of the information. Indeed, this information is likely to be inaccurate, putting into question the basis on which insurers must protect accountability. The goals of appropriateness of care and fiscal accountability are compatible if measures are devised to assure the confidentiality of information submitted and a review system based on a consensus of peers.

References

1. Marmor J, Scheidemandel P, Kanno C: Psychiatrists and Their Patients: A National Study of Private Office Practice. Washington, DC, Joint Information Service of the American Psychiatric Association and the National Association of Mental Health, 1975
2. Langsley DG: Comparing clinic and private practice of psychiatry. Am J Psychiatry 135:702-706, 1978
3. Office visits of psychiatrists: national ambulatory medical care survey, US, 1975-1976, in Vital and Health Statistics of the National Center for Health Statistics. Washington, DC, US Department of Health, Education, and Welfare, 1978

Table 46

OUTPATIENT DIAGNOSES FROM THE WASHINGTON PSYCHIATRIC SOCIETY STUDY AND THE MANDUC STUDY

Diagnosis	WPS Study (N=6,604)		MANDUCS		
	Number	Percent	Number	Percent of 11,232 Individuals	Percent of 13,409 Diagnoses
Schizophrenia	685	10.4	722	6.4	5.4
Major affective disorders	849	12.9	434	3.9	3.2
Psychotic organic brain syndrome	93	1.4	29	0.3	0.2
Neuroses	1878	28.4	9464	84.3	70.6
Personality disorders	1375	20.8	1065	9.5	7.9
Alcoholism	363	5.5	119	1.1	0.9
Drug dependence	183	2.8	13	0.1	0.1
Psychophysiologic	318	4.8	149	1.3	1.1
Transient situational	400	6.1	945	8.4	7.1
Nonpsychotic organic brain syndrome	83	1.3	19	0.2	0.1
Mental retardation	61	0.9	5	0	0
All other diagnoses	316	4.8	445	4.0	3.3

Concerns of One Company's Medical Director: A Confidential Case Study

Our total medical claims cost per employee increased 194 percent from 1971 through 1981 . . . without any major benefit plan changes. Major medical costs which include physician fees alone went up by 389 percent. On a per employee basis, we have about an 11 percent compound growth rate in our total medical plan costs each year. In 1981, our medical claims costs increased by 15.3 percent over 1980. This does not include the costs of absenteeism, disability, workers compensation, life insurance, etc.

Our goal is to improve employees' and their families' health and safety, and *to address the problems of rapidly rising health care costs.* Particularly those associated with the treatment of mental illness. Our health care strategy includes health education and communication, early detection of illness, a substance abuse program, individual involvement in community service and health care organizations, and the exploration of possible alternative forms of health care delivery for our employees.

We are concerned that each patient receive appropriate care in the appropriate setting for the appropriate price with minimal duplication and efficient use of high cost technical equipment and facilities. We have focused on the potential for the redesign of health care insurance and our own benefit plans to correct coverage situations that are not in the best interests of providing cost effective, quality health care.

We feel strongly that all our employee health programs should be voluntary to emphasize that the responsibility for the health of an individual rests with the individual—not the company, the physicians, and not the government.

I am *not* a benefits expert nor have I any great expertise on insurance matters. I do however, see a very close relationship between the optimum functioning of any work organization and a reasonably high level of medical benefits for employees and their dependents. I deeply believe that a healthy work force tends to be a productive work force. This means the provision of adequate care for all illnesses, for preventive medical services, for occupational health services, and, for a safe work environment.

Psychiatric Benefits

What are our psychiatric benefits? Our inpatient psychiatric coverage provides full payment for up to 365 days of care during a period of hospitalization ordered by a physician in any 36 consecutive months. Our outpatient psychiatric coverage provides for reimbursement of 80 percent of eligible charges which exceed $150 (all causes deductible) in eligible expenses incurred by a family in a calendar year. The reasonable and customary charges for mental health care which are covered include: psychiatric care and treatment rendered by a licensed physician; treatment by a licensed psychologist, or a licensed mental health clinic (which is under the full time direction and supervision of a physician or licensed psychologist).

The lifetime maximum in benefit payments for charges for outpatient treatment for psychiatric disorders is $15,000 for each eligible individual family member. (This individual $15,000 maximum is included in an overall major medical plan family maximum of $250,000.) There is no contribution by employees for medical coverage.

Compared to other employers, our benefits package for psychiatric care (both inpatient and outpatient) ranks fairly high. On the inpatient side we are generally far ahead of other employers.

Experience

We have become increasingly concerned about the rising cost implications of our mental health benefits and the future direction of these benefits as part of our overall concern about increasing health care costs. In 1980, our mental health benefit costs were $26.6 million, $14.9 million for inpatient care (which was 15.4 percent of our total hospital plan costs) and $11.7 million for outpatient care (which was 22.2 percent of our total major medical plan costs). In 1978, only two years earlier, our mental health benefit costs were $19.3 million, $10.6 million for inpatient care (14.1 percent of total hospital plan costs) and $8.7 million for outpatient care (21.9 percent of our total major medical plan costs).

One of the most startling facts to me is that if we go back to 1967 our costs for inpatient psychiatric care represented only 6.4 percent of total hospital plan benefits. In other words in thirteen years inpatient psychiatric bills have very nearly tripled as a percentage of the total hospital bills we pay.

In 1980 our average hospitalization per claim costs for a psychiatric patient was 100 percent higher than the next average cost diagnostic category (cardiac disorder) and 562 percent higher than our national average cost for all diagnostic categories.

One may break down such data in several ways. One is by the compound growth rate of these expenses. For the period from 1976 to 1980 the overall compound growth rate for hospital costs for psychiatric disorder rose at an annual percentage of 16.1 percent—about double the rate of our hospital costs for physical illness.

Another intriguing finding about inpatient costs is a *wide geographic spread* in the range of such benefits. If one looks at the cost per employee per year in locations where we have significant populations, we note that in one location the cost is $169.41 and that at another it is $18.13 (the average is $73.35). To me, such a finding is startling to say the least. And I have no ready explanation for this extraordinary spread.

My data on outpatient costs are not quite so comprehensive. The total was $11.7 million which represented 22.2 percent of our total major medical plan expenditures in 1980. Again we see a wide geographic distribution ranging from $139.36 per employee per year to $9.21 per employee per year at selected locations, with an overall average of $57.29.

The combined 1980 (inpatient and outpatient) mental health costs averaged

$130.64 per employee with a geographic range from $231.64 to $27.34. This represented an increase from 1979 to 1980 of 19.31 percent—far in excess of the increase for the care of physical illness under hospitalization and major medical plans for that period.

The bottom line seems to be that we have a serious cost management problem when it comes to expenditures for mental health treatment.

Concerns

We are concerned about what appears to be the general lack of review of inpatient length of stay for mental illness as compared to purely physical problems. While we recognize that it is difficult to establish a "standard" length of stay for a specific psychiatric disorder, there is increasing evidence that our length of stay for mental illness (including alcohol and drug abuse) is considerably higher than the national average for patients with the same diagnosis. We tend to feel that the company's comprehensive coverage is an influencing factor.

We sense an overall need within the mental health field to account for the results of the variety of treatments being used to treat patients.

Of particular concern to us today are benefits relating to psychiatric hospitalization. We clearly recognize that the staff of psychiatric hospitals want the absolute best possible care for their patients. Many these days are limited by the insurance benefits available to their patients and attune the treatment program to the twenty days, thirty days or two months which are the maximum allowable under some plans. With essentially unlimited stay allowed by our plan, quite clearly hospital staff, patients and patients' family will seek the *optimum* in hospital benefits. All are concerned with obtaining the best possible care for the patient. If a few more days or weeks or months will apparently contribute to that optimum result, there are no constraints at present to limit such treatment so long as benefits are available. Neither our medical department nor our insurance management system require mental health treatment reports nor other approvals. The only limitation is the 365 days of full cost care.

But things seem to be getting out of hand. When that 365 days of treatment costs in excess of $350 a day for a patient with a psychiatric disorder, I must put on my management hat and raise some questions. Similar patients are being treated for one or two months in community hospital psychiatric units and, on discharge, seem to be doing neither better nor worse than those who spend a year or more definitive inpatient therapy. To a large degree the psychopathology dictates that outcome. (One might well make a case for multiple short term hospitalizations in a semi-crisis supportive environment which could be equally beneficial to the patient and much less costly to the payor.)

It is also interesting to note that different hospitals under our plan manage patients with similar psychiatric disorders in markedly different ways. One hospital for instance utilizes 12 percent of our inpatient psychiatric benefits—favoring as you would expect extremely long term, intensive, and excellent care.*

*1979: $1.5 million of $11.6 million total inpatient costs.

And it has one of the highest per diem costs of any hospital covered by our benefit plans.

Cost containment of *all* medical benefits is a major concern of employers today. Psychiatric benefits seem the least concrete and least manageable and, for us, the most rapidly growing cost. The general reaction in industry has been to place arbitrary caps on the amount of treatment and/or total benefit dollars for a given period of time. We may be forced to move in that direction.

REASONS/PROBLEMS:

- The large number of individual patients who present no overt disability to their employers and who seem to lead essentially healthy lives but who are in therapy.
- Claims for four times weekly psychoanalytic treatment in employees who are outstanding in their work performance and manifest no disability. How often is the service non-essential and of high cost?
- Exorbitant claims for questionable therapy such as "primal scream," various questionable group process techniques, megavitamin therapy, etc., cloud the reality of effective medical psychotherapy.
- Hospital charges for inpatient treatment often seem to be based on the number of hospital days allowed for psychiatric care by the policy.
- Some individual practitioners seem to feel industry has unlimited funds and submit exorbitant fees for consultations and reports.
- Many concepts and treatment programs are difficult to explain and results hard to measure.
- Outcome studies have not clearly demonstrated efficacy or cost effectiveness.
- The chronic schizophrenic who vitally needs support on at least a weekly basis along with medication management for a lifetime.
- The spouse of an employee who is in psychoanalytic training and, at the halfway mark, expires the company maximum.
- The individual who has a moderately disabling chronic anxiety and has been shopping among therapists for years applies for an extension of benefits and the therapist reports the individual needs at least three or four more years of twice weekly therapy but offers neither treatment plan nor specific diagnosis.
- The employee who has a psychotic spouse who is housebound and indeed requires ongoing support.

The implementation of our health care strategy continues to evolve. We are searching for ways to encourage and educate our employees to make wise choices about their health and about using the health care system. Mental health costs are clearly one of our most significantly growing costs and we are looking for alternatives to solve this problem. Two options include:

- Mental health treatment reports with care review, through a third party organization.
- Medical Staff involvement with required approval of continued treatment when in hospital length of stay for mental illness exceeds "x" days, weeks or months. Far more mental health education/training/communication activities for employees.

Analysis of Utilization of Psychiatric Services by Employees of a Large Company, 1978-1980

Assuming that this company's insurance coverage (cost data attached) did not change over this three year period, the claims data indicate that utilization per capita in constant price terms did not change very much. (A net increase of 5 percent over 3 years.) Given the likelihood of a claims reporting error (claims data sometimes combined more than one treatment under diagnostic category), this 5 percent increase is too small to be considered as a trend.

As to absolute amounts, the company's benefit payments per covered person were higher than Blue Cross-Blue Shield's experience under FEHBP. In fact, the company's benefit payments per covered person were about 28 percent higher. This is accounted for by the fact that a greater share of employees (and dependents) used psychiatric services in a given year than BC/BS FEHBP enrollees (a 3-3.5 percent utilization rate for the private company's employees as compared to 1.5-2 percent for federal employees). This calculation assumes that the number of claims reported equals number of persons utilizing psychiatric care.

While the percentage of the total covered population of the company using psychiatric services has increased, the average claim per beneficiary declined in constant price terms for both inpatient and outpatient settings. In other words, if the figures submitted are reasonably accurate, this increase in utilization was offset by a decrease in the dollar value of services used per beneficiary.

The pertinent data are presented below. All dollar figures are in constant prices using 1980 dollars. (The hospital room and board component of the CPI was used to translate inpatient costs to a constant cost basis; the physician's service component of the CPI was used for outpatient costs):

Table 47.
DISAGGREGATED UTILIZATION EXPERIENCE

	1978	1979	1980
Inpatient benefits paid per claim	$4,449.00	$4,111.00	$4,182.00
Inpatient benefits paid per covered person	21.70	20.75	22.94
Inpatient claims per covered person	49%	50%	55%
Outpatient benefits paid per claim	650.00	601.00	576.00
Outpatient benefits paid per covered person	17.16	17.28	17.92
Outpatient claims per covered person	2.6%	2.9%	3.1%
Total claims per covered person	3.0%	3.4%	3.7%
Total benefits paid per covered person	38.86	38.03	40.86

Percentage change of total benefits paid per covered person from 1978-1980 equals +5.1%. The increases in benefits paid as reported by the company shows a 30 percent increase ($31.44 in 1978 to $40.87 in 1980).

Table 48
MEDICAL PLANS-UTILIZATION EXPERIENCE MENTAL/NERVOUS DISORDERS (AS SUBMITTED BY A LARGE U.S. COMPANY)

INPATIENT

Year	Number of Claims	Current Dollars Benefits Paid	Constant $ Benefits Paid
1978	2,995	$10,580,465	$13,325,523
1979	3,189	11,590,609	13,111,549
1980	3,567	14,919,147	14,919,147

OUTPATIENT

Year	Number of Employees, Dependents, Retirees Receiving Benefits	Current Dollars Benefits Paid	Constant $ Benefits Paid
1978	16,209	$ 8,726,033	$10,538,687
1979	18,180	9,886,033	10,923,793
1980	20,235	11,651,749	11,651,749

TOTAL ELIGIBLE POPULATION

Year	Number of Employees, Dependents, Retirees
1978	614,021
1979	632,008
1980	650,194

Constant Prices 1980 = 100

Cost Sharing and the Demand for Ambulatory Mental Health Services

By the Rand Corporation, Santa Monica, CA

A REVIEW AND SELECTED TABLES

Mental Health Benefits Studied

Santa Monica, California—Widespread coverage for mental health problems would only increase overall health care costs by a small amount, according to a new study by Rand Corporation.

Researchers found that only 9 percent of the people who were offered full mental health coverage for up to 52 doctor's office visits a year sought such treatment. And only 5 percent of those underwent psychotherapy.

At the same time, according to the federally funded study, those who did receive the generous mental health benefits sought therapy twice as often as those whose plans required they pay all costs up to $1,000 before coverage began.

"These figures at first may seem contradictory," said Willard G. Manning, Jr., an economist who conducted the study for Rand. "What they tell us is that generous coverage sharply increases the demand for mental health services."

"But, the fact remains that only a small percentage of those with such generous coverage draw upon it," Dr. Manning said.

According to the study, a full-coverage health care plan, which includes full mental health benefits, paid out only an average of $24 a year for mental health claims.

That was just 5 percent of the amount paid for all other health services by the plan.

However, the researchers emphasized that such low mental health plan utilization can only be anticipated where mental health coverage is widespread.

"Any employer or insurance company offering more generous mental health benefits than others in the community might find that those desiring mental health services would flock to those plans," Dr. Manning said.

Although those who receive more generous mental health benefits than others increased their spending for mental health care, that in spending was about equal with the increase in spending on traditional health care services when people are given more generous medical care benefits, the survey noted.

(Note: Rand is already revising the study as a result of internal and external recommendations.)

Table 49
SAMPLE IN HEALTH INSURANCE STUDY AT INITIAL ENROLLMENT (Rand)

Site	Insurance Plan						Total
	Free	25/25	25/50	50/50	95	Deductible	
Dayton, OH	301	260	0	194	280	105	1140
Seattle, WA[a]	431	132	121	0	253	285	1222
Fitchburg, MA	241	37	88	56	113	188	723
Franklin Co., MA	297	61	91	58	162	220	889
Charleston, SC[b]	72	23	25	9	42	37	208
Georgetown Co., SC[b]	91	26	33	9	35	68	262
Total	1433	539	358	326	885	903	4444

NOTE: This table excludes babies born or adopted into enrolled families after initial family enrollment; insurance plan refers to medical and mental health coinsurance rates, or the Individual Deductible Plan.

[a]Excludes enrollees in Group Health Cooperative of Puget Sound, a health maintenance organization (HMO).

[b]Excludes three-year enrollment group.

Table 50
USERS OF MENTAL HEALTH SERVICES, YEAR 2

Definition	Prevalence of Use of Mental Health Services							
	All Users		Users of Informal Providers Only		Users of Formal Providers Only		Users of Formal and Informal Providers	
	No. of Users	Enrollees (%)	No. of Users	Mental Health Users (%)	No. of Users	Mental Health Users (%)	No. of Users	Mental Health Users (%)
Conservative	302	7.1	139	46	134	44	29	10
Middle	390	9.2	227	58	128	33	35	9
Liberal	407	9.6	244	60	123	30	40	10

NOTE: Sample size = 4254.

Table 51
MEDIAN EXPENDITURES FOR MENTAL HEALTH USERS BY TYPE OF USE, YEAR 2 (Rand)

	Users of Any Formal Visit		Users of Any Informal Visit	
Definition	Formal Mental Health Expenditures[a] ($)	Prorated[b] ($)	Informal Mental Health Expenditures[a] ($)	Prorated[b] ($)
Conservative	280	280	22	14
Middle	280	280	20	11
Liberal	280	280	20	11

Note: Sample size = 4254.
[a]Includes all charges linked to any mental health diagnosis and the full office charge for any mental health visit.
[b]Includes all mental health charges and basic office visits prorated by proportion of associated diagnoses that are mental health diagnoses. Medication and reason for visit count as mental health diagnoses.

Table 52
PSYCHOTHERAPY VISITS, YEAR 2

Number of Visits	Percent of Enrollees
0	95.9
1-10	2.5
11-20	0.4
21-30	0.4
31-40	0.4
41-50	0.2
51+	0.2

Note: California Relative Value Studies codes 90801-90899 are used for mental health procedures. Sample size = 4254.

Table 53
PREVALENCE OF MENTAL HEALTH USE, YEAR 2 (Rand)

	Prevalence of Use	
Site	All Enrollees (%)	Users of Any Formal Visits (%)
Dayton	6.0	33
Seattle	8.2	69
Massachusetts	8.0	57
South Carolina	3.7	29

Note: Mental health use is identified by the conservative definition of a visit.

Table 54
USE OF FORMAL PROVIDERS OF MENTAL HEALTH SERVICES, YEAR 2

	Prevalence of Use (% of All Enrollees) (N=4254)		Prevalence of Use (% of Users of Any Formal Visit) (N=163)	
Category	Any Use	Modal	Any Use	Modal
Psychiatrist	2.0	1.8	53	47
Psychologist	1.0	0.9	25	23
Other mental health specialist	0	0	0	0
Miscellaneous individual	0.1	0.1	3	3
Mental health clinic[a]	0.4	0.3	11	9
Other clinic[a]	0.8	0.5	22	14
Psychiatric hospital[a]	0.2	0.2	6	4
Total[b]		3.8		100

Note: Mental health use is identified by the conservative definition of a visit.
[a]Type of individual provider is not known.
[b]Total is not applicable to "any use" categories because there is overlap in use between categories.

Table 55
MENTAL HEALTH DIAGNOSES BY TYPE OF USE, YEAR 2 (Rand)

	Prevalence of Use (%)					
	All Enrollees (N=4254)		Users of Any Formal Visits (N=163)		Users of Only Informal Visits (N=139)	
Category **Set 1 (specific)**	Any Diagnoses	Modal Diagnoses	Any Diagnoses	Modal Diagnoses	Any Diagnoses	Modal Diagnoses
Anxiety neurosis	2.4	1.9	32	20	35	34
Depressive neurosis	2.2	1.7	39	27	22	21
Other neuroses	0.6	0.4	11	6	5	4
Personality disorders	0.8	0.4	12	6	9	4
Major affective	0.3	0.2	6	4	1	1
Schiz./paranoia	0.1	0.1	3	1	0	0
Organic disorders	0.1	0.1	2	1	1	1
Child disorders	0.7	0.6	12	9	6	6
Other adult disorders	2.7	1.8	42	25	32	25
Other disorders	<0.1	<0.1	1	1	1	0
Any mental health diagnosis	7.1	7.1	100	100	96	96
No mental health diagnosis	NA	NA	1	1	3	3
Total[a]				101[b]		99[b]
Set 2 (aggregated)						
All minor	4.8	4.3	71	58	63	63
All major	1.2	0.9	23	16	9	9
All nonspecific	2.7	1.8	42	25	33	25
No mental health diagnosis	NA	NA	1	1	3	3
Total[a]				99[b]		100[b]

Note: Mental health use is identified by the conservative definition of a visit. For "modal" diagnosis, percentages of aggregate categories are the sums of the percentages of subordinate specific categories. NA = not applicable; enrollees can have no mental health diagnosis if they use no health services, no mental health services, or if they have no mental health diagnosis during all their mental health visits.

[a]Total is not applicable to "any use" categories because of overlap in users between categories.

[b]Total does not add to 100 due to rounding error.

IV. FEHBP

The Blue Cross Federal Employees mental health coverage is probably the most widely studied plan since good data existed, a large population was covered, and for years the benefits were essentially unlimited. Interpretation of the results depends on whether costs are adjusted for inflation and whether or not those costs are reported on a per capita basis.

The Mental Health Benefits Comparison (1980, 1983, 1984) chart was compiled from Health Benefits Comparison charts, individual plan brochures, and Addendum sheets issued by OPM. Any inconsistencies were checked through OPM actuaries.

Table 56
BLUE CROSS AND BLUE SHIELD FEDERAL EMPLOYEE PROGRAM
Number of Outpatient Psychotherapy Visits Per 1000 Contracts by Type of Provider, 1974-1980

	1974	1975	1976	1977	1978	1979	1980	Percent Increase 1974 to 1980
Psychiatrist								
Outpatient Visits Per 1000 Contracts	436.9	505.0	542.0	547.7	569.0	562.5	586.8	
Percent Increase Over Previous Year	—	15.6%	7.3%	0.9%	3.9%	(1.1%)	4.3%	34.3%
*Non-Medical Therapist**								
Outpatient Visits Per 1000 Contracts	84.0	142.2	193.2	237.4	244.4	254.4	316.3	
Percent Increase Over Previous Year	—	69.3%	35.9%	22.9%	2.9%	8.2%	19.6%	276.6%
Clinical Psychologist								
Outpatient Visits Per 1000 Contracts	—	—	95.6	141.1	155.3	174.5	209.3	
Percent Increase Over Previous Year	—	—	—	47.6%	10.0%	12.4%	19.9%	11%
Total Providers								
Outpatient Visits Per 1000 Contracts	520.9	647.2	735.2	785.1	813.4	826.9	903.1	
Percent Increase Over Previous Year	—	24.2%	13.6%	6.8%	3.6%	1.7%	9.2%	73.4%
Non-Medical Therapists as a Percent of Total	16.1%	22.0%	26.3%	30.2%	30.0%	32.0%	35.0%	

*Includes clinical psychologists, psychiatric social workers, and psychiatric nurses

Table 57
BLUE CROSS AND BLUE SHIELD FEDERAL EMPLOYEE PROGRAM
Average Cost Per Outpatient Psychotherapy Visit by Type of Provider, 1974-1980

	1974	1975	1976	1977	1978	1979	1980	Average Percentage Increase 1974 to 1980
Psychiatrist								
Average Cost Per Visit	$30.66	$33.95	$37.11	$39.03	$41.52	$44.40	$48.47	
Percent Increase Over Previous Year	—	10.7%	9.3%	5.2%	6.4%	6.9%	9.2%	7.95
*Non-Medical Therapist**								
Average Cost Per Visit	$26.51	$29.58	$31.63	$33.11	$34.96	$37.52	$40.54	
Percent Increase Over Previous Year	—	11.6%	6.9%	4.7%	5.6%	7.3%	8.1%	7.4
Clinical Psychologist								
Average Cost Per Visit	—	—	$34.45	$36.76	$38.36	$40.95	$44.16	
Percent Increase Over Previous Year	—	—	—	6.7%	4.4%	6.8%	7.8%	6.4**
Total Providers								
Average Cost Per Visit	$30.00	$32.99	$35.68	$37.24	$39.55	$42.21	$45.69	
Percent Increase Over Previous Year	—	10.0%	8.2%	4.4%	6.2%	6.7%	8.2%	7.3

*Includes clinical psychologists, psychiatric social workers, and psychiatric nurses
**1976-1980 Average

Table 58
FEDERAL EMPLOYEE HEALTH BENEFIT PROGRAM
BLUE CROSS AND BLUE SHIELD
Comparison of Mental and Nervous Benefits and Total Health Benefits Paid for All Covered Persons, United States, 1966-1980

	Total Mental Benefits Paid		Total Health Benefits Paid		
Year	**Amount (Millions)**	**Percentage Increase Over Previous Year**	**Amount (Millions)**	**Percentage Increase Over Previous Year**	**Percent Mental Benefit of Total Health Benefit**
1960-65	$40.2		$1040.4		3.9
1966	13.6		277.2		4.9
1967	18.5	37	336.8	22	5.5
1968	25.3	37	405.0	20	6.3
1969	31.0	22	480.9	19	6.5
1970	41.8	35	601.9	25	6.9
1971	49.8	19	698.9	16	7.1
1972	54.5	11	760.4	9	7.2
1973	61.7	13	848.2	11	7.3
1974	70.1	14	979.1	15	7.2
1975	90.8	30	1206.5	23	7.5
1976	108.4	19	1406.7	16	7.7
1977	116.4	7	1505.4	7	7.7
1978	123.5	6	1670.1	11	7.4
1979	135.7	9	1790.7	7	7.6
1980	155.5	15	2040.8	14	7.7

Table 59 (Histogram of Table 58)

Federal Employee Health Benefit Program Blue Cross and Blue Shield—by Percent that Mental and Nervous Benefits Payments Formed of Total Health Benefits Paid for all Covered Persons: United States, 1966-1980

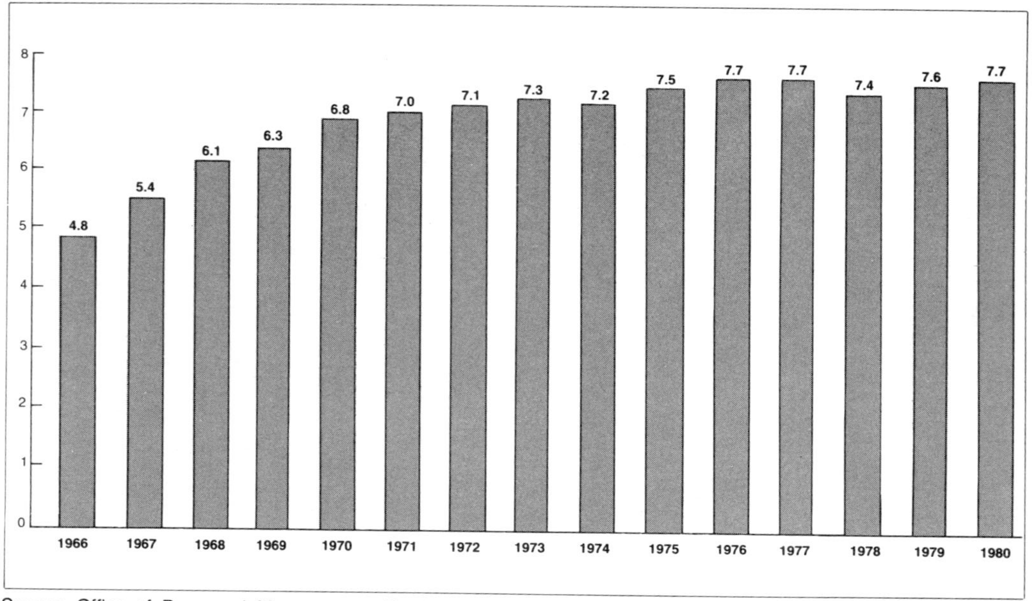

Source: Office of Personnel Management. Unpublished data from the Office of the Actuary. U.S. Civil Service Commission.

See Comment, Chart 44.

Table 60

Federal Employee Health Benefits Program BC and BS Total Mental Benefits Paid, By Year 1966-1980

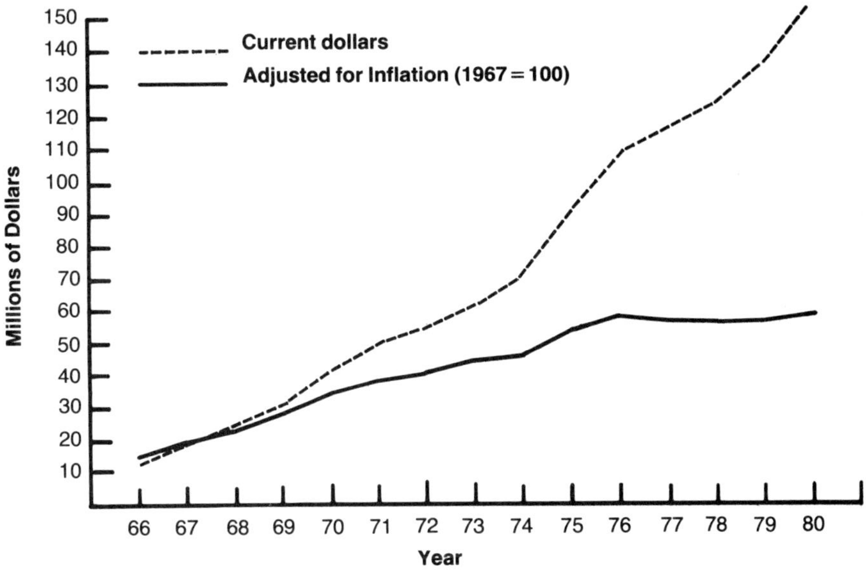

Table 61

Federal Employee Health Benefits Program BC and BS Total Mental Benefits Paid, By Year 1966-1980

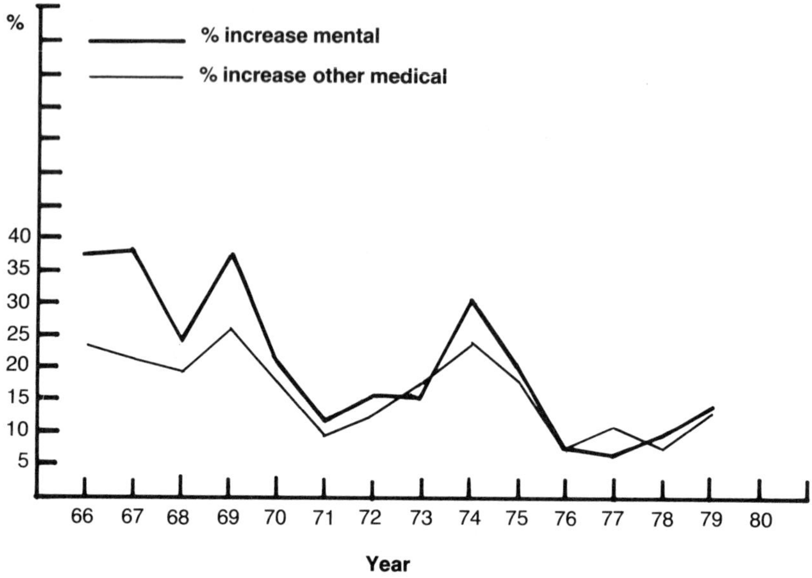

Table 62

Federal Employee Health Benefits Program BC and BS Total Mental Benefits Paid, By Year 1966-1980

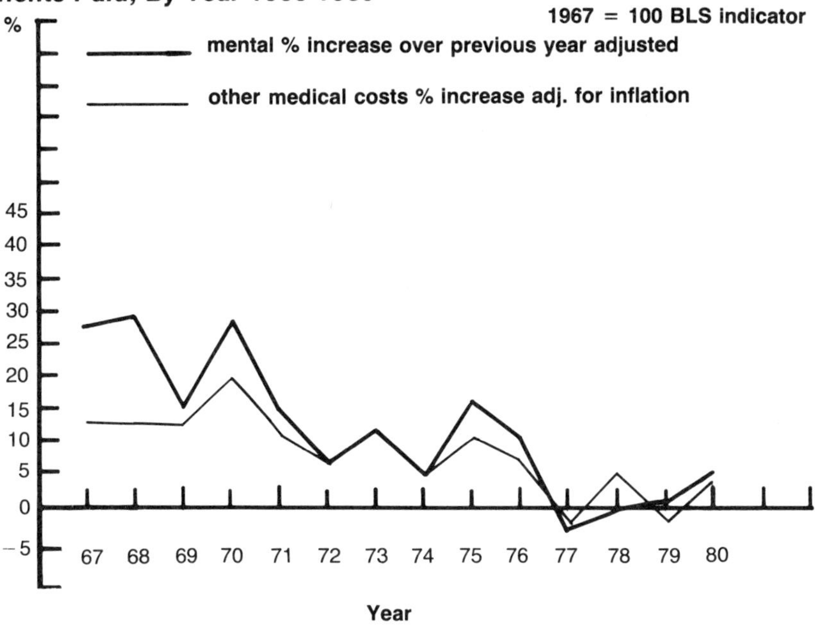

Table 63
FEHB MENTAL HEALTH BENEFITS COMPARISON CHART
For Years 1980, 1983, 1984
(Fee-for-Service Plans Open to All Employees and Annuitants)

LEGEND

LM	Lifetime maximum
DED	Deductible
CY	Calendar year
MHC	Mental health catastrophic
*	Applies to IP *and* OP care
Adm	Admission
i	Deductible included under catastrophic
R&B	Room and board
IP	Inpatient
OP	Outpatient

Indemnity Benefit (Aetna Life)		1980	1983	1984
General Deductible Per Person/Family/CY	Hi	$75/three	$200/three	$200/three
	Lo	$100/three	$250/three	$250/three
Inpatient Care	Hi	100% of 1st $2,000 R&B; 80% of all other to $20,000	80% to $20,000/CY	$1,000 CY DED; 80% to MHC; then 100% to $50,000 LM
	Lo	100% of 1st $1,000 R&B; 75% of all other to $15,000	75% to $15,000/CY	$1,000 CY DED, 75% to MHC; then 100% to $50,000 LM
Outpatient Care	Hi	80% to $1,000	80% to $1,000/CY	80% to $1,000/CY
	Lo	75% to $750	75% to $750/CY	75% to $750/CY
Mental Health Catastrophic Inpatient Only to LM Per Person	Hi	None	None	$5,000
	Lo	None	None	$5,000
Med/Surg Catastrophic Per Person/Family/CY	Hi	$1,000/$2,000	$2,500/$5,000	$2,000/$4,000
	Lo	$1,250/$2,500	$3,000/$6,000	$2,000/$4,000
Alcohol/Drug Abuse	Hi	Incl. in mental health	Same as Mental Health	Provided
	Lo	Incl. in mental health	Same as Mental Health	Provided

Table 63 (continued)
FEHB MENTAL HEALTH BENEFITS COMPARISON CHART

Service Benefit (Blue Cross/ Blue Shield)		1980	1983	1984
General Deductible Per Person/Family/CY	Hi	$100	$200/two	$200/two
	Lo	$200	$250/two	$250/two
Inpatient Care	Hi	100%/365 days to $50,000 LM*	$50 DED; up to 60 days @ 100% to $50,000 LM*	$50 DED/adm; 80% to MHC then 100% to $75,000 LM*
	Lo	100%/90 days $50,000 LM*	$100 DED; 100% to 30 days; to $50,000 LM*	$100 DED/adm; 75% to 30 days/CY; $50,000 LM*
Outpatient Care	Hi	$100 DED; 80% to LM*	70% to 50 visits/yr OP to LM	70% to 50 visits/CY to LM*
	Lo	$200 DED; 75% to LM*	75% to 25 visits/yr OP to LM	75% to 25 visits/CY to LM*
Mental Health Catastrophic Inpatient Only to LM Per Person	Hi	None	None	$4,000
	Lo	None	None	None
Med/Surg Catastrophic Per Person/CY	Hi	$1,000	$1,000/Basic	$1,500/$1,500
	Lo	$2,000	$1,000/Supplemental $2,500	$2,500/$2,500
Alcohol/Drug Abuse	Hi	None	Detox. IP same as mental health OP	Detox. only
	Lo	None	Detox IP same as mental health OP	Detox. only

Alliance	1980	1983	1984
General Deductible Per Person/Family/CY	$50	$150/two	$200/two
Inpatient Care	100%/30 days; then 80%	100% to 30 days	$750 CY DED; 100% for 30 days, then 50% to MHC; then 100% to $50,000 LM
Outpatient Care	85% to 50 visits/ CY	50% to $15/visit to 50 visits/CY	50% to $15/visit to 50 visits/ CY
Mental Health Catastrophic Inpatient Only to LM Per Person	None	None	$8,000[i]
Med/Surg Catastrophic Per Person/CY	None	$1,000/$1,000	$1,000/$2,000
Alcohol/Drug Abuse	—	Same as Mental Health	Provided

Table 63 (continued)
FEHB MENTAL HEALTH BENEFITS COMPARISON CHART

APWU	1980	1983	1984
General Deductible Per Person/Family/CY	None	$150/three	†$175/three
Inpatient Care	100% to 50 days	$23/day for 1st 10 days; 100% to 30 days	†$500 CY CED, 50% to MHC, then 100% to $25,000 LM*
Outpatient Care	100% from 2nd visit to $600 person/$1,400 family	80% to $300/person $800/family max.*	†$500 CY DED, 50% up to $50/visit; to $300 max.
Mental Health Catastrophic Inpatient Only to LM Per Person	None	None	$8,000[i]
Med/Surg Catastrophic Per Person/CY	None	$1,000/$1,000	$2,000/$2,000[i]
Alcohol/Drug Abuse	100% IP	Same as Mental Health	Provided

†$500 M.H. deductible in lieu of general deductible can be satisfied by inpatient and/or outpatient M.H. charges.
*IP and OP

GEHA	1980	1983	1984
General Deductible Per Person/Family/CY	$80/three	$200/three	$200/three
Inpatient Care	100% R&B + up to $25/Dr. visit; 80% of other	70% to 60 days	$500 CY DED, 50% to MHC; then 100% to $50,000 LM
Outpatient	30 visits to $25/visit	Up to $25/visit; to 30 visits/CY	Up to $25/visit; to 30 visits/CY
Mental Health Catastrophic Inpatient Only to LM Per Person	None	None	$8,000[i]
Med/Surg. Catastrophic Per Person/Family/CY	$1,000/$2,000	$2,000/$2,000	$2,000/$2,000[i]
Alcohol/Drug Abuse	Provided	Same as Mental Health	Provided

Table 63 (continued)
FEHB MENTAL HEALTH BENEFITS COMPARISON CHART

Mail Handlers	**1980**	**1983**	**1984**
General Deductible Per Person/Family/CY	None	None	None
Inpatient Care	100% to lesser of $2,500 or 50 days in 6 mo; to $7,500 LM*	$100 DED/ confinement; then lesser of $2,500 or 50 days in 6 mo.	$125 DED/confinement, then 100% to $2,500, then 0 to MHC; then 100% to $25,000 LM
Outpatient	75% to $450/CY; to $15/visit up to 15 visits + 5 adult or 20 child collateral visits to $15/visit	None	None
Mental Health Catastrophic Inpatient Only to LM Per Person	None	None	$5,000
Med/Surg Catastrophic Per Person/CY	None	None	$2,500/$5,000
Alcohol/Drug Abuse	Incl. in Mental Health	Same as Mental Health	Provided

NAGE	**1980**	**1983**	**1984**
General Deductible Per Person/Family/CY	$100/three	$200/two	$200/two
Inpatient Care	100% to $50,000 LM*	100% to 60 days	$100 DED/adm, 50% to MHC; then 100% CY to $50,000 LM*
Outpatient Care	50% to $1,000	50% to $1,000/CY	50% to $1,000/CY*
Mental Health Catastrophic Inpatient Only to LM Per Person	None	None	$7,500/$15,000
Med/Surg Catastrophic Per Person/Family/CY	$4,000	$1,000	$1,000
Alcohol/Drug Abuse	Provided	Same as Mental Health	Provided

Table 63 (continued)
FEHB MENTAL HEALTH BENEFITS COMPARISON CHART

NALC	1980	1983	1984
General Deductible Per Person/Family/CY	$50/three	$150/three	$150/three
Inpatient Care	100% to 90 days per CY	$12.50/day for 1st 5 days, then 100% to 60 days or $4,000	$500 DED/adm, 50% to MHC; then 100% to $50,000 LM
Outpatient Care	80% to $5,000 CY	Separate $150 DED, 50% to $1,250/CY	Separate $150 DED, 50% to $1,250/CY
Mental Health Catastrophic Inpatient Only to LM Per Person	None	None	$8,000[i]
Med/Surg Catastrophic Per Person/Family/CY	$1,000/$1,000	$1,000/$1,000	$1,000/$1,000[i]
Alcohol/Drug Abuse	100% to 30 days LM	50% to 30 days LM	Provided

NFFE	1980	1983	1984
General Deductible Per Person/Family/CY	$150/two	$175/two	$175/two
Inpatient Care	100%/30 days; then 85%	95% to 3 days, 100% for days 4 to 30 to $50,000 LM*	$175/DED/adm, 75% to MHC; then 100% CY to $50,000 LM*
Outpatient Care	50% to $20/visit to 50 visits/CY	50% to $20/visit up to 50 visits/CY	50% to $20/visit up to 50 visits/CY
Mental Health Catastrophic Inpatient Only to LM Per Person	None	None	$5,000[i]
Med/Surg Catastrophic Per Person/Family/CY	None	$2,000/$4,000	$2,000/$2,000
Alcohol/Drug Abuse	—	Same as Mental Health	Provided

Table 63 (continued)
FEHB MENTAL HEALTH BENEFITS COMPARISON CHART

NTEU	**1980**	**1983**	**1984**
General Deductible Per Person/Family/CY	$100	$175/three	$175/three
Inpatient Care	100%/30 days, then 80% to $50,000 LM*	90% to 10 days, 100% for days 11 to 30 to $50,000 LM*	$400 CY DED, 100% for 30 days, then 50% to MHC; then 100% CY to $50,000 LM*
Outpatient Care	50% to $20/visit up to 50 visits/CY	50% to $20/visit up to 50 visits/CY	50% to $20/visit to 50 visits/CY
Mental Health Catastrophic Inpatient Only to LM Per Person	None	None	$8,000[i]
Med/Surg Catastrophic Per Person/Family/CY	None	$2,000/$4,000	$2,000/$3,000[i]
Alcohol/Drug Abuse	Provided	Same as Mental Health at 50%	Provided

Postal Supervisors	**1980**	**1983**	**1984**
General Deductible Per Person/Family/CY	$100/two	$200/two (MM)	$200/two
Inpatient Care	R&B @ 100% to 31 days + $600 for other	$165 CY DED, then 100% R&B to 31 days, $600 for other	$800 CY DED, 100% for 31 days, then 50% to MHC, then 100% CY to $50,000 LM
Outpatient Care	80% to 50 visits	50% to $20/visit 50 visits/yr	50% up to $20/visit to 50 visits/CY
Mental Health Catastrophic Inpatient Only to LM Per Person	None	None	$8,000[i]
Med/Surg Catastrophic Per Person/Family/CY	None	$1,000/$1,000	$1,000/$1,000
Alcohol/Drug Abuse	Same as Mental Health	Same as Mental Health	Provided

Table 63 (continued)
FEHB MENTAL HEALTH BENEFITS COMPARISON CHART

Postmasters		1980	1983	1984
General Deductible Per Person/Family/CY	Hi	$100/two	$200/two	$200/two
	Lo	$150/two	$275/two	$275/two
Inpatient Care	Hi	R&B @ 100% 31 days/CY; $600 other than 80%	$25/day copay for 5 days, 100% to 60 days	$500 CY DED, 70% to MHC; then 100% CY to $40,000 LM
	Lo	R&B to $50 31 days/CY, other $300 then 80% of allowable	R&B to $50/day to 60 days, first $300 at 100% of ancill., then 80% to or of $5,000	R&B $50/day to 60 days, then 0 to MHC then 100% CY to $40,000 LM Other: Ancillaries same as '83
Outpatient Care	Hi	50% of charges	50% to $1,000/CY	50% to $1,000/CY
	Lo	50% of charges	50% to $1,000/CY	50% to $1,000/CY
Mental Health Catastrophic Inpatient Only to LM Per Person	Hi	None	None	$8,000[i]
	Lo	None	None	$8,000[i]
Med/Surg Catastrophic Per Person/Family/CY	Hi	N/A	$1,000/$2,000	$1,000/$2,000[i]
	Lo	N/A	None	None
	Lo	N/A	None	None
Alcohol/Drug Abuse	Hi	None	None	None
	Lo	None	None	None

V. CHAMPUS

Executive Summary

This series of nineteen reports describes the utilization of inpatient and outpatient psychiatric services by CHAMPUS beneficiaries throughout Fiscal Year 1980 (October 1, 1979 through September 30, 1980). This is the first time these annual reports have been produced. Comparisons with national data have not been prepared for this series of reports, but it is anticipated that they will be available for future reports.

Key Statistics

- $158 million were paid by all sources (government, other insurance, patient) for psychiatric care provided under CHAMPUS. Of this amount, 72 percent were CHAMPUS (government) dollars.
- $114 million or 16.8 percent of total CHAMPUS dollars spent on inpatient and outpatient medical care were spent on psychiatric care.
- 49 percent of the total professional services visits were for treatment of persons diagnosed with "neuroses."
- Of the total number of providers paid by CHAMPUS, 31 percent were psychiatrists and 16 percent were psychologists.
- There were 22,228 psychiatric hospital admissions (including care in Residential Treatment Centers) with an average length of stay of 31.1 days and 1.4 hospital admissions per hospitalized beneficiary.
- For each hospital admission, there were an average of 12.3 inpatient professional services visits, as compared with 11.5 outpatient visits per user beneficiary.
- The average amount paid for inpatient psychiatric care per hospital admission was $5,197, $514 of which were spent for inpatient professional services visits.
- The average amount paid from all sources for psychiatric care under CHAMPUS was $1,820 per user beneficiary. The average amount paid for inpatient care was $7,524 per user beneficiary and $538 for outpatient care.
- Slightly more than 50 percent of CHAMPUS user beneficiaries receiving psychiatric care were spouses; 21 percent were sons; 16 percent were daughters and more than 125 were retirees.
- California had 5,563 or 22 percent of the total number of all types of practitioners paid by CHAMPUS for psychiatric care rendered in Fiscal Year 1980.

Management Summary

The following analysis of the data is intended to summarize some of the most important findings contained in this series of reports. This information is presented under the following topical headings:

- Cost of psychiatric care;
- Utilization of mental health care under the CHAMPUS Program;
- Psychiatric care provided;
- Type of practitioner data;
- Characteristics of CHAMPUS user beneficiaries.

Cost of Psychiatric Care Under CHAMPUS

During Fiscal Year 1980, an estimated $679 million were spent by the government for inpatient and outpatient care under the CHAMPUS program excluding care in foreign countries. Of this amount, 16.8 percent or $114 million were spent for psychiatric care.

Further analysis indicates that $115.5 million were paid by all sources (CHAMPUS, other insurance and patient) for inpatient psychiatric care including hospital admissions and inpatient professional services visits. Of this amount, an estimated $88.5 million (76.6 percent) were paid by CHAMPUS (government). This amount represents almost 15.4 percent of CHAMPUS dollars paid for inpatient care in Fiscal Year 1980.

For outpatient psychiatric care, an additional $42.7 million were paid by all sources (CHAMPUS, other insurance and patient) for professional services visits. Of this amount, an estimated $25.8 million (60.3 percent) were paid by CHAMPUS (government). This amount represents almost 25 percent of CHAMPUS dollars paid for outpatient professional services in Fiscal Year 1980.

Table 64 shows the total average amount paid for inpatient psychiatric care for each psychiatric diagnostic code. The average amount paid per hospital admission (including hospital services and inpatient visits) was $5,196.60. By far the most costly admission was for "behavior disorders of childhood" which averaged about $12,900 per admission (including inpatient visits).

The average amount paid per visit to each type of practitioner varied according to the setting (inpatient or outpatient), the type of professional, as well as by diagnostic code or procedural code. Generally speaking, outpatient visits cost more than inpatient visits. Psychologists were paid the most per visit, whether inpatient or outpatient, followed by psychiatrists for both settings. Social workers ranked lowest in terms of the average amount paid for either inpatient or outpatient visit.

Psychologists were paid in the range of $50-$52 per visit, psychiatrists were paid from $43-$49 per visits and social workers were paid between $32-$39 per visit.

Table 64 shows the ranges for the average amount paid for inpatient and outpatient visits across the country by type of practitioner. For some types of practitioners there is a difference of as much as $40 per visit between the low and high ranking states. There appears to be more variance in the inpatient visits than in the outpatient visits where the difference between high and low is usually no more than $30.

The variation in the average amount paid per visit for the low-ranking states is difficult to categorize by region of the country since the states are fairly well distributed nationwide. However, at the high end of the range Alaska and California predominate.

Utilization of Psychiatric Care Under CHAMPUS

A total of 22,228 psychiatric hospital admissions accounted for 691,742 hospital days and 272,595 inpatient visits. Table 69 provides detailed hospital admissions data by psychiatric diagnostic code. The average hospital length of stay including care in residential treatment centers was 31.1 days with an average of 12.3 inpatient visits per admission. Thirty percent of the total number of hospital days and 44 percent of inpatient visits were for treatment of patients with neuroses.

CHAMPUS user beneficiaries had a total of nearly 2 million professional services visits by all types of practitioners in Fiscal Year 1980. Outpatient visits accounted for 77 percent of these visits with average amount paid per visit of $46.79. Fifty percent of the total outpatient visits were for treatment of patients with neuroses.

Psychiatrists accounted for 83 percent of the total number of inpatient visits with attending physicians having 11 percent of the total. Psychologists accounted for 3 percent of inpatient visits.

Regarding outpatient visits, psychiatrists had 40 percent of the total, psychologists 28 percent and social workers 19 percent of the total visits. See Table 65 for a complete listing of professional services visits as distributed among all types of practitioners.

Psychiatric Care Provided

Table 66 lists the most frequently used procedures for each type of practitioner's inpatient visits. Psychiatrists used verbal psychotherapy of 25 minutes duration in 21 percent of their visits. The average amount paid per visit for this procedure was $32.00. Psychologists used psychotherapy of 45-50 minutes duration in 26 percent of their visits and were paid an average of $57 per visit.

Regarding outpatient visits, verbal psychotherapy of 50 minutes duration was the most widely used psychiatric procedure. It accounted for 44 percent of psychiatrists' visits and 76 percent of therapists' visits. Fifty percent of all outpatient visits to psychologists were for psychotherapy of 45-50 minutes duration.

The average amount paid per outpatient visit for psychiatrists was $51 and for psychologists the amount was $57. Therapists received an average of $43 per visit. See Table 67 for more information on outpatient visits.

The most frequently diagnosed disorder was overwhelmingly "neuroses." Only therapists provided care for a different diagnosis, namely "drug dependence," most frequently. Table 68 indicates the most frequent diagnosis and the average amount paid per inpatient and outpatient visit by type of practitioner.

For inpatient visits, the average amount paid per visit ranged from $30-$50, with psychologists at the end of the range. Regarding outpatient visits, the average amount paid per visit was higher, ranging from $39-$53. Again, psychologists were paid the most per visit.

Table 69 provides a listing of the psychiatric diagnoses ranked from high to low for frequency of inpatient visits. Visits for treatment of "neuroses" comprised 43 percent of the total, with "schizophrenia" in second place with 20 percent of the total.

Similar data are presented for outpatient visits in Table 70. Again, treatment for "neuroses" ranked first with 49 percent of the total visits. "Transient situational disturbances" was second with 20 percent and "behavior disorders of childhood" ranked third with 11 percent of total outpatient visits.

Type of Practitioner Data

Of the total number of all types of providers of psychiatric care paid by CHAMPUS in Fiscal Year 1980, 31 percent were psychiatrists and 16 percent were psychologists. Table 71 shows the numbers of providers and percent of the total they represent for the other categories.

Data regarding the distribution of all types of providers by state show that California ranked number one with 22 percent of the total or 5,563 providers of all types paid by CHAMPUS for psychiatric care. Florida was second with 7 percent of the total, while 6 percent of the total providers were from Texas. More than half of all the providers paid by CHAMPUS for psychiatric care, 57 percent, were in ten states.

Characteristics of CHAMPUS User Beneficiaries

Of the total number of user beneficiaries, spouses comprised 50 percent of the total, 21 percent were sons, 16 percent were daughters and 12 percent were retirees.

Age category 35-44 had the highest percent of total user beneficiaries with 17 percent of the total. There was equal distribution for the 15-19, 25-34 and 45-54 age groups at 16 percent each. Treatment of children under ten years of age and those in the 20-24 age group each accounted for 8 percent of the total user beneficiaries. Almost 50 percent of the user beneficiaries were between the ages of 25 and 55.

Table 64
RANGES FOR AVERAGE AMOUNT PAID PER VISIT (PROFESSIONAL SERVICES ONLY) BY TYPE OF PRACTITIONER FOR ALL DIAGNOSTIC CODES COMBINED[1]

Type of Practitioner	Inpatient (Report 3)		Outpatient (Report 4)[2]	
Attending Physicians	Maine	$18.75	Mississippi	$32.25
	All States	34.54	All States	42.46
	Tennessee	55.29	Virginia	51.60
Psychiatrists	West Virginia	$24.32	Maryland	$28.49
	All States	43.00	All States	48.72
	California	61.37	Nevada	58.00
Psychologists	Wisconsin	$22.94	South Dakota	$34.92
	All States	49.82	All States	52.12
	Louisiana	58.55	California	57.98
Social Workers	Missouri	$ 6.17	Wisconsin	$ 9.62
	All States	31.93	All States	38.68
	California	47.31	California	45.98
Therapists (All Types)	NONE		New York	$38.82
			All States	43.87
			Alaska	50.63
All Others	Arkansas	$12.37	West Virginia	$27.57
	All States	36.51	All States	40.64
	Virginia	55.48	California	47.87

[1]The ranges shown for each type of practitioner indicate the states with the lowest and highest average amount paid per visit for each type of practitioner in column 1. The average amount paid per visit for all states combined, all diagnostic codes combined, is shown between the low and high values. The edit was a minimum of ten visits per each type of practitioner.

[2]The State of Alaska was highest for average amount paid per visit for every type of practitioner. Therefore, the states listed are actually second highest, with the exception of therapists (all types).

Table 65

UTILIZATION BY TYPE OF PRACTITIONER AND PERCENT OF TOTAL VISITS
(Professional Services Only—All Diagnostic Codes Combined)

	Inpatient (Report 3)		Outpatient (Report 4)	
Type of Practitioner	Number of Visits	Percent of Total Visits	Number of Visits	Percent of Total Visits
Attending Physicians	29,752	10.9%	45,393	5.0%
Psychiatrists	225,133	82.6	360,959	39.5
Psychologists	7,099	2.6	257,607	28.2
Social Workers	2,997	1.1	171,759	18.8
Therapists (All Types)	—	—	71	*
All Others	7,614	2.8	77,374	8.5
Total Visits	272,595		913,163	

*Less than 0.1%

Table 66
MOST FREQUENTLY USED PROCEDURES FOR EACH TYPE OF PRACTITIONER AND AVERAGE AMOUNT PAID PER VISIT
(Inpatient Professional Services—Report 1)

Type of Practitioner	Procedural Code No.	Description	Frequency	Percent of Total Procedures*	Average Amount Paid Per Visit For Procedure Indicated
Attending Physicians	90855	Psychotherapy, Inpatient care, 20-30 minutes	4,710	15.5%	$26.39
Psychiatrists	90806	Psychotherapy—verbal, 25 minutes	49,147	21.3	31.77
Psychologists	92804	Psychotherapy, adult or child, 45-50 minutes, Hospital or other facility	1,866	25.7	56.91
Social Workers	98622	Individual Therapy/ Counseling by a Social Worker—46-60 minutes	605	19.8	39.61
All Others	90805	Psychotherapy—verbal, 50 minutes	986	12.3	51.34

*Percentages are based on the total number of psychiatric visits provided by the type of practitioner indicated in Column 1.

Table 67
MOST FREQUENTLY USED PROCEDURES FOR EACH TYPE OF PRACTITIONER AND AVERAGE AMOUNT PAID PER VISIT
(Outpatient Professional Services—Report 2)

Type of Practitioner	Procedural Code No.	Description	Frequency	Percent of Total Procedures*	Average Amount Paid Per Visit
Attending Physicians	92803	Psychotherapy, adult or child, 45-50 minutes, in office	14,417	30.9%	$49.73
Psychiatrists	90805	Psychotherapy—verbal, 50 minutes	163,688	44.4	50.82
Psychologists	92803	Psychotherapy, adult or child, 45-50 minutes, in office	129,562	49.8	55.75
Social Workers	03030	Individual Counseling	96,448	55.8	44.77
Therapists (All Types)	90805	Psychotherapy—verbal, 50 minutes	62	75.6	43.47
All Others	90805	Psychotherapy—verbal, 50 minutes	47,498	59.9	43.24

*Percentages are based on the total number of psychiatric visits provided by the type of practitioner indicated in Column 1.

Table 68
MOST FREQUENTLY DIAGNOSED DISORDER FOR EACH TYPE OF PRACTITIONER AND THE AVERAGE AMOUNT PAID PER VISIT
(Inpatient Professional Services Only—Report 3)

Type of Practitioner	Diagnosis No.	Description	Average Amount Paid Per Visit
Attending Physicians	300	Neuroses	$36.20
Psychiatrists	300	Neuroses	41.44
Psychologists	300	Neuroses	49.88
Social Workers	300	Neuroses	30.14
All Others	300	Neuroses	35.53

Table 68A
MOST FREQUENTLY DIAGNOSED DISORDER FOR EACH TYPE OF PRACTITIONER AND THE AVERAGE AMOUNT PAID PER VISIT
(Outpatient Professional Services Only—Report 4)

Type of Practitioner	Diagnosis No.	Description	Average Amount Paid Per Visit
Attending Physicians	300	Neuroses	$44.85
Psychiatrists	300	Neuroses	49.70
Psychologists	300	Neuroses	52.88
Social Workers	300	Neuroses	39.75
Therapists (All Types)	304	Drug Dependence	50.63
All Others	300	Neuroses	40.89

Table 69
RANK ORDER OF DIAGNOSTIC CODES BY NUMBER OF VISITS AND PERCENT OF TOTAL VISITS
(Inpatient Professional Services—Report 3)

Diagnostic Code Number	Description	Number of Visits	Percent of Total Visits
300	Neuroses	118,300	43.4%
295	Schizophrenia	54,517	20.0
307	Transient situational disturbances	23,621	8.7
296	Active psychoses	19,299	7.1
308	Behavior disorders of childhood	17,523	6.4
301	Personality disorders	9,211	3.4
298	Other psychoses	8,549	3.1
303	Alcoholism	3,867	1.4
294	Psychosis associated with other physical condition	2,639	1.0
299	Unspecified psychosis	2,531	0.9
290	Senile and presenile dementia	2,144	0.8
293	Psychosis associated with other cerebral condition	1,983	0.7
309	Mental disorders not specified as psychotic, associated with physical conditions	1,691	0.6
304	Drug dependence	1,595	0.6
297	Paranoid states	1,282	0.5
306	Specified symptoms not elsewhere classified	1,252	0.5
305	Physical disorders of presumably psychogenic origin	1,106	0.4
302	Sexual deviation	796	0.3
291	Alcoholic psychosis	475	0.2
292	Psychosis associated with intracranial infection	214	0.1
	Total Visits =	272,595	

Table 70
RANK ORDER OF DIAGNOSTIC CODES BY NUMBER OF VISITS AND PERCENT OF TOTAL VISITS
(Outpatient Professional Services—Report 4)

Diagnostic Code Number	Description	Number of Visits	Percent of Total Visits
300	Neuroses	449,117	49.2%
307	Transient situational disturbances	185,243	20.3
308	Behavior disorders of childhood	99,968	10.9
301	Personality disorders	51,430	5.6
295	Schizophrenia	48,721	5.3
296	Active psychoses	26,294	2.9
309	Mental disorders not specified as psychotic, associated with physical conditions	6,957	0.8
306	Special symptoms not elsewhere classified	6,850	0.8
299	Unspecified psychosis	6,333	0.7
298	Other psychoses	5,720	0.6
305	Physical disorders of presumably psychogenic origin	5,420	0.6
303	Alcoholism	4,553	0.5
290	Neuroses	3,987	0.4
294	Psychosis associated with other physical condition	3,630	0.4
304	Drug dependence	2,531	0.3
297	Paranoid states	2,118	0.2
293	Psychosis associated with other cerebral condition	1,717	0.2
302	Sexual deviation	1,711	0.2
291	Alcoholic psychosis	702	0.1
292	Psychosis associated with intracranial infection	161	*
	Total Visits =	913,163	

*Less than 0.1%

Table 71
PERCENT OF TOTAL PROVIDERS PAID BY CHAMPUS IN FISCAL YEAR 1980 BY TYPE OF PRACTITIONER

Type of Practitioner	Total Number	Percent of Total Number of Providers
Attending Physicians	6,424	25.3%
Psychiatrists	7,763	30.5
Psychologists	3,969	15.6
Social Workers	1,910	7.5
Therapists	17	0.1
All Others	5,340	21.0
Total	25,423	100.0%

CHAMPUS UTILIZATION DATA—1980: COMPARISON WITH CERTAIN FEHBP PLANS AND A LARGE PRIVATE SECTOR PLAN*

An analysis of a very complete collection of CHAMPUS data for the year 1980 indicates that CHAMPUS eligibles are *not* heavy users of psychiatric services. This conclusion applies both to *per capita* charges incurred and to the percentage of the total eligible population that uses mental health services of any form under CHAMPUS in a given year.

In 1980, total amounts paid by all CHAMPUS users† amounted to:

All outpatient services	$ 43,379,766
All inpatient therapy services	11,760,679
All hospital charges (in addition to inpatient services)	104,068,326
	$159,208,771

Vector Research—on contract with DOD—estimated that there were a total of 8,191,124 eligibles in FY 1981 (overlapping FY 80 & 81). This estimate is not likely to vary significantly from the actual 1980 figure. Dividing this number into the total level of charges for 1980 yields a *per capita* dollar utilization rate of $19.44, which, adjusted to 1982 prices by the All Medical component of the CPI, comes to $24.13 per covered person.

A comparison of this utilization rate with utilization rates of various federal employee programs in 1979—similarly adjusted to 1982 prices—shows that

*Private sector plan asked not to be identified.
†Includes all DOD beneficiaries plus non-DOD beneficiaries of the Coast Guard, Commissioned Corps of the U.S. Public Health Service, Commissioned Corps of NASA. Excluded are CHAMPVA, contractor denials, deductible only claims, cancellation claims, and all other claims.

CHAMPUS eligibles use mental health services at a dollar rate in the range of federal employee plan members with very restricted psychiatric coverage:

	Per Capita Charges	Quality of Coverage
American Foreign Svc.	$89.46	Liberal—Exc.
Blue Cross/Blue Shield	46.35	Liberal—Exc.
National Alliance	33.73	Restricted—Fair
Aetna	29.09	Restricted—Good
CHAMPUS	24.13	Liberal—Exc.
AFGE	21.24	Restricted—Fair
GEHA	18.60	Restricted—Fair
Rural Letter Carriers	9.22	Restricted—Fair

The number of users as a percentage of the total eligible population is also very low compared to FEHBP members. Only 1 percent (actually 0.99 percent) of all eligibles received benefits for mental health services in 1980, compared to 1.8 percent of Blue Cross/Blue Shield eligibles and 1.7 percent of Aetna covered persons.

A comparison with a large private sector plan offering similar liberal mental health coverage is also favorable. Persons eligible for benefits under this large plan incurred charges of $50.71 per covered person in 1980 (adjusted to 1982 price levels) and slightly more than 3 percent of all eligibles were users of this coverage.

It should be noted that many CHAMPUS eligibles use "on-base" services which are not included in these computations. "On-base" psychiatric services are not extensive, however, being confined to acute, very short-term therapy and evaluations leading to referral or discharge from service. The "on-base" usage of other medical services is much more extensive, however, and it is this phenomenon that has distorted the perception of usage of psychiatric services under CHAMPUS. There is a tendency to measure usage in terms of percent of total benefits paid. Obviously, percent of benefits paid for mental health services under CHAMPUS would be large since such a large part of other medical services are provided "on-base" and, hence, outside CHAMPUS. Per capita usage is a more accurate measurement, and, when applied to this program, reveals a much more modest utilization pattern than commonly believed.

Prepared by:
John Krizay, Economic Consultant

VI. Health Maintenance Organizations: Utilization and Coverage of Mental Health Services

Excerpts from a Study Sponsored by APA, 1983

The HMO concept won acclaim in the early 70s as an economical way of providing medical services, and, it was on this basis, that the HMO Act was passed setting guidelines for federal qualification and offering incentives to the medical and health insurance industries to organize and to offer more medical services in their settings. Since the HMO is both insurer and provider, it has a built-in inducement to economize. However, a common criticism of HMOs has been that, in the interest of economy, chronic patients may be "short-changed" and, while evaluations based on mortality and morbidity data show HMOs to be effective and competent health care providers, such data do not reveal the extent to which personal suffering and pain of chronic patients may go unattended. It is in this regard that treatment of mental illness in HMO settings is of interest. As with many chronic ailments, treatment of mental illness has an indeterminate quality. Progress in treatment is not dramatic and positive results may only be noted over a long period. Given the budget constraints under which medical practitioners must operate in HMOs, how is an expensive course of treatment such as psychotherapy dealt with?

Toward this end the authors undertook an examination of utilization rates in federally qualified HMOs operational in 1979-1980 as they relate to coverage offered by the plans. The groups were observed at a time when many new HMOs were being introduced and, hence, had low membership levels.

However, the years 1979 and 1980 provide the only complete comparative data available since 1980 was the last year for which HMOs were required to submit utilization data to DHHS. The analysis was enhanced by a presentation of coverage and *modus operandi* of HMOs in the "Report of the Task Force on Health Maintenance Organizations", Daniel Y. Patterson, M.D., chairperson (1983). Typically, HMOs impose limitations on psychiatric care that are as severe as the weakest psychiatric coverage of conventional plans. According to the Task Force Report, 30 days inpatient psychiatric care and 20 outpatient psychiatric visits are the norm. Examination of the plans included in this study confirm this observation: 25 plans covered 30 inpatient days or less, 6 covered 45 days, 3 covered 60 days and only 1 covered 120 days.

But, while coverage variations are few, utilization rates vary considerably. Indeed there was no correlation observed between outpatient coverage and total psychiatric utilization rates nor were there any other observed cause and effect relationships. The range of per capita benefits paid out by HMOs is very wide in contrast to conventional plans where groups with similar coverage and confined to a geographic area tend to show much narrower variation in utilization. A question thus arises as to what extent the variations in HMO plans are attributable to limitations in coverage or to other factors.

Since HMOs do not charge for individual services, finding a measure of utilization comparable to private sector services paid for on a fee-for-service basis involves some assumptions. For this analysis, the number of outpatient encounters plan members had with psychiatrists and other mental health professionals—on a per capita basis—was multiplied by $60.00 to arrive at a figure representing outpatient charges per covered person. By using the $60 figure we arrive at an outpatient cost approximating mid-1982 prices. This could be a bit high depending upon the extent to which group therapy was resorted to or non-M.D. therapists employed by HMOs. CHAMPUS, for example, estimated average charges for all types of outpatient therapy in 1980 at $47.00. While there is no longer an official index of price of services of mental professionals, the index of all physician services rose by approximately 25 percent from 1980 to mid-1982, and it is likely that mental health professionals raised their fees similarly. The $60.00 factor, therefore, should provide a good first approximation of equivalent HMO charges for outpatient services at 1982 prices.

Hospital charges were arrived at by multiplying the number of discharge days per capita by $250—a widely reported average room and board charge in mid-1982. This figure may be on the low side since hospital charges, although varying greatly from region to region, are generally higher in heavily populated urban areas where the largest HMOs are located. Other charges—including medication and inpatient physician services—are based only on an average share of total costs revealed by Federal Employee Plans. According to that experience, "other" psychiatric costs averaged about 12½ percent of the total. However, the percentage varied tremendously from plan-to-plan and from year-to-year, and there is no way of knowing if HMOs generally should fit at the top or the bottom of the range. Since the charges for "other" services constitute a relatively small part of the total, however, distortions due to the use of this arbitrary factor should be minimal.

A thorough review and testing of the data suggests that the observed variations in mental health utilization rates among HMOs are not at all related to stated coverage limits. Based on coverage information for 53 federally qualified plans for the years 1979-1980 (years for which utilization data were available) the most significant finding was the wide variations in utilization levels among plans imposing like limitations; plans of similar size, similar age and operating in the same regions. Utilization varied in unusual ways including from year to year in the same plan, i.e. outpatient care up one year but down the next while inpatient care showed reverse behavior. One is tempted to conclude that budget constraints may have been as important in determining course of treatment as clinical judgment. As implied in the task force report, HMOs seem to make use of management decisions to establish "medical necessity" in the treatment of mental illness as well as in general medicine. Do HMOs without a strong pro-psychiatric voice on the board deny care on the basis of limiting definitions (e.g. chronic vs. acute cases)?

The experience, whatever the explanation for these unusual utilization patterns, illustrates the irrelevance of coverage design in HMOs. Group Health of South Central Wisconsin offered exceptionally high inpatient coverage (120 days) but experienced relatively low inpatient utilization during the two years under study (Table 72). Curiously, this plan experienced extremely high outpatient utilization. Group Health Plan of Southeast Michigan covered 45 days inpatient care (reinstated after 60 days if for a different diagnoses) but had a utilization rate of $.78 per covered person per year in 1980 and zero in 1979 whereas Marion Health Foundation of Ohio with only 20 days of inpatient coverage had an inpatient utilization cost of $6.60 and $10.83 per covered/year (Table I.A.). Among plans with similar benefits coverage, even within plans from year to year, wide ranges of utilization and seemingly random changes in utilization rates cause one to suspect different management philosophies and concerns at work. A plan like Kaiser of Southern California with liberal outpatient coverage, had average total costs no greater than that of Kaiser of Northern California which had much more restrictive outpatient psychiatric benefits. Both plans had the same inpatient coverage.

Curiously, the large plans, as a group, have the highest average utilization rate ($14.65 per covered person) but the lowest maximum ($35.41 per covered person). The maximum per capita cost of medium sized HMOs was $44.10 while, among the "small" HMOs, the highest utilization rate was $44.43—comparable to the Blue Cross-Blue Shield FEP experience with coverage far more extensive. A more revealing comparison is by type of plan: Group, IPA, or Staff. The HMOs reporting were about equally divided among these three types, although in terms of total membership, Group plans are dominant (nearly 80 percent of total membership). Staff plans—the second largest category—produced the highest utilization rate estimated at $15.66 per capita, ranging up to $44.43. IPAs had the lowest average utilization rate ($9.68 per capita) and the lowest maximum as well as $25.05. This is somewhat surprising since IPAs are a looser affiliation and are thought to have less discipline over their provider force than Groups or Staff plans.

Two other factors may influence utilization: one factor is geographic/regional differences and a second factor is that, for various reasons noted in the literature, HMOs attract a different population than do private insurance plans. A survey sponsored by the American Medical Association (Background Information Supplemental to Council on Medical Service Report A (A-80)) found significant differences in age, sex and socioeconomic backgrounds between HMO membership and private insurance plans. HMOs have a slightly younger membership with larger families and more children, and they enroll fewer senior citizens and fewer single workers. The ratio of females to males is higher in HMOs than in the general population. A discussion of economic and cultural motivations underlying individual choices is beyond the scope of this paper, but this phenomenon and its implications for mental health utilization deserves further study.

A typical assumption in insurance studies particularly those pertaining to psychiatric coverage is that higher benefits result in higher utilization. It was expected that this assumption would hold true for HMOs. However, unlike conventional plans (review studies of FEHBP utilization), HMO outpatient coverage available does not correlate with outpatient utilization. In fact, after running numerous statistical tests on combinations of factors (e.g., outpatient coverage against total utilization, etc.) there were very few correlations observed and *none* of any statistical significance. One hypothesis examined in this study, was the expectation that good outpatient coverage would result in lower hospital admissions. Conversely, it was anticipated that poor outpatient coverage would cause the hospital admissions rate to be higher than average. The hospital admissions rate correlated *very* weakly (correlation coefficient .1) with outpatient coverage but since the variation in outpatient coverage is narrow, not even tenuous inferences can be drawn at this point.

The inconsistency of the utilization experience as it relates to coverage and the variations in utilization from year to year and among similar plans are, nonetheless, significant phenomena. These observations suggest a wide range of treatment options applicable to HMO patients with the choice, perhaps influenced as much by budget restraints as clinical preference. Of course, the rate of financial constraints in determining treatment modes is not an unusual occurrence in medical practice of all kinds. Indeed, this issue has been at the root of the argument regarding health insurance and national health care systems everywhere. The significance regarding psychiatric utilization in HMO settings, however, is in interpreting the data, for it is evident that other forces are at work that the typical analytical approach will not reveal. Comparison with utilization experience in other settings may be particularly hazardous.

Table 72
UTILIZATION OF MENTAL HEALTH SERVICES SELECTED HMOs
1979-1980

Plans		Dollar Value Utilization* (per covered person)		Imputed Dollar Maximum Coverage**	
By State	**Year**	**Outpatient**	**Inpatient**	**Inpatient**	**Outpatient**
California					
Comprecare	'79	1.76	1.73	7500	1200
	'80	—	—		
Family Health Program	'79	—	—	6000	1160
	'80	10.05	0.69		
Family Health Services	'79	1.67	4.20	N/A	
	'80	2.10	1.62		
Foundation Health Plan	'79	3.53	1.05	N/A	
	'80	2.84	2.35		
INA	'79	5.70	2.35	11,250	700
	'80	5.17	2.57		
Kaiser—Northern California	'79	7.11	0.86	1,250	1,180
	'80	9.41	0.89		

Table 72 (continued)

Plans		Dollar Value Utilization* (per covered person)		Imputed Dollar Maximum Coverage**	
By State	**Year**	**Outpatient**	**Inpatient**	**Inpatient**	**Outpatient**
Kaiser—Southern California	'79	8.08	1.61	1250	3510
	'80	10.96	2.07		
Maxicare	'79	—	—	N/A	
	'80	3.53	2.12		
Colorado					
Comprecare	'79	8.43	10.10		
	'80	11.58	8.49	7,500	1,200
San Luis Valley	'79	—	—		
	'80	7.04	-0-	6,750	1,000
Kaiser	'79	4.19	2.03	5,000	1,000
Connecticut					
Community Health Care Center	'79	10.43	9.15	5625	975
	'80	13.45	14.22		
Florida					
American Health Plan	'79	4.83	1.22	7,750	1,000
	'80	6.40	1.49		
Av-Med	'79	N/A	N/A		
	'80	2.53	3.10	2625	800
Florida Health Care Plan	'79	4.27	5.63	7,750	1,200
	'80	N/A	N/A		
Illinois					
Intergroup	'79	1.80	8.20	N/A	
	'80	2.88	14.86		
Michael Reese	'79	5.17	4.51	7300	1200
	'80	4.58	8.95		
Indiana					
Metro Health Plan	'79	3.48	5.16	15,000	1,100
	'80	2.65	5.48		
Kentucky					
Health Care, Louisville	'79	3.74	10.50	250	1200
	'80	4.91	13.67		
Louisiana					
HMO, Baton Rouge	'79	2.16	5.78	Revoked/N/A	
	'80	N/A	N/A		

Table 72 (continued)

Plans By State	Year	Dollar Value Utilization* (per covered person) Outpatient	Inpatient	Inputed Dollar Maximum Coverage** Inpatient	Outpatient
Massachusetts					
Harvard Com. H.P.	'79	23.45	7.54	15,000	1,180
	'80	N/A	N/A		
Michigan					
Group Health Service Michigan	'79	4.88	6.67	11,250	1,200
	'80	N/A	N/A		
Health Central	'79	N/A	N/A	7,500	1,200
	'80	14.09	5.75		
Michigan HMO Plans, Inc.	'79	4.88	6.67	7,500	1,200
	'80	N/A	N/A		
Minnesota					
Share	'79	6.02	10.03	7,050	1,100
	'80	5.70	8.14		
Missouri					
Prime Health	'79	7.14	3.50	7,500	1,200
	'80	6.05	7.95		
New Hampshire					
Matthew Thornton	'79	11.60	5.88	7,500	1,200
	'80	11.46	10.13		
New Jersey					
CoMed	'79	N/A	N/A	7,500	1,000
	'80	5.53	6.15		
Cross Roads	'79	1.13	1.50	5,000	930
	'80	0.37	2.51		
Rutgers	'79	4.92	11.06	7,500	2,648
	'80	N/A	N/A		
Southshore	'79	1.05	2.68	N/A	
	'80	N/A	N/A		
New York					
Genessee Valley	'79	8.01	10.48	11,250	600
	'80	N/A	N/A		
Health Care, Buffalo	'79	4.48	3.64		
	'80	8.06	2.71	N/A	

Table 72 (continued)

Plans		Dollar Value Utilization* (per covered person)		Inputed Dollar Maximum Coverage**	
By State	**Year**	**Outpatient**	**Inpatient**	**Inpatient**	**Outpatient**
Manhattan Health Plan	'79	1.95	3.58	7,500	1,200
	'80	—	—		
Weschester	'79	6.85	4.62	7,500	1,200
	'80	—	—		
Ohio					
Kaiser	'79	7.38	8.09	7,500	1,045
	'80	7.80	8.31		
Marion	'79	4.88	6.60	7500	1020
	'80	5.02	10.83		
Oregon					
Capitol	'79	6.86	2.63	N/A	
	'80	3.10	1.20		
HMO Oregon	'79	N/A	N/A	Revoked/N/A	
	'80	21.71	11.06		
Pennsylvania					
Greater Delaware Valley	'79	2.74	4.06	15,000	795
	'80	N/A	N/A		
HMO, Pennsylvania	'79	9.25	4.49	8,750	870
	'80	12.67	9.55		
Rhode Island					
R.I. Group Health Association	'79	11.64	10.38	11,250	300
	'80	N/A	N/A		
South Carolina					
Piedmont Health Care	'79	4.14	9.53	7,500	600
	'80	N/A	N/A		
Texas					
CompCare (GHP)	'79	N/A	N/A	N/A	
	'80	7.61	5.38		
Group Health El Paso	'79	1.06	-0-	Revoked/N/A	
	'80	N/A	N/A		
Prucare Houston	'79	1.99	8.54	3,750	900
	'80	1.42	3.16		

Table 72 (continued)

Plans By State	Year	Dollar Value Utilization* (per covered person) Outpatient	Inpatient	Inputed Dollar Maximum Coverage** Inpatient	Outpatient
Wisconsin					
Group Health Cooperative South Central Wisconsin	'79	34.03	4.85	30,000	1,200
	'80	25.67	10.30		
D.C.-Maryland (Combined)					
GHA	'79	12.79	3.41	7,500	1,100
	'80	9.24	2.73		
Health Plus, Inc.	'79	N/A	N/A	7,500	800
	'80	2.08	3.87		
Kaiser Georgetown	'79	7.91	8.31	7,500	1,200
	'80	N/A	N/A		
Metropolitan Baltimore	'79	10.64	5.67	0	900
	'80	N/A	N/A		

*Outpatient encounters valued @ $60, inpatient days valued @ $250, 12.5 percent of total added for "other" services (e.g., inpatient ancillary costs).
**Value of total Mental Health Services covered in any one year.

VII. Evaluation and Prediction Models

Several qualitative and quantitative scales have been proposed as researchers try to evaluate mental health coverage in plans and make comparisons across plans.

The Hay-Huggins computer model described below gives average dollar costs per enrollee of various benefit designs (based on national utilization experience). The Value Point System is a qualitative approach developed by John Krizay of Health Data Associates to compare mental health benefit coverages. Relative value scales are proposed by some sources.

The American Psychiatric Association has used both quantitative and qualitative scales to compare plan designs but the first step in making comparisons is the collection of accurate raw data. More and more public and private groups are beginning to systematically collect and store data, but an integrated effort is needed to avoid duplication of expense and time and to yield a comprehensive and accurate picture.

A. *Value Point System*

Outpatient Coverage

Values for Services Provided:

Maximum—20 visits per person covered per year	15 points
21–49 visits per person covered per year	25 points
50–100 visits per person covered per year	35 points
>100 visits per person covered per year	50 points

Values for Choice of Treatment Modes Permitted:

Group sessions—same bases as individual therapy	10*
Group sessions—allowing 2 sessions = 1 individual session	15*
Collateral visits and/or family therapy	10
Treatment includes alcoholism & drug abuse	5
Treatment by other members of mental health team (in case of RN's, MSW's and ACSW's under supervision of M.D. only)	10

*where visit limitation >100, add 15 points in any case.

Penalties for Restrictions on Outpatient Coverage:

If patient required to pay 50 percent or more of charges of:
(test to *lowest* visit level)

41-50 individual visits (or equivalent) per person/year .... 10 points
31-40 individual visits (or equivalent) per person/year .... 15 points
21-30 individual visits (or equivalent) per person/year .... 20 points
<20 individual visits (or equivalent) per person/year .... 30 points

Bonus points (add) (test to *highest* level)
Where co-payment averages 25 percent or less for
50 visits or more add .... 5 points
100 visits or more add .... 10 points

Average per visit charges used in calculating penalties and bonuses for years 1973 through 76 are as follows:

1973	$28	individual visit charge
1974	31	
1975	34	
1976	37	
1982	70	

Inpatient Coverage

Values for Inpatient Services Provided:
Up to 30 days hospital expenses annually .... 15 points
Up to 60 days hospital expenses annually .... 30 points
Up to 90 days hospital expenses annually .... 45 points
Up to 120 days hospital expenses annually .... 60 points

["Per confinement" restrictions are interpreted in terms of maximum annual allowance, e.g., 90 per confinement where "new" confinement starts after 90 day interval from last discharge, means effective annual coverage of 185 days.]

Inpatient Treatment Options:

Permits day (or night) treatment but applies co-payment of not more than 20 percent .... 10 points
Substitute day (or night) treatment on equal basis (or 2 for 1 basis where hospital days restricted) .... 20 points

Penalties for Restrictions on Inpatient Coverage:
(test to *lowest* hospital day level)

where plan covers:

<75% of normal inpatient costs for 61-90 days, deduct .... 10 points
<75% of normal inpatient costs for 40-60 days, deduct .... 15 points
<75% of normal inpatient costs for 31-45 days.............................. 20 points
<75% of normal inpatient costs for 30 .... 30 points

Bonus Points (add)

Covers all normal costs for *more than* 90 days	10 points
Covers all normal costs for *one year* or *more*	20 points

Computations or penalties and bonuses include co-payment, dollar maximums as percent of average daily cost of given year, days covered, and any other restrictions increasing patient's share of liability. The following average daily hospital cost figures are used:

1973	70.00
1974	76.25
1975	87.75
1976	98.50
1982	300.00

General

Penalty Points Applied to Mean of Inpatient, Outpatient Values

(Dollar values are for 1976. For comparisons with other years, adjust by medical component of Consumer Price Index)

1973 Schedule (rounded)	**Points**
Maximum dollar coverage $1500 life, $750 annual	−50
Maximum dollar coverage $1501-3500 life; $751-1750 annual	−30
Maximum dollar coverage $3501-7500 life; $1750-3750 annual	−20
Maximum dollar coverage $7501-19,000 life; $3751-9500 annual	−10
Maximum dollar coverage $19,000-37,500 life; $9501-18,750 annual	− 5
Maximum dollar coverage >$37,500 life; >18,750 annual	0

1974 Schedule

Maximum dollar coverage $1650 life; $825 annual	−50
Maximum dollar coverage $1651-3825 life; $826-1900 annual	−30
Maximum dollar coverage $3826-8200 life; $1901-4100 annual	−20
Maximum dollar coverage $8201-20,750 life; $4101-10,375 annual	−10
Maximum dollar coverage $20,750-41,000 life; $10,376-20,500 annual	− 5
Maximum dollar coverage >$41,000 life; >$20,500 annual	0

1975 Schedule

Maximum dollar coverage $1800 life; $900 annual	−50
Maximum dollar coverage $1801-4200 life; $901-2100 annual	−30
Maximum dollar coverage $4201-9000 life; $2101-4500 annual	−20
Maximum dollar coverage $9001-23,000 life; $4501-11,500 annual	−10
Maximum dollar coverage $23,001-45,000 life; 11,501-22,500 annual	− 5
Maximum dollar coverage >$45,000 life; >$22,500 annual	0

1976 Schedule

Maximum dollar coverage $2,000 life; $1,000 annual	−50
Maximum dollar coverage $2000-4499 life; $1000-2499 annual	−30
Maximum dollar coverage $5000-9999 life; $2500-4999 annual	−20
Maximum dollar coverage $10,000-24,999 life; $5000-9999 annual	−10
Maximum dollar coverage $25,000-49,999 life; $10,000-24,999 annual	− 5
Maximum dollar coverage >$50,000 life; >$25,000 annual	0

B. Hay Associates Model for Determining Cost of Mental and Nervous Care Insurance

Hay Associates has developed a model that will enable employers to measure the cost of establishing, or revising, an insurance package for the coverage of mental health care. The model permits analysis of variations in any of the following areas:

- Inpatient deductible
- Inpatient per day deductible
- Maximum inpatient days
- Inpatient coinsurance
- Maximum inpatient bill
- Limit on outpatient visits covered
- Outpatient deductible
- Outpatient coinsurance
- Limit of dollars allowed per outpatient visit
- Maximum out-of-pocket limit
- Maximum bill in a year
- Maximum bill in a lifetime

The Hay model includes a state-of-the-art analysis incorporating the most recent data on mental and nervous care. An important aspect of the model is that it permits measurement of the interactive effect of variations.

Description of Model

The inpatient part of the model includes a distribution of the average days per stay in eleven different day categories. Since care varies significantly between adults and children, these claims are examined separately. On the outpatient side the model evaluates the cost, the number of claimants, and average visits for 22 visit categories. These categories range from one to five visits in a year to 200 or more visits in a year. By specifying each of the parameters involved in a program, the model develops a base line cost for the program. Then, by variation of one or more factors, the model can analyze the impact of any change in the program.

Validation of Model

The model was carefully constructed by Hay primarily using information from the Blue Cross/Blue Shield coverage of Federal employees. This plan, which covers over 5,000,000 people—employees and annuitants and their dependents—has been closely monitored for the last two decades. With the large Federal data base and valid data gathering technique, the system gives the best possible information that we know of on the distribution of mental and nervous health care benefits. Further, since the Federal program has seen three major changes in plan design in the last ten years, the data on that program gives a good indication of the effect of variations in covered care.

Two main sources were used to develop the distributions in the Hay model, and these were then fitted to the expected 1982 total Blue Cross/Blue Shield mental and nervous claims costs. The two main sources were a detailed study of all 1973 claimants[1] and the MANDUCS[2] study. MANDUCS was an extensive study of 1977 claims in the Washington area for outpatient mental and nervous treatment. In order to integrate the MANDUCS analysis with the total FEHB study, the Washington area claims utilization and cost were modified to reflect the total country. Information in the earlier study had shown that the Washington area utilization rates were substantially higher than those observed in the country as a whole.

To bring the information up to date, the model was modified to produce a total inpatient cost of $113 million and a total outpatient cost of $79 million for calendar 1982. These totals were obtained from statements by Blue Cross/Blue Shield officials. The model assumes that the average cost of an outpatient visit in 1982 will be $65 and that the average inpatient day will cost $270. These data were based on discussions with the professional organizations, using their surveys when possible. In any particular case, actual unit costs can be substituted if they are known to be different.

Applicability to Non-Federal Programs

In using the model for a particular program, it is important to understand the potential differences between the Federal population utilization and that of any other insured group. Because of two characteristics of the Federal population covered by Blue Cross/Blue Shield, it is likely that the changes as measured by the model will be the maximum that could be experienced by any other plan of statistically significant size.

First, Federal employees were covered by a program, during the time of the two studies on which the model is based, that provided the maximum possible benefits in most cases. Therefore, there was no reduction in demand because of benefit limitations. Thus, any plan with limits on mental health care in any

[1] *Utilization of Mental Illness Benefits under the Federal Employees Health Benefits Program*—U.S. Civil Service Commission, June 1, 1977.

[2] *Mental and Nervous Utilization and Cost Survey*—M.R. VonKraff and Morton Carmer—NIMH and U.S. OPM—May 1979.

area would have a lower demand factor than that reflected in the Federal program.

Second, most studies have shown that the Federal employees use care to a greater extent than the country at large. For instance, the outpatient part of the model predicts that 36 percent of claimants will use more than 15 visits in a year and that the average claimant will use 20 visits. Studies of private sector care show significantly lower usage. A review of Michigan Blue Shield data in 1975 showed an average of 10 visits per claimant. A review of 20 years of Kaiser experience showed that only 15 percent of claimants used more than 15 visits a year.

Because of these two factors, Hay believes that the model based on Federal data is the maximum that any particular employer could anticipate. Therefore, it will be safe to assume that the cost changes derived from the model would be at least as large as most employers will experience.

Comparison to Insurance Company Data

Since most employer programs are underwritten by insurers, or the employers rely on insurers to price the effect of a change of program, it is important to relate the Hay model to the measures that insurers may use. For instance, it might be necessary to explain why an insurer would estimate a rise in cost for a particular option that is substantially different from the rise in cost shown by the Hay model.

Most large insurers use models that are similar to, but not as refined as, the Hay model. For instance, an insurance rate manual might show the increase in cost of raising a 30 day inpatient limit to 60 days but not the cost of going to 45 days. We believe that the cost shown by our model will be close to the cost shown by an insurer using a sophisticated up-to-date model. However, since insurers are inclined to err on the side of conservatism in setting costs for changing a limit, it is possible that some may estimate cost changes higher than those stated by the Hay model. For instance, even if insurance companies studies show the same costs that the model does, the insurers will often add a further safety margin as high as 25 percent or 50 percent to allow for potential adverse selection.

While much of the insurers' safety margin will be offset by the fact that Federal employees are higher users than experienced in the private sector, it must be recognized that some insurers might quote higher premiums than shown by the Hay model. This will be particularly true of insurance companies which do not have existing valid statistics on the cost of raising mental and nervous limits. For instance, if an insurance company's practice has always been to limit mental and nervous outpatient care reimbursement to 50 visits a year, the company will not be too sure of the effect of raising a limit to 75 or 100 visits. In these cases, they are likely to substantially overestimate the cost of moving to the higher limit. In fact, overestimates on the order of two or three times actual cost would not be unexpected. Where an insurance company does give a cost that is significantly higher than the Hay model cost, it will be well to inquire as to the basis for the cost. If insurers' anticipated claims costs are not derived from a valid data base, the employer might be convinced to negotiate a lower rate increase with the insurer based on the Hay model.

Edwin C. Hustead, F.S.A., M.A.A.A.
Hay Associates
August 20, 1982

Table 73
1982 BLUE CROSS/BLUE SHIELD HIGH OPTION FORMULA

Plan Mental and Nervous Benefit Formula (For outpatient professional care)
Plan Pays 70 Percent After $200 Deductible

LIMITS
No More Than 47 Visits A Year (Assuming three visits for physical care)
No More Than $50,000 Lifetime

Visit Range	Clmts	Avg Bill	Pd By Plan	Pd By Clmt
1-5	17,718	$ 163	$ 44	$ 119
6-10	12,994	488	271	216
11-15	7,859	845	521	324
16-20	4,502	1,170	749	421
21-25	3,286	1,495	976	519
26-30	2,395	1,820	1,204	616
31-35	1,909	2,145	1,431	714
36-40	1,396	2,470	1,659	811
41-45	1,221	2,795	1,886	909
46-50	810	3,120	2,068	1,052
51-55	577	3,445	2,068	1,377
56-60	569	3,770	2,068	1,702
61-65	482	4,095	2,068	2,027
66-70	459	4,420	2,068	2,352
71-75	405	4,745	2,068	2,677
76-80	482	5,070	2,068	3,002
81-85	397	5,395	2,068	3,327
86-90	347	5,720	2,068	3,652
91-95	276	6,045	2,068	3,977
96-100	195	6,370	2,068	4,302
101-200	1,587	8,775	2,068	6,707
201-365	133	14,625	2,068	12,557

Total Bill = $79.3 million
Plan Pays = $39.1 million
Employee Pays = $40.2 million

Note: The utilization over 47 visits will drop in 1982 because many patients will not be able to afford continuation of treatments. However, this will not affect the amount paid by the plan.

Table 74
1980 BLUE CROSS/BLUE SHIELD HIGH OPTION FORMULA
IN 1982 DOLLARS

Plan Mental and Nervous Benefit Formula (For outpatient professional care)
Plan Pays 80 Percent After $100 Deductible

LIMITS
No More than $50,000 Lifetime

Visit Range	Clmts	Avg Bill	Pd By Plan	Pd By Clmt
1-5	17,718	$ 163	$ 90	$ 73
6-10	12,994	488	350	138
11-15	7,859	845	636	209
16-20	4,502	1,170	896	274
21-25	3,286	1,495	1,156	339
26-30	2,395	1,820	1,416	404
31-35	1,909	2,145	1,676	469
36-40	1,396	2,470	1,936	534
41-45	1,221	2,795	2,196	599
46-50	810	3,120	2,456	664
51-55	577	3,445	2,716	729
56-60	569	3,770	2,976	794
61-65	482	4,095	3,236	859
66-70	459	4,420	3,496	924
71-75	405	4,745	3,756	989
76-80	482	5,070	4,016	1,054
81-85	397	5,395	4,276	1,119
86-90	347	5,720	4,536	1,184
91-95	276	6,045	4,796	1,249
96-100	195	6,370	5,056	1,314
101-200	1,587	8,775	6,980	1,795
201-365	133	14,625	11,660	2,965

Total Bill = $79.3 million
Plan Pays = $61.0 million
Employee Pays = $18.3 million

Table 75
1981 BLUE CROSS/BLUE SHIELD HIGH OPTION FORMULA IN 1982 DOLLARS

Plan Mental and Nervous Benefit Formula (For outpatient professional care)
Plan Pays 70 Percent After $150 Deductible

LIMITS
No More Than $50,000 Lifetime

Visit Range	Clmts	Avg Bill	Pd By Plan	Pd By Clmt
1-5	17,718	$ 163	$ 61	$ 101
6-10	12,994	488	289	199
11-15	7,859	845	539	306
16-20	4,502	1,170	766	404
21-25	3,286	1,495	994	501
26-30	2,395	1,820	1,221	599
31-35	1,909	2,145	1,449	696
36-40	1,396	2,470	1,676	794
41-45	1,221	2,795	1,904	891
46-50	810	3,120	2,131	989
51-55	577	3,445	2,359	1,086
56-60	569	3,770	2,586	1,184
61-65	482	4,095	2,814	1,281
66-70	459	4,420	3,041	1,379
71-75	405	4,745	3,269	1,476
76-80	482	5,070	3,496	1,574
81-85	397	5,395	3,724	1,671
86-90	347	5,720	3,951	1,769
91-95	276	6,045	4,179	1,866
96-100	195	6,370	4,406	1,964
101-200	1,587	8,775	6,090	2,685
201-365	133	14,625	10,185	4,440

Total Bill = $79.3 million
Plan Pays = $52.4 million
Employee Pays = $26.9 million

Cost of Mental and Nervous Care for High User Population with Full Benefits in 1983

Data Source

The most recent solid data is for expenses incurred in 1980 for the high option of the Blue Cross/Blue Shield Federal Employee Health Benefits Program (FEHBP).

This option covered 1,520,000 employees and annuitants and the families of 970,000 of the enrollees. The plan covered all inpatient care and 80 percent of outpatient care after a $100 annual deductible. The only limit on coverage was an individual lifetime limit of $50,000 on mental and nervous benefits. Only 114 patients had reached this limit by 1980.

Thus, only a very few of the claims costs were not reported either because they totalled less than $100 or more than $50,000.

Enrollment Base

The enrollment of 1,520,000 included 550,000 self-only enrollments and 970,000 family enrollments. Using the traditional Blue Cross/Blue Shield assumption that each family contract includes 2.9 dependents, the total covered population would have been 4,330,000 people. However, other data indicates that this is an overstatement and that a factor of no more than 2.0 should be used. Thus, the total population was probably around 3,460,000.

Total Expenses Incurred in 1980

Blue Cross/Blue Shield reported a total of $162,300,000 in mental and nervous expenses incurred in the high option in 1980. This included a total of $104,600,000 inpatient and $57,700,000 outpatient charges. Thus, the expenses incurred were as follows:

	Per Enrollee	Per Covered Person
Inpatient	$ 68.80	$30.20
Outpatient	38.00	16.70
Total	$106.80	$46.90

Benefits Paid in 1980

Section III presents expenses (the total bill) incurred during the year (i.e., the patient entered the hospital and saw the doctor in 1980 but the bill may have been in 1981). Blue Cross/Blue Shield also reported the benefits (the amount reimbursed by the carrier) paid in 1980. Because of the application of the deductible and coinsurance and the payment lag this amount is less than $162,300,000.

The total benefits paid in 1980 for mental and nervous treatment were

$147,900,000. This was 7.9 percent of the total benefits paid for all care for this population in 1980.

Projection to 1983

Since 1980, the average cost of medical care has increased 13 percent a year. Using this assumption, a total per enrollee cost of $154 would be expected for a population with utilization similar to that expected for Blue Cross/Blue Shield enrollees in 1980. Alternatively, this could be expressed as $68 per covered person.

C. A Review of Studies of Demand and Utilization of Specialty Mental Health Services

(AN EDITED SUMMARY)

Richard G. Frank, Ph.D.
University of Pittsburgh
Thomas G. McGuire, Ph.D.
Boston University and
The Health Data Institute

1. The rate of utilization of mental health services depends on many factors. Insurance coverage is probably not the most important.

The rates at which insured populations use health care differ greatly. This is illustrated by Table 76, which reports utilization statistics for 35 studies of large populations insured for inpatient and outpatient mental health care. On any dimension, utilization statistics may vary by as much as ten times. Even grouping studies by type of coverage, accomplished in Table 77, does not eliminate large variations within the groups. The limited ability of the type of insurance to explain utilization is also true in the econometric studies. The list of other factors that determine use is long: personal characteristics, health status, and characteristics of the local mental health sector.

The large fluctuation in use regardless of insurance coverage has important implications for groups considering coverage for mental disorders as well as for the APA and others who would offer advice on the right coverage. For instance, an insurance company, a benefit consulting firm, or the APA might consider developing an actuarial model which could predict use and costs at different levels of insurance. This model could be based on national averages or the experience of a covered population, such as enrollees in a Blue Cross and Blue Shield plan. Because coverage only partly determines use, however, a simple model tying utilization to benefits—even if based on a single group that represents the national average—will not accurately forecast use in another group.

Advice to a group considering changes in coverage for mental disorders must be based on the group's past utilization. This approach to benefit consultation is much more relevant to the group at hand. A disadvantage, however, is that the approach requires a lot of data. Currently, many corporations do not know what they spend on their employees' care or what the money buys. Most insurer reports on mental health costs calculate the average costs per eligible individual. This statistic is of limited use, however, in considering the impact of changing the benefit. For example, an average annual cost of $20 per person for outpatient psychiatric benefits could be the result of 20 employees in 1,000 using $1,000 in benefits each, or the result of 80 cases in 1,000 at an average cost of $250 per case. A benefit change, such as imposing a $500 limit on coverage, would have a very different effect in each circumstance. A more informative description of experience is required to make progress in assisting groups to design benefit changes.

2. Heaviest use of ambulatory mental health services occurs when there are no restrictions on supply and the benefits have been place for some time.

There are studies of several populations with negligible supply restrictions which have had benefits in place for a number of years, including Blue Cross and Blue Shield enrollees in Massachusetts and Michigan, federal employees, and CHAMPUS (a health insurance program for the uninformed services) beneficiaries. In the studies reviewed, these groups show some of the highest rates of ambulatory cases and visits per thousand population covered. Perhaps illustrating this best are reports from Blue Cross and Blue Shield in Massachusetts and Michigan. For both of these plans, the insurers large market share and fairly uniform policies minimize the chance that consumers who need mental care the most will flock to the best coverage, skewing utilization rates. This phenomenon is called adverse selection.

Since 1976, Massachusetts has mandated that an annual $500 worth of outpatient psychiatric benefits be available in every health insurance policy written in the state. Groups in Michigan have had outpatient psychiatric benefits since the late 1960's. Although the Michigan Blues confine payments to psychiatrists and approved outpatient clinics for the bulk of its business, there have been few supply restrictions to limit use. Both plans feature first-dollar coverage and limits on total outpatient benefits.

The high rates of use in these two states stemmed from the large number of people using mental health benefits: 51 per thousand in Michigan and 29 per thousand in Massachusetts. These were among the highest rates in non-HMO populations, and recent unpublished reports from these two plans show even higher rates of use than are listed in this table. This high use exists even though these plans exclude intensive long-term therapy because dollar limits on coverage are low.

Coverage for federal employees and CHAMPUS beneficiaries generally has not been curtailed by dollar limits (recent changes in Federal Employees Health Benefits put limits on use) but has featured cost sharing of 20-25 percent. In general, fewer people in these plans sought treatment, but those who did averaged more visits per year than people in other Table 77 plans. In plans with generous limits on covered visits, a high proportion of use is accounted for by the most intensive users. In reports both on federal employees and the Rand Health Insurance Study, 75 percent of the ambulatory mental health visits are made by individuals seeing providers 20 or more times a year.

Taken together, these findings have a number of implications. First of all, because such a large portion of visits in an insured group is accounted for by few people making many visits, dollar limits, such as setting the yearly maximum at $500 or $1,000, or limiting the number of covered visits, can control costs. Small copayment, in the range of 20-25 percent, may also deter use.

3. Constraints on supply can significantly affect outpatient use.

In most fee-for-service settings, the availability of services does not seriously hamper utilization. Organized care settings, however, such as community mental health centers or prepaid group practices may purposely hold down use by restricting the supply. Use of benefits under such circumstances does not really represent demand, or what the enrollees would like to use given the coverage. It instead represents the interaction of what enrollees demand and what management decides they can have. The utilization experiences of prepaid group practice plans are therefore hard to interpret.

The difficulties in interpreting utilization in prepaid groups are illustrated by the Hankin et al. report on what happened after the Columbia Health Plan in Maryland increased the copayment for a mental health visit. The higher copayment could be expected to curb the use of benefits use were determined by consumer demand. If visits were already being rationed, however, as evidence suggests they were, the copayment increase would only reduce the need for rationing. Critically confounding the Hankin study was a concomitant increase in mental health staff, probably further reducing the rationing of demand. Thus, the small change in use reported by the study may say little about demand responsiveness.

4. Econometric studies have found that demand for ambulatory mental health care responds to cost-sharing. The degree of response is at least as great as demand for other medical care.

Studies by Frank, McCall et al., McGuire, and Wells et al. all use a multivariate statistical model to estimate the effect of insurance on demand for office-based mental health care. The McCall et al. study,which shows little responsiveness, is so seriously flawed (see below) that it should be disregarded. The other studies find a moderate to high response of demand to cost sharing, meaning consumers use for fewer services as their costs go up.

Probably the single most important investigation of how insurance reacts to demand is the Rand Health Insurance Study. In a recent report, Wells et al. found that expenditures on ambulatory mental health care fell 47 percent in a plan with the most cost sharing compared with those under a free care plan. In the case of overall ambulatory medical expenses, the drop was 33 percent. According to this comparison, the demand for outpatient mental health care is at least as responsive to cost sharing the demand for other ambulatory medical care. Wells et al. apparently believe the difference between 47 and 33 percent is not important; they characterize the responsiveness of demand for outpatient mental health care as "roughly" the same as demand for ambulatory medical care. This contrasts with earlier studies which found demand for such mental health care to be more responsive.

We have serious reservations about the Rand group's interpretations of these findings as indicated in a paper by Ellis and McGuire included with this report. This analysis points out that due to the structure of benefits in the Rand experiment, the actual cost sharing by some people in the *different* plans is the same. Causing this homogenization is the "maximum dollar expenditure" (MDE) feature, which stipulates free care after patients have paid a specified amount out of their own pockets. This means that comparing the use among different plans can give a misleadingly low estimate of the actual responsiveness to cost sharing.

How critical this MDE effect is in the results of Health Insurance Study is an empirical matter. Ellis and McGuire believe it may be quite significant, while Rand researchers, who dismissed the issue in their report, appear to believe it matters little. It is safe to say, at this point, that the effect is of some importance. Controlling for this effect might accentuate patients' response to coinsurance or might heighten the difference between demand responsiveness to insurance for health and mental health. Recognizing the effect of the MDE may make the Rand report more consistent with earlier studies.

5. Reports do not allow estimation of the effects of expanding eligible mental health providers.

Insurers perceive that expanding coverage to psychologists or social workers will increase the costs of office-based mental health care. Nearly 40 states require some independent coverage for psychologists, and a growing number of states stipulate "vendorship" for social workers. In plans that have allowed these three providers to "compete" on nearly equal footing for some time, nonphysician providers have gained a substantial market share. In Massachusetts, in CHAMPUS, and in Blue Cross/Blue Shield plans for federal employees, these other providers have cornered from 25-40 percent of the market. It is not known what proportion of these services would otherwise have been provided by psychiatrists and other physicians.

Table 76

Study	Ambulatory Cases/1000	Inpatient Cases/1000	Ambulatory Visits/1000	Visits/Case	Inpatient Days/1000	Inpatient Days/Case	Unit Cost	Cost Per Case	Cost Enrollee
Dorken (1976)	17.40	14.28	154.55	8.8	197.05	13.80			17.48
Spiro et al (1975)[1]	4.00	3.00						172/970[2]	
Spiro et al (1975)[3]	6.00	3.00	51.00	8.5				141/974	
Penn Jer Del (1981)[4]		2.90			70.2	24.2			
Richman & Brown (1979)	35.00		111.00	3.2[5]					
Wallen et al (1982)[6]			60.07			10.01			
Goldensohn (1972)				14.5					7.50[7]
Jameson et al (1978)[8]	11.10	4.90	58.90	5.3	71.1	14.50			4.08
Fullerton et al (1976)[9]			103.00		30.5				
Liptzin et al (1980)	51.31		445.03	8.6					21.00
Hankin et al (1980)	68.70		404.70	5.9					
Glasser & Duggan (1969)	6.70	4.20	56.90		52.9	12.60			3.40
Craig & Patterson (1981)[11]		1.29	192.00		9.78	7.58			7.28
Cohen & Hunter (1978)[12]					20.80			245.73	35.72
Cohen & Hunter (1972)[13]					31.33			452.70	3.88
D'Arcy et al (1981)	20.00	10.00							
Giacolone (1970)[14]	6.65	3.28	99.05	14.90	38.28	11.64		245.57	1.61[15]
Green (1969)				7.80					
Goldensohn et al (1969)[16]	11.00	0.43	88.70	8.06[17]	7.77	18.00			
Blue Cross of Mass. (1982)	28.60		306.40	10.71					11.91
Von Korff & Kramer (1979)	20.40		667.46	32.71				1299	
Wash Psychiatric Soc (1980)									
Williams et al (1979)[18]	138.00	0.43	299.00	2.16	0.8	20.2			8.74

Table 76 (continued)

Study	Ambulatory Cases/1000	Inpatient Cases/1000	Ambula-tory Visits/1000	Visits/Case	Inpatient Days 1000	Inpatient Days Case	Unit Cost	Cost Per Case	Cost Enrollee
Williams et al (1979)[19]	61.50	0.12	255.00	4.15	2.0	16.70			6.53
Social Security (1971)	2.00	3.30			50.8	15.39			
D'Arcy (1973)	85.2								
Avnet (1962)	5.80	0.35	54.55	9.40	8.0	22.8			
Weiss et al (1973)[20]	57.0		125.60	2.20[21]					
Hustead & Sharfstein[22]	7.27	1.40	256						12.30
Rice et al (1971)[23]		156.6			1237	7.9			
Diehr et al (1983)[24]	54		577.50	10.6					23.19
Diehr et al (1983)[25]	89		293.30	3.3					8.78
Diehr et al (1983)[26]	80	187.80	2.5						7.57
Towery et al (1980)	20.4		667.40	32.7					26.50
Blue Cross of Mich (1979)		7.93			143.05	18.05			22.86

1. 1970 data reported for fee for service plan
2. outpatient/inpatient
3. 1970 data reported for prepaid plan
4. 1980 day for manufacturing enrollees reported
5. This is the authors approximation
6. 1979 data after copayment change is reported
7. Ambulatory care only
8. 1973 data reported
9. 3rd year of experiment reported
10. 1976 data reported
11. 1976 data reported
12. Local 770
13. Local 889
14. 1968 data reported for inpatient, 1969 for outpatient
15. estimates made by authors
16. 1966 data reported
17. This figure is the authors estimate because reported data were inconsistent
18. PPG reported
19. IPP reported
20. Non-poverty cases reported
21. Authors estimate due to reporting inconsistency
22. Aetna Experience & Blues Cost
23. 1967 Data reported
24. Blue Cross Data
25. Group Health Data
26. United Health Care Data

†Prepaid Plans

Table 77
AMBULATORY UTILIZATION BY PRESENCE OF 1ST DOLLAR COVERAGE

Study	Case/1000	Visits/1000	Visits/Case
1st dollar coverage			
Spiro et al (1975)	6.00	51.00	8.50
Richman and Brown	35.00	111.00	3.20
Jameson et al (1978)	11.10	58.90	5.30
Liptzin et al (1980)	51.31	445.03	8.60
Glasser & Duggan (1969)	6.70	56.90	8.50
Giacolone (1970)	6.65	99.05	14.90
Goldensohn et al (1969)	11.00	88.70	8.06
BC/MASS (1981)	38.60	306.40	10.71
Williams et al (1979)†	138.00	299.00	2.16
Diehr et al (1983)†	89.00	293.00	3.30
Mean	38.33	180.89	7.32
No 1st dollar coverage			
Dorken (1976)	17.40	154.55	8.80
Hustead & Sharfstein (1978)	7.27	256.00	35.00
Hankin et al (1980)	68.70	404.70	32.71
Von Korff & Kramer (1979)	20.40	667.40	32.71
Weiss et al (1973)	57.00	125.60	2.20
Avnet (1962)	5.80	54.55	9.40
Diehr et al (1983)	54.00	577.50	10.60
Mean	32.93	320.04	14.9

WELLS ET AL. (1982)—THE RAND STUDY

In 1971, Rand Corporation began work on the Health Insurance Study (HIS), eventually to enroll 2,756 families (7,706 persons) from six sites across the country in a set of insurance plans for three to five years. By experimentally assigning families to insurance plans, Rand sought to avoid selection biases. Plans varied in the percent of cost paid by the enrollee from 0 to 95 percent. All plans featured a maximum dollar expenditure (MDE) per family of $1,000 or less, limiting the financial liability of the family. The HIS was thus a study of "catastrophic" health insurance, popular in some quarters in the early 1970's as a model for national health insurance. The HIS has great potential for answering questions about the response of demand for medical care to cost-sharing.

Empirical results from the HIS have begun to appear. Newhouse et al. (1982) presented interim results from one year of the experiment showing that health expenditures respond to cost sharing. Total expenditures per person per year were 60 percent greater in the plan with no cost sharing ($401) in comparison to the plan with 95 percent cost sharing ($254). Ambulatory expenditures made up slightly less than one-half of the total and exhibited a similar response to cost-sharing. Wells et al. (1982) focus on ambulatory mental health expenditures. The main finding of this report is that, "The percentage response of ambulatory mental health care expense to cost sharing on HIS coinsurance plans is *roughly* the same as that for ambulatory medical health care expense."

There are many other findings of this report. Among the more important:

- Expenditures on ambulatory mental health services were about $24 per person in the free care plan, or 5 percent of total expenditures, excluding dental care. Mental health was 17 percent of the ambulatory total when all care was free.
- Most of the response to cost-sharing was in the probability of some use, rather than the extent of use given same treatment.
- No difference in response to cost-sharing was found among income groups.
- Cost-sharing has no significant effect on the choice between mental health specialties and general medical providers.

In this report we discuss the most important and controversial finding, that demand for ambulatory mental health care is only as responsive to cost-sharing as is demand for general ambulatory medical care. Our discussion draws from the Ellis and McGuire paper included with this report.

Table 4, adapted from Wells et al. (1982), compares expenditures for ambulatory health and mental health care by insurance plan for Year 2 of the HIS study. These comparisons form the basis of the conclusions in the Rand report. All families in the insurance plans had maximum dollar expenditure levels (MDE's) experimentally assigned to be either a dollar amount ($750 or $1,000) or a percent of the previous year's family income (5, 10, or 15 percent), whichever was less.

Rand's conclusions that cost sharing for ambulatory mental health care has a moderate impact on total expenditures and that this response is comparable with the response of other ambulatory medical care are based on comparisons of the free care plan with the 95 percent plan. Expenditures for mental health are cut nearly in half, from $24.28 to $12.83, moving from free care to 95 percent coinsurance, subject to the MDE. This is roughly similar to the reduction in expenditures by a third, from $138.15 to $92.05, for other ambulatory medical care.

If we were to compare behavior in the 50 percent plan with free care, however, the conclusions would be quite different. For mental health, use drops to 13 percent of the free care amount when individuals pay 50 percent of the costs, subject to the MDE, indicating a very high response to cost sharing. The drop in use for mental health is, furthermore, much greater than the reduction for other medical services.

The Rand results contain an anomaly. Expenditures "ought" to fall continually as the percentage of costs borne by the individual rises. This is true up to the 50 percent plan, but then a reversal occurs and use in the 95 percent plan is higher than the 50 percent plan. Is the free care/50 percent comparison a better test of the impact of cost sharing? Or is the free care/95 percent comparison to be preferred? It is critical to address this question fairly; interpretations of the Rand report turn on the answer.

Wells et al. base their interpretation of their finding totally upon the 95 percent plan, disregarding the 50 percent plan because, "the mental health use estimate on the 50 percent does not appear to be reliable because site and plan are confounded" (p. 108). The culprit, according to the authors, is Dayton, Ohio, which has more than its share of 50 percent plan members and whose members use mental health care at lower rates.

We find this site-plan confounding argument unconvincing for the following reasons. First, effects of site differences on mental health expenditures are explicitly analyzed in the report and the results are found to be quite mixed. Statistically significant site differences are found only in the probabilities of and expenditures on informal versus formal providers. Second, even if we accept their argument and make the extreme assumptions that all of the 50 percent plan participants live in Dayton, and that Dayton residents spend only half of the national average on mental health, this would at most double the expenditures level for the 50 percent plan from $3.10 to $6.20 per enrollee per year. Expenditures would remain only 26 percent of expenditures under the free plan and still less than half of total expenditures under the 95 percent plan. Third, this site-effect explanation for mental health does not explain why a similar reversal should hold true for other medical services. As Table 78 shows, expenditures for all ambulatory services other than mental health are also lowest in the 50 percent plan. Finally, the reversal occurs for ambulatory expenses when site-effects cannot possibly explain this anomaly. In Newhouse et al. (1982, p. 17) a reversal is reported for all ambulatory expenses within a single site. The explanation offered there is, "The misordering between the 50- and the 95-percent coinsurance plans is insignificant and appears to reflect random fluctuation."

There is another explanation for the reversal between the 50 percent and 95 percent plans. The explanation is based on the fact that the MDE is reached more quickly by a family in the 95 percent plan, causing the coinsurance rate at the margin to drop to zero. With average annual health expenditures of around $1,400 for a family of four during this period, reaching the MDE would have been quite common for families in the 95 percent plan. With the marginal incentives the same for many families in the free care and 95 percent plans, it is not surprising there is not much difference in use.

The way the MDE can build in a reversal is shown in Tables 80 and 81. Table 80 shows a demand curve for all medical care with the dollars of expenditure dependent on the share of costs paid by the consumer. For simplicity here we ignore the impact of uncertainty and assume that medical care is just like any other good, with more of the good consumed as its price (here cost shared) decreases. If there were no MDE, then this consumer (which could be thought of as a family or a single individual) would choose an expenditure level of A if he were required to pay 95 percent of total costs. For the two other plans shown, expenditures would be B (50 percent plan) and C (free care). The shaded bars in Table 81 show that without an MDE, expenditures would fall monotonically as coinsurance rises.

Now consider the effect of a $1,000 MDE. In the 95 percent plan, after expenditures of $1,053 (the amount necessary to bring the consumer's contribution to $1,000), the marginal price falls to zero. Now the choice of the consumer is to use C, taking advantage of the fact that after $1,053, expenditures are fully covered. The unshaded bar in Table 81 is expenditures in the 95 percent plan in the presence of the MDE. These now exceed expenditures in the 50 percent plan. Rand's experiment, of course, has the MDE. The "reversal" in Table 81 and possibly in Table 78 is simply due to the structure of incentives in the plans.

The simulation analysis reported in Ellis and McGuire's paper strongly suggests that the maximum dollar expenditure (MDE) feature of the insurance plans causes serious difficulty for interpretation of the HIS results. Incentives introduced by the MDE can account for the otherwise anomalous "reversal" in expenditure levels seen for both mental health and other medical ambulatory expenditures in Table 78. Recognition of the effect of the MDE means that the Rand results are consistent with the hypothesis that the demand for ambulatory mental health care is quite responsive to cost sharing, and more responsive than demand for other ambulatory medical expenses. Discarding the 95 percent plan on the grounds that it is severely contaminated by the MDE and focusing attention instead on the 25 and 50 percent plans leaves a set of results that confirms rather than contradicts previous research and third-party experience. Rand's conclusion that the demand for ambulatory mental health care is roughly as responsive to cost sharing as is demand for other ambulatory medical services appears to be premature.

Table 78
EXPENDITURES ON AMBULATORY CARE PER ENROLLEE RAND'S HIS, YEAR 2

	Ambulatory Medical Care[1]		**Ambulatory Mental Health Care**	
Plan	**Sample Mean (Standard Error)[3]**	**Percent of Free Plan**	**Unstandardized[2] Predicted Expense (Standard Error)**	**Percent of Free Plan**
Free Care	$138.15 (5.74)	100	$24.28 (5.07)	100
25% Coinsurance	104.72 (6.82)	76	17.97 (6.17)	74
50% Coinsurance	79.74 (7.61)	58	3.10 (1.89)	13
95% Coinsurance	92.05 (6.65)	67	12.83 (4.44)	53

Source: Wells et al. (1982), Table 6.3, p. 107.

Notes:

[1]These numbers differ from those from Table 3 of Newhouse et al. (1983) in the following respects: the data are from Year 2 only for all six sites and expenses for drugs and supplies and informal mental health (prorated) have been excluded.

[2]The unstandardized prediction is used in order to be comparable with the samples mean for ambulatory medical expenses.

[3]Standard errors are unadjusted for intra-family correlation so are biased downward.

Table 79
DISTRIBUTION OF PSYCHOTHERAPY VISITS—YEAR 2

(1) Number of Visits	(2) Percent of Sample[1]		(3) Approximate Percentage of Visits[2]	
0	95.5		0	
1-10	2.5		17	
11-20	.4		10	
21-30	.4	1.2	17	73
31-40	.4		23	
41-50	.2		15	
51+	.2		18	

NOTES:
[1]The percent of sample was taken from Wells et al. (1982), Table 4.3, p. 59.
[2]The percent of visits was calculated by assuming sample means for the seven different intervals to be 0, 4, 14, 24, 34, 44, and 52, respectively. Weighting these interval means by the percent of sample and dividing by the average number of visits (.58) yields an approximation of the distribution of visits.

Table 80

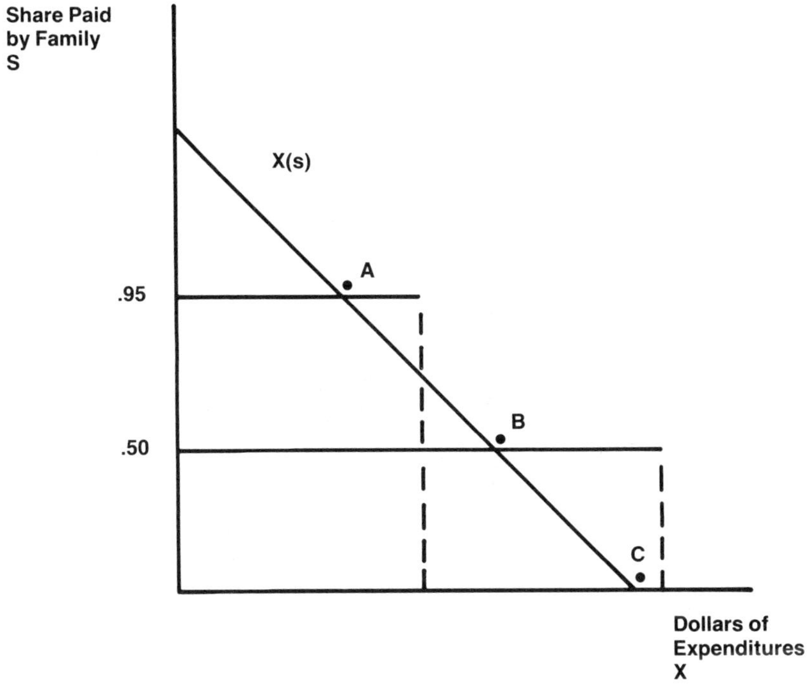

Table 81

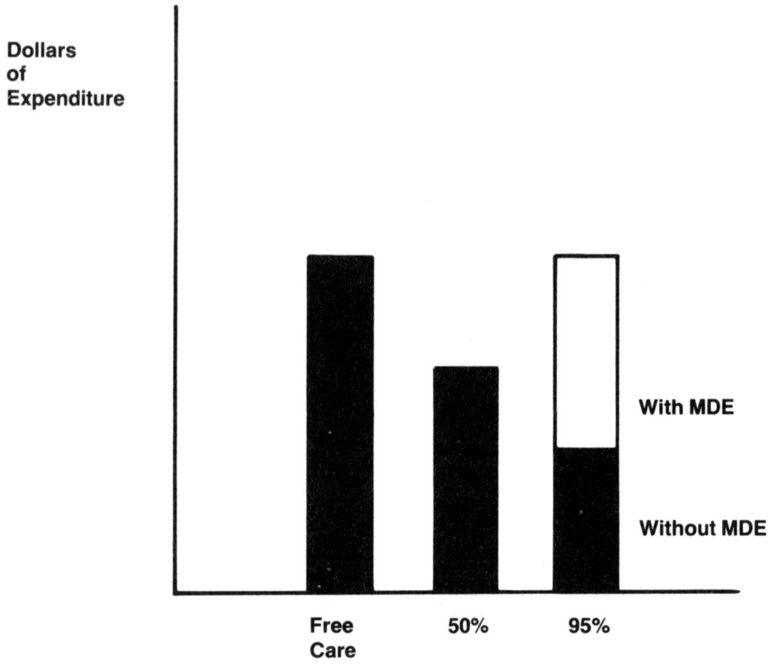

References and Bibliography

Alander R, Campbell: An evaluative study of an alcohol and drug recovery program. Human Resource Management, Spring 1975.

American Hospital Association Advisory Panel on Financing Health Care Financing Mental Health Care in the U.S.: A Study and Assessment of Issues and Arrangements. Rockville: National Institute of Mental Health (HSM73-9117), 1973.

American Medical Association: Economic Grand Rounds. Chicago: American Medical Association 1983a.

American Medical Association: A Physician's Guide to Preferred Provider Organizations. Chicago: American Medical Association 1983b.

American Psychiatric Association: Position statement on Public Law 92-603 (PSRO). American Journal of Psychiatry 131:1072, 1974.

American Psychiatric Association: Manual of Psychiatric Peer Review. Washington: 1976.

American Psychiatric Association: Diagnostic and Statistical Manual of Mental Disorders, Third Edition. Washington: American Psychiatric Association, 1980.

American Psychiatric Association: 1982 Changes in Plans Participating in the FEHBP—Provisions Affecting Treatment of Psychiatric Illness. Unpublished.

American Psychiatric Association: Psychiatric Peer Review—Insuring Quality, Managing Costs, and Promoting Standards. Washington: American Psychiatric Association, 1983a.

American Psychiatric Association: Survey, Psychiatric Benefits Project. Unpublished, 1983b.

American Psychiatric Association Commission on Psychotherapies: Psychotherapy Research: Methodological and Efficacy Issues. Washington: American Psychiatric Association, 1982.

American Psychiatric Association Commission on Psychotherapies: Somatic Therapies. Washington: American Psychiatric Association, 1984.

American Psychiatric Association Commission on Psychotherapies: Psychosocial Therapies. Washington: American Psychiatric Association, 1984.

American Psychiatric Association and Health Insurance Association of America: Psychiatric Coding System for Insurance Claims Reporting. Washington: American Psychiatric Association, 1982.

Andersen R, Francis A, Lion J, Daughety V: Psychologically related illness and health services utilization. Medical Care 15:(5), 1977.

Armer JE: Mental Wellness and the Cost of Health Care. In Mental Wellness Programs for Employees. (Eds) RH Egdahl, DC Walsh, and WB Goldbeck. New York: Springer Verlag, 1980.

Asher J: Assuring Quality Mental Health Services: The CHAMPUS Experience. Washington: Government Printing Office (ADM81-1099), 1981.

Astrachan BM, Levinson DJ, Adler DA: The impact of National Health Insurance on the tasks and practices of psychiatry. Archives of General Psychiatry 33:785-794, 1976.

Avnet HH: Psychiatric Insurance. New York: Group Health Insurance, Inc., 1962.

Barrie K, Smirnow B, Webber A, Kiefhaber A, Goldbeck WB: Mental Distress as a Problem for Industry. In Mental Wellness Programs for Employees. (Eds) RH Egdahl, DC Walsh, and WB Goldbeck. New York: Springer Verlag, 1980.

Bennett AE, Hargrove EA, Engle B, Voluntary health insurance and nervous and mental disease. JAMA 151:(3), 1953.

Bergin AE, Lambert MJ: The Evaluation of Psychotherapeutic Outcomes. In Handbook of Psychotherapy and Behavior Change. 2nd Ed. (Eds) SL Garfield and AE Bergin. New York: Wiley & Sons, 1978.

Berry CA: Good Health for Employees and Reduced Health Care Costs for Industry. Washington: Health Insurance Association of America, 1981.

Blue Cross of Greater Philadelphia: Joint Health Cost Containment Program, Hospital Utilization Report. Philadelphia: 1981.

Blue Cross-Blue Shield of Massachusetts: Outpatient Psychiatric Payment Experience. Boston: April 1982.

Bockoven JS: Moral Treatment in Community Mental Health. New York: Springer Publishing Company, 1972.

Braceland FJ: The Institute of Living 1822-1972. Hartford, CT: The Institute of Living, 1972.

Chodoff P, Santora P: Psychiatric peer review: The Washington, D.C. experience 1972-1975. American Journal of Psychiatry 134:121–125, 1977.

Cockrell DK: The inflating factors in health care. Business Insurance 17:(42), 1983.

Cohen J, Hunter H: Mental health insurance: a comparison of a fee-for-service indemnity plan and a comprehensive mental health center. American Journal of Orthopsychiatry 42:(1), 1972.

Congressional Budget Office: Catastrophic Medical Expenses: Patterns in the Non-Elderly, Non-Poor Population. Washington: CBO, 1982.

Corrigan JD, Koyanagi C: For Ayes Only—Legislating Mental Health Insurance Coverage in Your State. Washington: National Association of State Mental Health Program Directors, National Council of Community Mental Health Centers, and National Mental Health Association, 1982.

Craig TJ, Patterson DY: A comparison of mental health costs and utilization under three insurance models. Medical Care 19:(2), 1981.

Cruze AM, Harwood HJ, Kristiansen PL, Collins JJ, Jones DC: Economic Costs to Society of Alcohol and Drug Abuse and Mental Illness, 1977. Rockville, MD: National Institute of Mental Health (ADM contract no. 283-79-001), 1981.

Culpepper BW: Statement to the Subcommittees on Alcoholism and Drug Abuse, Employment and Productivity. Committee on Labor and Human Resources, U.S. Senate. July 14, 1982.

Curran G, Kiefhaber A: Mental wellness programs in industry: A survey report. Alcohol Health and Research World, Fall 1980.

D'Arcy C, Bold G, Schmitz JA: Psychiatric health care and costs under comprehensive public health insurance: Experience in a Canadian province. Medical Care 19:(9), 1981.

Deutsch A: The Shame of the States. New York: Harcourt, Brace, 1948.

Dickerson OD: Health Insurance. Homewood, IL: Richard D. Irwin, Inc., 1963.

Dorken H (Ed): CHAMPUS: Ten-state claims experience for mental disorder. In The Professional Psychologist Today. San Francisco: Jossey Bass, Inc., 1976.

Duehrssen A-M: Die Beurteiling des behandlungserfolges in der psychotherapie. Zeitschrift der Psychosomatischen Medizin 3:(3), 1957.

Duehrssen A-M: Katamnestische ergebnisse bei 1004 patienten nach analytischer psychotherapie. Zeitschrift der Psychosomatischen Medizin 7:(2), 1972.

Edwards DW, Greene LR, Abramowitz SL, Davidson CV: National health insurance, psychotherapy, and the poor. American Psychologist 34:(5), 1979.

Ellis RP, McGuire TG: Rand study analysis. Boston University Department of Economics, 1983. Unpublished.

Faris REL, Dunham HW: Mental Disorders in Urban Areas. Chicago: University of Chicago Press, 1939.

Faulkner EJ: Health Insurance. New York: McGraw-Hill, 1960.

Fenton WS, Leaf PJ, Moran NL, Tischler GL: Trends in psychiatric practice, 1965-1980. American Journal of Psychiatry 141:346–351, 1984.

Flaherty JA, Meagher R: Measuring racial bias in inpatient treatment. American Journal of Psychiatry 137:679-682, 1980.

Foley HA, Sharfstein SS: Madness and Government: Who Cares for the Mentally Ill? Washington: American Psychiatric Press, Inc., 1983.

Follette W, Cummings NA: Psychiatric services and medical utilization in a prepaid health plan setting. Medical Care 5:(1), 1967.

Follmann JF Jr.: Insurance Coverage for Mental Illness. New York: American Management Association, 1970.

Follmann JF Jr.: Helping the Troubled Employee. New York: American Management Association, 1979.

Foote A, Erfurt JC, Strauch PA, Guzzardo TL: Cost effectiveness of Occupational Employee Assistance Programs. Ann Arbor, MI: Institute of Labor and Industrial Relations, University of Michigan—Wayne State University, 1978.

Ford CV: The Somatizing Disorders: Illness As a Way of Life. New York: Elsevier Biomedical, 1983.

Fox RP: A Primer on the Issue of Insurance Coverage for Psychotherapy. Unpublished, 1976. (1538 E. 4 St., Santa Ana, CA 92701.)

Frank RG: Cost-benefit analysis in mental health services: A review of the literature. Administration in Mental Health 8:161-176, 1981a.

Frank RG: Physician Pricing and Location in Mental Health. Unpublished doctoral dissertation, Boston University, 1981b.

Frank RG, McGuire TG: A Review of Studies of Demand and Utilization of Specialty Mental Health Services. Washington: American Psychiatric Association, 1983.

Fullerton DT, Lorenz FN, Nyca GR: Utilization of prepaid services by patients with psychiatric diagnoses. American Journal of Psychiatry 133:1057–1060, 1976.

Gaeta E, Lunn R, Grey L: AT&T looks at program evaluation. EAP Digest: May-June, 1982.

General Motors Corporation: Statement on Drug Abuse and Alcoholism. An invited submission to the Committee on Labor and Human Resources, U.S. Senate, July 14, 1982.

Gibson RW (Ed): Professional responsibilities in peer review and psychiatry: A conference report. Washington: American Psychiatric Association, 1970.

Ginzberg E: Remarks at the annual meeting of the Association of American Medical Colleges, Washington DC, Nov. 1983. The Blue Sheet, Nov 10, 1983.

Glasscote R, Sanders D, Forstenzer HM, Foley AR: The Community Mental Health Center: An Analysis of Existing Models. Washington: Joint Information Service of the American Psychiatric Association and the National Association for Mental Health, 1964.

Glasser MA, Duggan T: Prepaid psychiatric care experience with UAW members. American Journal of Psychiatry 126:675–681, 1969.

Goldberg FD: State laws mandating mental health insurance coverage. Hospital and Community Psychiatry 28:759-763, 1977.

Goldberg ID, Krantz G, Locke BZ: Effect of a short-term outpatient psychiatric therapy benefit on the utilization of medical services in a prepaid group practice program. Medical Care 8:(5), 1970.

Goldensohn SS, Fink R, Shapiro S: Referral, utilization, and staffing patterns of a mental health service in a prepaid group practice program in New York. American Journal of Psychiatry 126:689–697, 1969.

Goldensohn SS: Cost utilization and utilization review of mental health services in a prepaid group practice plan. American Journal of Psychiatry 134:(11), 1977.

Goldman HH, Sharfstein SS, Frank RG: Equity and parity in psychiatric care. Psychiatric Annals 13:487-491, 1983.

Granatir WL: Psychotherapy and national health insurance. American Journal of Psychiatry 131:267–270, 1974.

Greenspan SI, Sharfstein SS: Efficacy of psychotherapy: Asking the right questions. Archives of General Psychiatry 38:1213-1219, 1981.

Grob GN: Mental Institutions in America. New York: Free Press, 1973.

Group for the Advancement of Psychiatry Committee on Therapy: Psychotherapy and Its Financial Feasibility Within the National Health Care System. New York: GAP, 1978.

Guillette W: Claims review. National Association of Private Psychiatric Hospitals Journal 8:(4), 1976.

Guillette W: Is psychotherapy insurable? National Association of Private Psychiatric Hospitals Journal 9:30-32, 1977.

Guillette W, Crowley B, Savitz SA, Goldberg FD: Day hospitalization care: A pilot study. Hospital and Community Psychiatry 29:(8), 1978.

Hall CP: Financing mental health services through insurance. American Journal of Psychiatry 131:1079–1088, 1974.

Hall RCW, Beresford TP, Gardner ER, et al: The medical care of psychiatric patients, Hospital and Community Psychiatry 33:25-34, 1982.

Hankin JR, Steinwachs DM, Charmian E: The impact of utilization of a copayment increase for amubulatory psychiatric care. Medical Care 18:(8), 1980.

Hay-Huggins Group: Survey of Private Sector Health Insurance Coverage. Washington: Hay-Huggins, 1981.

Hay-Huggins Group: Non-cash Compensation Comparison, Health Care Plans. Washington: Hay-Huggins, 1983.

Health Data Institute: Claims Analysis in Mental Health. Washington: American Psychiatric Association, 1983.

Health Insurance Association of America: New Group Health Insurance. Washington: HIAA, 1981.

Health Insurance Association of America: Prospective Payment: A Sound Approach to Containing Hospital Costs. Washington: HIAA, 1983.

Hogan DB: The Regulation of Psychotherapists (4 volumes). Cambridge, MA: Ballinger Publishing Co., 1978.

Hollingshead AB, Redlich FC: Social Class and Mental Illness. New York: John Wiley & Sons, 1958.

Horgan CM: The Utilization and Expenditure Patterns for Ambulatory Mental Health Services. Hyattsville, MD: National Center for Health Services Research, 1981.

Iglehardt JK: Medicaid in transition. New England Journal of Medicine 309:868-872, 1983.

Jones KR, Vischi TR: Impact of alchohol, drug abuse, and mental health treatment of medical care utilization: A review of the research literature. Medical Care, Supplement 17:1-82, 1979.

Klerman GL: The efficacy of psychotherapy as the basis for public policy. American Psychologist 38:929-934, 1983.

Krizay J: Mental Illness and the Community's Responsibility. Unpublished monograph prepared for the American Psychiatric Association, 1980.

Krizay J: Federal employees' experience as a guide to the cost of insuring psychiatric services in the various states. American Journal of Psychiatry 139:866-871, 1982.

Krizay J, Braun EL: Report on Utilization Characteristics of the FEHBP Mental Health Benefits. Washington: Washington Psychiatric Society, 1980.

Krizay J, Braun EL: Health Insurance Coverage for Treatment of Mental Illness: Full-time Employees of Medium- and Large-size Establishments in the Private Sector, 1981. Unpublished monograph prepared for the American Psychiatric Association, 1983.

Langsley DG: Comparing clinic and private practice of psychiatry. American Journal of Psychiatry 135:702–706, 1978.

Levin BL, Glasser JH: Mental health within prepaid health plans. Administration in Mental Health 7:(4), 1980.

Levin BL, Glasser JH: A survey of mental health service coverage within HMOs. American Journal of Public Health 69:(11), 1979.

Levenson AI: The growth of investor-owned psychiatric hospitals. American Journal of Psychiatry 139:902-906, 1982.

Levitan SJ, Kornfeld DS: Clinical and cost benefits of liaison psychiatry. American Journal of Psychiatry 138:790-793, 1981.

Liebowitz B: Employee assistance programs as an employee benefit and risk management. Employee Benefits Journal, March 1982.

Lippman DH, Lowry FH, Rickhi B: Attitudes of Ontario psychiatrists toward health insurance. Canadian Medical Association Journal 125:(7), 1981.

Liptzin B: The effects of national health insurance on Canadian psychiatry: The Ontario experience. American Journal of Psychiatry 134:248–252, 1977.

London P, Klerman GL: Evaluating psychotherapy. American Journal of Psychiatry 139:709-717, 1982.

Luft LL, Sampson LM, Newman DE: Effects of peer review on outpatient psychotherapy: Therapist and patient follow-up survey. American Journal of Psychiatry 133:891–895, 1976.

Maclntyre DM: Voluntary Health Insurance and Rate Making. New York: Cornell University Press, 1962.

Manuso J: Corporate Mental Health Programs and Policies. In Strategies for Public Health. (Eds) LY Ng and DL Davis. New York: Van Nostrand Reinhold, 1980.

Marmor J, Scheidemandel PL, Kanno CK: Psychiatrists and their Patients: A National Study of Private Office Practice. Washington: Joint Information Service of the American Psychiatric Association and the National Association for Mental Health, 1975.

Marshall E: Psychotherapy works, but for whom? Science 207:506-508, 1980.

May P: Cost efficiency of treatments for the schizophrenic patient. American Journal of Psychiatry 127:1382-1385, 1971.

Mayo JA: Utilization of a community mental health center by Blacks: Admission to inpatient status. Journal of Nervous and Mental Disease 158:202-207, 1974.

McCall N, Parker S, Rice T: Colorado Psychology Expanded Mental Health Benefit Experiment. Washington: Health Care Finance Administration (HCFA contract no. SSA-600-76-0168), 1981.

McGuire TG: Financing Psychotherapy: Cost Effects and Public Policy. Cambridge, MA: Ballinger Publishing Company, 1981.

McGuire TG: Financing and Demand for Mental Health Services. In Economics and Mental Health. (Eds) McGuire TG and Weisbrod BA. Washington: Government Printing Office (ADM)81-1114, 1981.

McGuire EG, Frisman LK: Reimbursement policy and cost-effective mental health care. American Psychologist 38:935-940, 1983.

McGuire TG, Montgomery JT: Mandated mental health benefits in private health insurance policies: A legal and economic analysis. New Haven, CT: Yale University, Institute for Social and Policy Studies, 1981.

McKinley R: Electric company's EAP works! EAP Digest, Sept-Oct 1981.

McLellan T, Luborsky L, O'Brien CP, Woody GE, Druley KA: Is treatment for substance abuse effective? JAMA 247:(10), 1982.

Mehr RI, Cammack E: Principles of Insurance. Homewood, IL: Richard D. Irwin, Inc., 1976.

Miller L: Giving a healing hand with personal problems. S.A.M. Advanced Management Journal, Spring 1981.

Modern Health Care: Quality assurance may be major health issue by 1990. Vol. 131:(9), 1983.

Mollica RF, Redlich FC: Equity and changing patient characteristics 1950 to 1975. Archives of General Psychiatry 37:1257-1263, 1980.

Mollica RF: From asylum to community: The threatened disintegration of public psychiatry. New England Journal of Medicine 308:367-373, 1983.

Muller C, Schoenberg M: Insurance for mental health: A viewpoint on its scope. Archives of General Psychiatry 31:(6), 1974.

Mumford E, Schlesinger HJ, Glass GV: The effects of psychological intervention on recovery from surgery and heart attack: An analysis of the literature. American Journal of Public Health 72:141-151, 1982.

Mumford E, Schlesinger HJ, Glass GV, Patrick C, Cuerdon T: A new look at evidence about reduced cost of medical utilization following mental health treatment. American Journal of Psychiatry, in press.

Muszynski S, Brady J, Sharfstein SS: Coverage for Mental and Nervous Disorders: Summaries of 300 Private Sector Health Insurance Plans. Washington:

American Psychiatric Press, Inc., 1983.

Myers ES (Ed): National Health Insurance. Psychiatric Annals 4:(1), 1974.

National Association of State Mental Health Program Directors: NIMH grants and contracts affecting mental health care at state and local levels. Washington: NASMHPD, February 3, 1983.

National Center for Health Services Research: National Health Care Expenditure Study. Rockville: NCHSR, 1981.

National Center for Health Services Research: Research on Competition in the Financing and Delivery of Health Services: A Summary of Policy Issues. Washington: Government Printing Office (PHS 83-3328-1), 1982.

National Governors Association Center for Policy Research: Recent and Proposed Changes in State Medicaid Programs: A Fifty-State Survey. Washington: NGA, 1982.

Nelson SH: Standards affecting mental health care: Review and commentary. American Journal of Psychiatry 136:303-307, 1979.

Page BI: Who Gets What From Government. Berkeley: University of California Press, 1983.

Panzetta AF: Cost benefit studies in psychiatry. Comprehensive Psychiatry 14:(5), 1973.

Parloff MB: Psychotherapy and research: An anaclitic depression. Psychiatry 43:(4), 1980.

Parloff MB: Psychotherapy research evidence and reimbursement decisions: Bambi meets Godzilla. American Journal of Psychiatry 139:717-718, 1982.

Parloff MB, Wolfe B, Hadley S, Waskow IE, et al: Assessment of Psychosocial Treatment of Mental Disorders: Current status and prospects. Invited submission to the President's Commission on Mental Health, February 1978. Unpublished.

Patterson DY, Bise B: GHA Study of Cost Offsets of Mental Health Service Provision in an HMO. Unpublished; NIMH contract no. 282-77-0219-MS, February 1978.

Pelletier KR: Healthy People in Unhealthy Places—Stress and Fitness at Work. New York: Delacorte Press/Seymour Lawrence, 1984.

Piasecki JR, Pittinger JE, Rutman ID: Determining the Costs of Community Residential Services for the Psychosocially Disabled. Washington: Government Printing Office (ADM77-504), 1978.

President's Commission for the Study of Ethical Problems in Medicine and Biomedical and Behavioral Research: Securing Access to Health Care: The Ethical Implications of the Differences in the Availability of Health Services. Volume 1: Report. Washington: Government Printing Office, 1983.

Prospective Payment Guide: Non-government PPS plans likely to multiply. Vol. I. (2), 1983. (Key Communications Group, Chevy Chase, MD)

Psychiatric Viewpoints Report: Health Insurance and the Practice of Psychiatry. Roche Products Inc., 1983.

Psychotherapy Finances: Reimbursement: Will insurance help build your practice in the 1980s? 8:(8), 1981.

Punch L, Johnson DEL: HMOs predict rapid enrollee growth as consumer cost concerns mount. Modern Health Care 14:(1), 1984.

Rafferty J, Rafferty EL: Health Insurance and the Utilization of Mental Health Services. (NIMH Small Grant #1 R03 MH 36939-01.) Phoenix, AZ: Metrecon Research Inc., 1983.

Raichel T: Letter to V Smaller, American Hospital Association, re mental health coverage, dated 6 February 1981.

Richman A, Brown MB: Reimbursement by Medicare for Mental Health Services by General Practitioners—Clinical, Epidemiologic, and Cost Containment Implications of the Canadian Experience. Washington: Institute of Medicine, 1979.

Reed LS: Coverage and Utilization of Care for Mental Conditions Under Health Insurance—Various Studies 1973-74. Washington: American Psychiatric Association, 1975.

Reed LS, Myers ES, Scheidemandel PL: Health Insurance and Psychiatric Care: Utilization and Cost. Washington: American Psychiatric Association, 1972.

Regier DA, Goldberg ID, Taube CA: The de facto U.S. mental health services system. Archives of General Psychiatry 35:685-693, 1978.

Reifman A, Wyatt RJ: Lithium: A brake in the rising cost of mental illness. Archives of General Psychiatry 37:385-388, 1980.

Robert Wood Johnson Foundation: Special Report: Updated Report on Access to Health Care for the American People. RWJF, 1983.

Rothman DJ: The Discovery of the Asylum. Boston: Little, Brown, 1971.

Scheidemandel PL, Kanno CK, Glasscote RM: Health Insurance for Mental Illness. Washington, D.C.: Joint Information Service of the American Psychiatric Association and the National Association for Mental Health, 1968.

Schlesinger HJ, Mumford E, Glass GV, Patrick C, Sharfstein SS: Mental health treatment and medical care utilization in a fee-for-service system. American Journal of Public Health 73:422-429, 1983.

Schulberg HC: Quality-of-care standards and professional norms. American Journal of Psychiatry 133:1047-1051, 1976.

Sharfstein SS: Third-party payers: To pay or not to pay. American Journal of Psychiatry 135:1185-1188, 1978.

Sharfstein SS: Reductions in insurance for mental disorders: Adverse selection, moral hazard, and consumer demand. American Journal of Psychiatry 139:1425-1430, 1982.

Sharfstein SS: Third-party payments, cost-containment, and DSM-III. Presented at an American Psychiatric Association workshop, "An Interim Appraisal of DSM-III," October 1983.

Sharfstein SS, Magnas HL: Insuring intensive psychotherapy. American Journal of Psychiatry 132:1252-1256, 1975.

Sharfstein SS, Beigel A: Less is more: Today's economics and its challenge to psychiatry. American Journal of Psychiatry, in press.

Sharfstein SS, Michels R: A Formal Statement from the Negative Point of View. Paper prepared for an American Psychiatric Association debate, "A Scientific Debate: Should Third-party Reimbursement be Reserved for Treatments Proven Safe and Effective?" May 1983a.

Sharfstein SS, Taube CA: Reductions in insurance for mental disorders: Adverse selection, moral hazard, and consumer demand. American Journal of Psychiatry 139:1425-1430, 1982.

Sharfstein SS, Muszynski S, Gattozzi A: Maintaining and Improving Psychiatric Insurance Coverage: An Annotated Bibliography. Washington: American Psychiatric Press, Inc., 1983b.

Sharfstein SS, Towery OB, Milowe ID: Accuracy of diagnostic information submitted to an insurance company. American Journal of Psychiatry 137:70-73, 1980.

Shepherd M: Psychoanalysis, psychotherapy, and health services. British Medical Journal. Vol:1557-1559, 1979.

Smith ML, Glass GV, Miller TI: The Benefits of Psychotherapy. Baltimore: Johns Hopkins University Press, 1980.

Sonne JC: Insurance and family therapy. Family Practice 12:(4), 1973.

Sorensen JE, Zelman WN: CHAMPUS experience with concurrent peer review: Case studies, utilization, and cost effectiveness analysis. Rockville, MD: National Institute of Mental Health, March 1980.

Spiro HR, Siassi I, Crocetti G: Cost-financed mental health facility. Parts I, II, and III. Journal of Nervous and Mental Diseases 160:(3), 1975.

Steering Committee: Toward a National Plan for the Chronically Mentally Ill. Report to the Secretary by the DHHS Steering Committee on the Chronically Mentally Ill. Washington: Government Printing Office (ADM)81-1077, 1981.

Stein LI, Test MA, Weisbrod BA: Alternative to mental hospital treatment: I-conceptual model, treatment program, and clinical evaluation; II-Economic benefit-cost analysis; III-Social cost. Archives of General Psychiatry 37:392-397, 1980.

Stoddard FJ, Altman HG, Sheldon M, Senger H, Van Buskirk D: Psychiatric benefits and insurance regulation in Massachusetts: A national model? American Journal of Psychiatry 140:327-331, 1983.

Sue S: Community mental health services to minority groups: Some optimism, some pessimism. American Psychologist 32:616-624, 1977.

Sullivan FW: Peer review and PSRO: An update. American Journal of Psychiatry 133:51–55, 1976.

Sullivan FW: Peer review and professional ethics. American Journal of Psychiatry 134:186–188, 1977.

Taube CA, Thompson JW, Rosenstein MJ, Rosen BM, Goldman HH: The "chronic" mental hospital patient. Hospital and Community Psychiatry 34:611-615, 1983.

Technology and Health Care et al: Medical Technology and the Health-Care System: A Study of the Diffusion of Equipment-Embodied Technology. Washington: National Academy of Sciences, 1979.

Tibbitts SJ, Marizano AJ: Preferred Provider Organizations. Pluribus Press, Inc., 1984.

Towery OB, Sharfstein SS: Fraud and abuse in psychiatric practice. American Journal of Psychiatry 135:92–94, 1978.

Towery OB, Sharfstein SS, Goldberg ID: The mental and nervous disorders utilization and cost survey (MANDUCS): An analysis of insurance for mental disorders. American Journal of Psychiatry 137:1065–1070, 1980.

Upton D: Mental Health Care and National Health Insurance: A Philosophy of and an Approach to Mental Health Care for the Future. New York: Plenum Press, 1983.

U.S. Chamber of Commerce: A National Health Care Strategy: How Business Can Stimulate a Competitive Health Care System: How Business Can Use Specific Techniques to Control Health Care Costs. Washington: Government Printing Office, 1978a and 1978b.

U.S. Chamber of Commerce: Managing Health Costs: Strategies for Coalitions and Businesses. Clearinghouse on Business Coalitions for Health Action (Pub. no. 6615), 1982.

U.S. Congress Office of Technology Assessment: Assessing the Efficacy and Safety of Medical Technologies. Washington: Government Printing Office, 1978.

U.S. Senate, 93rd Congress: Hearings before the Permanent Subcommittee on Investigations of the Committee on Government Operations, Parts 1 and 2; July 23-26, 1974. Washington: Government Printing Office, 1974.

U.S. House of Representatives: Tax Reform Act of 1983, Report of the Committee on Ways and Means. Washington: Government Printing Office (98-432, Vol. I), 1983.

VandenBos GR: Health financing, service utilization, and national policy: A conversation with Stan Jones. American Psychologist 38:948-955, 1983.

Vaughn WT Jr., Becker D: Mental Health Services Delivery and Financing. Annotated bibliography. Burlingame, CA: Center for Collaborative Studies, 1978.

Veroff J, Kulka RA, Douvan E: Mental Health in America: Patterns of Help-Seeking from 1957 to 1976. New York: Basic Books, 1981.

VonKorff MR, Kramer M: Mental and Nervous Disorders Utilization and Cost Survey. Rockville, MD: National Institute of Mental Health and U.S. Office of Personnel Management, 1979.

Wallen J, Roddy P, Fahs M: Cost sharing, mental health visits, and physical complaints in retired miners and their families. Working paper for the National Center for Health Services Research, presented at the APHA, Montreal, 1982.

Washington Psychiatric Society (sponsor): Report on Utilization Characteristics of the FEHBP Mental Health Benefits. Washington: WPS, 1980.

Weaver CA: EAPs—How they improve the bottom line. Risk Management 27:(7), 1979.

Weisbrod BA: A guide to benefit-cost analysis, as seen through a controlled experiment in treating the mentally ill. Discussion paper of The Institute for Research on Poverty, University of Wisconsin, 1979.

Wells KB, Manning WG, Duan N, Ware JE, Newhouse JP: Cost Sharing and the Demand for Ambulatory Mental Health Services. R-2960-HHS. Santa Monica, CA: Rand Corporation, 1982.

Wilensky GR, Farley PJ, Taylor AK: Variations in Health Insurance Coverage: Benefits Versus Premiums. Unpublished monograph prepared for the National Center for Health Services Research, Washington, 1983.

Williams SJ, Diehr P, Drucker WL, Richardson WC: Mental health services: Utilization by low-income enrollees in a PGP and in an IPP. Medical Care 17:(2), 1979.

Witkin MJ: Trends in Patient Care Episodes in Mental Health Facilities 1955-1977. Rockville, MD: Division of Biometry and Epidemiology, National Institute of Mental Health (Stat. Note 154), 1980.

Zitrin A, Klein H: Can psychiatry police itself effectively? The experience of one District Branch. American Journal of Psychiatry 133:653–656, 1976.

Index